TAKE TODAY

The Executive as Dropout

Other books by Marshall McLuhan

The Mechanical Bride: Folklore of Industrial Man

Explorations in Communications
    (*with E. S. Carpenter*)

The Gutenberg Galaxy: The Making of Typographic Man

Understanding Media: The Extensions of Man

Voices of Literature
    (*with R. J. Schoeck*)

The Medium Is the Massage: An Inventory of Effects

War and Peace in the Global Village

Through the Vanishing Point: Space in Poetry and Painting
    (*with Harley Parker*)

Counterblast
    (*with Harley Parker*)

Culture Is Our Business

From Cliché to Archetype
    (*with Wilfred Watson*)

TAKE TODAY

The Executive as Dropout

Marshall McLuhan and Barrington Nevitt

HARCOURT BRACE JOVANOVICH, INC. / NEW YORK

901.94
M22π
80212
Oct 1972

Contents

PRO-LOG TO EXPLORATION   3

BRIDGES FOR EVERYMAN   7

SAMPLER FOR EAGER READERS   12

MANAGEMENT AS BORROWING, BURROWING, BARROWING   13

Chapter 1.   Postures and Impostures of Managers Past   15

     1 / *Role Becomes Job*   17
     2 / *New Resumes Old*   21
     3 / *"Ground" Remakes "Figure"*   24

Chapter 2.   Tribal Community to Magnetic City: Irresistible
Force By-passes Immovable Object   27

     1 / *Evolving*   27
     2 / *Developing*   28
     3 / *Petrifying*   31
     4 / *Fragmenting*   32
     5 / *Diversifying*   34
     6 / *Retrieving*   36

Chapter 3.   Households to World Shopping Centers: The
Real McCoy and Genuine Fakes   37

     1 / *Make-for-All*   38
     2 / *Money-for-All*   41
     3 / *Free-for-All*   48
     4 / *All-for-Money*   58
     5 / *All-for-Free*   68
     6 / *Fake-for-All*   79

Chapter 4.   The Etherealization of "Hardware" by "Software":
              From Wired Connections to Resonant Interfaces   86

              1 / *Designing*   87
              2 / *Secreting*   92
              3 / *Innovating*   95
              4 / *Extending*   108
              5 / *Probing*   113
              6 / *Gaming*   118

Chapter 5.   The Quantum Leap from Science to Art   123

              1 / *Unraveling*   123
              2 / *Unveiling*   128
              3 / *Reducing*   129
              4 / *Forecasting*   131
              5 / *Modeling*   135
              6 / *Re-cognizing*   138

Chapter 6.   Old Wars and New Overkill   149

              1 / PNR   149
              2 / EXP   152
              3 / TOP   155
              4 / GHQ   157
              5 / ENV   160
              6 / ART   164
              7 / GNP   169
              8 / SVC   173
              9 / MAD   175
             10 / DRE   176
             11 / EAR   179
             12 / EYE   181

Chapter 7.   Tribal Chiefs and Conglomerate Emperors   186

              1 / *Tribal Chiefs on Changing Premises*   188
              2 / *East to West to East*   198
              3 / *Heroes as Villains*   206
              4 / *Services as Disservices*   211
              5 / *Hard Experience v. Soft Knowledge*   225
              6 / *Conglomerate Emperors in Global Theater*   244

Chapter 8. The Crisis of Identity   258

       1 / *Off-spins and In-spins*   259
       2 / *Identity Through Violence*   266
       3 / *Effluents from Affluence*   275

Chapter 9. Everyman as Dropout and Drop-in   279

       1 / *Speed-up via Job Mobile*   280
       2 / *Specialist Ills v. Specialist Cures*   284
       3 / *Old as New and New as Old*   290

ECO-LOG FOR NAVIGATION   296

BIBLIOGRAPHY   299

TAKE TODAY

The Executive as Dropout

PRO-LOG TO
EXPLORATION

There is, it seems to us,
At best, only a limited value
In the knowledge derived from experience.
The knowledge imposes a pattern, and falsifies,
For the pattern is new in every moment
And every moment is a new and shocking
Valuation of all we have been. We are only undeceived
Of that which, deceiving, could no longer harm. . . .

Old men ought to be explorers . . .

T. S. Eliot, *Four Quartets*

Probing and ECO-sounding

The art and science of this century reveal and exploit the resonating bond in all things. All boundaries are areas of maximal abrasion and change. The interval or gap constitutes the resonant or musical bond in the material universe. This is where the action is. To naïve classifiers a gap is merely empty. They will look for connections instead of bonds. They will seek the authors' points of view instead of their probing of processes. Such readers will expect value judgments instead of understanding. With medieval dread they abhor vacuums. But by directing perception on the interfaces of the processes in ECO-land, all gaps become prime sources of discovery. Today's ecological awareness is echo recognition in boundless acoustic space (Greek *echo*: returned sound, personified in mythology as a mountain nymph).

Nothing has its meaning alone. Every *figure* must have its *ground* or environment. A single word, divorced from its linguistic *ground*, would be useless. A note in isolation is not music. Consciousness is corporate action involving *all* the senses (Latin *sensus communis* or "common sense" is the translation of all the senses into each other).

The "meaning of meaning" is relationship. When young activists harp on "relevance," they are asking for interface or the abrasion of dialogue; they are ECO-sounding to discover *where it's at*.

Truth is not matching. It is neither a label nor a "mental reflection." It is something we make in the encounter with a world that is making us. We "make sense," not in cognition but in recognition or re-*play*: Swimming as a cause of drowning is dubious, but only poor fish need boats.

PARADOX OF POWER

This book tells of hang-ups and explorations. The dropouts today are those determined to keep *in touch* with a fast-changing scene. Touch, as the Japanese know best of all, is created by space between and around figures and situations. The natural interval between the wheel and axle is where action and "play" are one. The aware executive is the one who "steps down" when the action begins to "seize up." He maintains his autonomy and his flexibility. This strategy may well be the key to understanding the "generating gap" of our entire epoch.

Looking to the role rather than to the individual, we can see that specialized jobs of managers are universal casualties of the age of electric-information speed.

"DIE HARD" (General Inglis)

(Diehards: Appellation of the Fifty-seventh Regiment of Foot in the British Army)

Dying hard is the worst way of keeping in touch. The new way is dropping out: "He who fights and runs away will live to fight another day."

Until now mangement studies have involuntarily supported the "diehards" and have been concerned with improvement of performance in servicing the physical needs of essentially nineteenth-century producers and consumers. At electric speeds the consumer becomes producer as the public becomes participant role player. At the same time, the old "hardware" is *etherealized* by means of "design" or "software."

Meanwhile, within the very same structure in which the public has become participant, the old management cast finds itself merely holding a fort that is no longer on the frontier of action. They automatically become "diehard" defenders of an old "movie set," as it were, expertly assuming a heroic stance and grimace: "Theirs not to reason why." Meantime, "the reason why" has become both plain and accessible to the new actors. The new cast is inclined to switch roles, as costumes, in order to keep in touch with the new action. The old cast of "diehards," on the other hand, is holding a "phony fort," much as the administrative "establishment" now finds itself in the role of "office boy" and "caretaker" of an abandoned operation.

What's Your Bag?

In passing, it might be noted that Women Liberationists seek to direct their energies toward capture of this abandoned fort of male prerogatives.

They thus become the "diehards" of the moment. They might be succeeded by Children Liberationists at any time as heads of fate and state.

> Beneath the bludgeonings of Chance,
> My head is bloody but unbowed.
> I am the master of my Fate.
> I am the captain of my soul.
>
> W. E. Henley, "Invictus"

The "diehard" as anesthetized man becomes the *touchstone*, the means of anticipating change. *In every situation metamorphosis depends on the frozen arrest of an action.* The "diehard," paradoxically, can be read as an epitaph on his own tombstone.*

The problem of the "diehard" is that he is unable to attain the role of continuing the complex process of transmitting tradition. He freezes on the controls.

VERTEX V. VORTEX

Fallacies of the Paraphernalia of Power

If the "diehard" fails to understand the *processes of power,* the "revolutionary," in seizing the *positions of power,* mistakes "the state apparatus" for the actual controls of power. The *effect* is the setting up of a "police state" regardless of ideology or intent. Power is always a relationship, the putting on of the vortex of the living community by becoming an acceptable service environment. The components that go into this *mask of power* must, therefore, vary according to the character of the communities. A wearable or bearable "mask of power" must comprise all the principal features and postures inherent in the life of the community. Today, on the other hand, it is a natural mistake of revolutionaries to take over the new service environments of press, radio, and TV. These cannot possibly wear the recognizable visage of deep currents of experience or feeling.

Numerous shortcuts to power now loom as we learn to do more with less. Actually, this is the time when more and more awareness is demanded of everybody. When everyone is more and more involved in the information environment and in the creative process of discovery and innovation, the old divisions of work, play, and idleness disappear. The creative worker is never more powerful or more at leisure, never more the dropout from the specialist job, than when using all his faculties. We are entering a time of dialogue and heightened human awareness that plagues many as the specter of "pollution." The etymology of this word (from Latin *pro-luere:* wash forth) reveals a hidden process that is entirely applicable to the present situation: pushed to extreme, dilution becomes pollution. It is like the rich

* For more on this theme of transformation and innovation, see "Narcissus and Narcosis" in *Understanding Media* by Marshall McLuhan.

Texan: whenever he cashed a check, the bank "bounced." *Every process pushed far enough tends to reverse or flip suddenly.* This is the *chiasmus pattern*, perhaps first noted by ancient Chinese sages in *I Ching: The Book of Changes.**

EVITABLE FATE

Since the satellite surround, beginning with Sputnik in 1957, there has come the sudden awareness that nature itself has dropped out. Old experience is no longer relevant, and man must now assume responsibility for the total programming of his planetary environment through new knowledge. "Experience," said Erasmus, "is the schoolmaster of fools." That is, the rates charged by this ruthless pedagogue are outrageous, and few have ever survived his instruction. As the criminal said on his way to execution: "This will teach me a lesson!" Today, effects and causes merge because they almost coincide in time and space in the new information environment. *Change itself has become the main staple.*

The literate Greeks abstracted visual order out of preliterate oral chaos and called their artifact "Nature" (*phusis*). This "natural" order consciously relegated the ancient gods and magic to the irrational "unconscious" and "chaotic." Magic played existence by ear. In today's electric world, man becomes aware that this artificial "Nature" of the Greeks is an extension of himself, just as he is an extension of nature—*all* that exists.

In this book there is no intent to endorse or condemn what has happened. Our concern is to explore and to reveal the process patterns of current happenings. Since it is no longer safe to wait for the harsh judgment of results, we must discover how to *anticipate effects with their causes* in order to avoid the "inevitable" by "programming Fate."

---

* The laws and history of chiastic patterns of action are traced through the Old Testament and classical Greek literature by Nils W. Lund in *Chiasmus in the New Testament.*

BRIDGES FOR
EVERYMAN

The intent of our book is to discuss and illustrate the sudden change from the industrial world of assembly-line "hardware" and visual space into the electric world of orchestrated programming. Twenty-five hundred years of rational culture are in the process of dissolution. Age-old habits of conceptualization will not serve to train observation on the *effects* of the new man-made forms of energy. Since Plato, philosophers and scientists have attributed constant forms and patterns of action only to the world of "Nature." Both Plato and Aristotle, and their followers, as well as all the other schools of philosophy, have refused to recognize any patterns of energy arising from man-made technologies. Having invented "Nature" as a world of rigorous order and repetition, they studied and observed only "natural" forms as having power to shape and influence psyche and society. The world of man's artifacts was considered neutral until the electric age. As the electric environment increasingly engulfed the old Greek "Nature," it became apparent that "Nature" was a *figure* abstracted from a *ground* of existence that was far from "natural." Greek "Nature," which sufficed until Einstein, excluded most of the chaotic resonance of the great Sound-Light Show of existence itself. Most of the pre-Socratic magic and ESP and all the Oriental and "primitive" Natures were pushed into the "subconscious." Civilized man exists by dumping most of his experience into *that* convenient bin. Electric man has discovered that it is his major resource center.

Perceiving Process Patterns by Inventories
of Their Effects

While dealing with the old Greek and Newtonian Nature, men found concepts and points of view useful for the framing of theories of causes that could be tested by measurement. At electric speeds, points of view disappear automatically and concepts have to yield to percepts, for concepts arise from endlessly repeated percepts—ossifications of percepts, as it were, which frequently obscure discovery. Percepts are not hypotheses that can be tested quantitatively, but percepts and observations do yield patterns which can be regarded as "causes" although, in fact, they are *processes*. Paradoxically, electronic man has no choice but to understand processes, if he is to be free. To free himself from servitude to his own artifacts has become the main program of the new ecological age that began with Sputnik. For twenty-five hundred years Western science and philosophy have ignored everything that we now consider to be ecological and mandatory.

The new information environment tends to supplant Nature, whereas the old mythic wisdom tried to explain nature. Thus modern man has to *live* mythically, in contrast to his ancient forebears, who sought to *think* mythically. Myth is the record of a simultaneous perception of effects with causes in a complementary process. It is possible to see a history of world art today in thirty seconds. A newspaper under a single date line gives you "Your World Today." These are mythic forms by virtue of speed and compression. When we hear that King Cadmus sowed the dragon's teeth and they sprang up armed men, we are given an instantaneous history of the effects of the phonetic alphabet on man and society. Myth does not limp but leaps.

In this book we turn to the study of new patterns of energy arising from man's physical and psychic artifacts and social organizations. The only method for perceiving process and pattern is by *inventory of effects* obtained by the comparison and contrast of developing situations.

Beyond Exposition for Exploration

Civilized, rationally educated people expect and prefer to have problems described and analyzed sequentially. They try to *follow* your argument to a conclusion. They expect the conclusion to be your *point of view*, illustrative of your *values*. In contrast to the method of exposition is the method of exploration. This begins by the admission of ignorance and difficulties. Such statement will tend to be a tentative groping. The blind man's cane picks up the *relation* of things in his environment by the quality of resonance. His tapping tells him what objects are adjacent to his stick. If his stick were *connected* to any of these objects, he would be helpless so far as orientation was concerned. This is always the plight of the logical method. It is useless for exploration. Its very strength makes it irrelevant. "Proof" of sanity is available only to those discharged from mental institutions.

"Seeing Them Off the Premises"

It is difficult to make a mistake in logic, once the premises are granted. Psychologists report that madmen are rigorously logical, but their premises are irrelevant. The method of exploration seeks to discover adequate premises. This book does not question the structures existing in our world as much as the hidden premises that are supposed to support them. When the *ground* changes, the *figures* may disappear. The *expository method* of system presentation serves very well to package preconceptions. The *exploratory method* encounters surprise and discovery at every turn. Only dead processes can be packaged.

BRIDGES ARE INTERVALS OF RESONANCE AS MUCH AS MEANS OF CON-
NECTION. LIKE ANY RESONATING INTERVAL, THEY TRANSFORM BOTH
AREAS THEY TOUCH.

The popular game of "bridge" originated in a major social breakdown.
When suburbia was new, community was buried. "Bridge," like booze,
served as a ghostly paradigm of community. Bridges mark breakdowns in
human communication. Every new slang phrase marks wit's end. It is a
frantically devised bridge over an unexpected break in the order of human
perception. In "hardware" terms, it is obvious that where roads end,
bridges begin. Confronting the wide diversity of breaks in the organization
structures of our time, this book throws bridges across every kind of gap in
our social fabric.

Consider human artifacts as bridges between areas of experience. Bridges
are metaphors (from Greek *metaferein:* "to carry across"). *Bridges as extensions of man are resonating vortices of power.*

THE GREATEST BRIDGE KNOWN TO MAN IS SPEECH AND LANGUAGE. AS
CLICHÉS, WORDS ABRIDGE TIME AND SPACE BY RECORDING AND STOR-
ING THE MULTITUDINOUS MATTERS OF PRIVATE AND CORPORATE IM-
PRESSION.

The language of a people is not only the resonant bridge that binds them
in space and time; it is also the medium that shapes and processes their
sensory and mental lives. The poet is concerned with releasing and controlling the corporate linguistic and traditional experience of the race by ever-
new resonance and rhythms. He bridges the latest and most ancient aware-
nesses by the interface that T. S. Eliot speaks of in *The Use of Poetry and
the Use of Criticism.*

THE AUDITORY IMAGINATION

What I call the "auditory imagination" is the feeling for syllable and
rhythm, penetrating far below the conscious levels of thought and
feeling, invigorating every word: sinking to the most primitive and forgotten, returning to the origin and bringing something back, seeking
the beginning and the end. It works through meanings, certainly, or
not without meanings in the ordinary sense, and fuses the old and
obliterated, and the trite, the current, and the new and the surprising,
the most ancient and the most civilized mentality.

Auditory imagination is the mind's ear—the complement of visual imagination. Less familiar as "bridge" is the "tragic flaw" (hamartia), of which
Aristotle speaks in the *Poetics.* Without this interval of ignorance or awareness in his character, the tragic hero cannot bridge one state to another.
The flaw is an area of interface and mutation, without which he cannot get
better, but can only be hung up.

When Lewis Carroll's Alice went through the looking glass, she bridged the inner and outer worlds of fancy and imagination just at the time when the French biologist Claude Bernard bridged the inner and outer fields of medical science by his exploration of *le milieu intérieur,* creating internal medicine. Alice went through the vanishing point into the "total field" that bridges the worlds of visual and acoustic, civilized and primal spaces.

SYMBOLISM IS PRE-EMINENTLY THE WORLD OF THE INTERVAL, OR RESONANT EFFECTS MINUS CAUSES (Greek *sym-ballein:* "to put together without connection"). Edgar Allan Poe's rediscovery of the transforming power of the interval was a retrieval of the Ovidian technique of metamorphosis by the use of double plots or actions. W. B. Yeats had discussed it as the technique for creating "the emotion of multitude." This "magical" parallelism was the mode beloved by Dante and Shakespeare. It is the pattern used by James Joyce in *Ulysses* to bridge the ancient and modern worlds by a continuous parallel of interface between myth and realism, order and anarchy. In the detective story Poe discovered the missing clue as the bridge for all scientific research: the Cyclopean and encyclopedic scanning of the total field by the omission of the private point of view. The bridge between the corporate scientific probe and the personal viewpoint was made by the deliberate organization of ignorance, by the suppression of data. The detective sets out to re-create an action that is perceived as flawed or breached. IT IS THE MISSING LINK THAT INSPIRES THE PARTICIPATION OF THE READER, AS IT IS THE ANARCHY OF DISEASE AND DISORDER THAT INSPIRES THE SCIENTIFIC QUEST.

Since Heisenberg and Linus Pauling, the only remaining material bond is resonance. The continuum of visual space of the Euclidian kind is not to be found in the material universe. There are no connections among "particles of being" such as appear in mechanical models. Instead, there is a wide range of resonating intensities that constitute an equally wide variety of "auditory" spaces. Ancient philosophers have often imagined God as a Being whose center was everywhere with boundaries nowhere. Such also is the nature of puns and of acoustic space itself.

> To define is to kill,
> To suggest is to create.
>   Stéphane Mallarmé

Walter Pater recognized that "the arts aspire to the condition of music," just as Poe invented the symbolist interval or gap that became the bridge between the structures of art and science in the twentieth century. The Japanese view the artist as one who makes bridges between old and new experience. So, in a changing world, new art is always needed to tune our perceptions to "where it's at." The artist of the preliterate society is a bridge between the visible and the invisible worlds. He is a "pontiff." His work may be in dance, music, or varied materials. His art is to create designs, masks, or vortices of power and energy, which "put on" the public.

As the detective reconstructs events, so the artist by retracing the processes of cognition (mimesis) bridges the world of sense and the world of awareness. James Joyce presents this cognitive bridge in monumental and dramatic form in *Finnegans Wake:* the entire tribal cycle of society now begins again, but awake. ENVIRONMENTAL AWARENESS CREATES A BRIDGE BE-TWEEN THE OLD ACCIDENTAL AND THE NEWLY PROGRAMMED EVENTS OF HUMAN EXISTENCE FOR ENRICHMENT THROUGH DIVERSITY.

Hypnotized by their rear-view mirrors, philosophers and scientists alike tried to focus the *figure* of man in the old *ground* of nineteenth-century industrial mechanism and congestion. They failed to bridge from the old *figure* to the new. It is man who has become both *figure* and *ground* via the electrotechnical extension of his awareness. *With the extension of his nervous system as a total information environment, man bridges art and nature.*

TODAY "NATURE" IS THE MESS-AGE
BUT MAN IS STILL THE CONTENT

SAMPLER FOR
EAGER READERS

Where to elect there is but one,
'Tis Hobson's choice—take that or none.
Thomas Ward, *England's Reformation*

	Page		*Page*		*Page*
AUTOMOBILIST	244	*Accountant*	79	Actor	274
BUSINESSMAN	252	*Bureaucrat*	220	Builder	34
COMPREHENSIVIST	293	*Consultant*	215	Critic	7
DEVELOPER	28	*Designer*	87	Detective	92
ECONOMIST	53	*Engineer*	135	Ecologist	145
FORECASTER	131	*Fashionmonger*	273	Faker	79
GENERAL	157	*Gentleman*	209	Griper	13
HOUSEWIFE	229	*Hijacker*	80	Historian	15
INNOVATOR	101	*Indian*	183	Insurer	113
JOBLESS	227	*Jester*	120	Jack-of-all-trades	291
KILLJOY	278	*King*	20	Kibbutznik	266
LIBERATIONIST	4	*Lawyer*	94	Librarian	105
MANUFACTURER	77	*Marketeer*	87	Marxist	60
NEGRO	242	*Newsman*	173	Nobody	268
ORGANIZER	255	*Original*	269	Oldster	290
PARENT	260	*Politician*	217	Publisher	142
QUESTIONER	201	*Queen*	231	Quack	241
RELIGIOUS	191	*Revolutionary*	263	Rationalizer	137
SCIENTIST	121	*Sport*	145	Stockholder	222
TEACHER	286	*Transporter*	241	Telecommunicator	248
UNDERTAKER	48	*Unionist*	182	University student	231
VALUATOR	234	*Visionary*	236	Videophonist	251
WARRIOR	152	*Writer*	139	Welfare agent	213
XENOPHOBE	178	*Xeroxer*	52	X factor	128
YOUTH	259	*Yankee*	206	Yogi	151
ZPG	101	*Zealot*	129	Zoologist	10

Every man has a right to defend his own ignorance.

Are you trying for answers before you've got the questions? Our questions follow.

MANAGEMENT AS BORROWING,
BURROWING, BARROWING

Toborrow and toburrow and tobarrow! That's our crass, hairy and ever-grim life, till one finel howdiedow Bouncer Naster raps on the bell with a bone and his stinkers stank behind him with the sceptre and the hourglass. James Joyce, *Finnegans Wake*

> To-morrow, and to-morrow, and to-morrow,
> Creeps in this petty pace from day to day,
> To the last syllable of recorded time;
> And all our yesterdays have lighted fools
> The way to dusty death.
> Shakespeare, *Macbeth*

Point of view is failure to achieve structural awareness. No static view-point is possible in the vortex of process. Nor can the effects of human organization be understood in terms of single isolated causes. All processes whatever involve clusters of interacting effects with causes. As a *figure*, every manager creates a service environment or *ground* that is an extension of himself. He puts on his organization like "The Emperor's New Clothes." The managing process is both a creation and an extension of man. As such, it is a *medium* that processes its users, who are its *content*. Whereas the *meaning* of management is the set of relationships engendered by the user, the *message* of management is the totality of its effects. IN THE WORLD OF ELECTRIC INFORMATION, ALL CENTERS OF POWER BECOME MARGINAL.

The keys to comprehending the data, the "keys to given," in any headache are also the "keys to heaven": when the hang-up is recognized as comic, it opens doors of perception that can transform all previous relationships and release tensions. Thus, a random inventory of gripes and jokes, culled from the irritant problems of any form of human organization whatever, will serve as structural clue or pattern illuminator.

The following chapters explore both the gradual variations and the sudden transformations that occur in the *figure-ground* interplay of man and his artifacts, as each remakes the other. Our chief resources are the gripes and jokes, the problems and breakdowns, of managers themselves; for therein lie the solutions and breakthroughs via pattern recognition of the processes involved. Managing *The Ascent from the Maelström* today demands awareness that can be achieved only by going *Through the Vanishing Point*.

When a man-made environment circumvents the entire planet, moon, and galaxy, there is no alternative to total knowledge programming of all human enterprise. Any form of imbalance proves fatal at electric speeds with the superpowers released by the new technological resources representing the full spectrum of the human senses and faculties. Survival now would seem to depend upon the extension of consciousness itself as an environment. This extension of consciousness has already begun with the computer and has been anticipated in our obsession with ESP and occult awareness.

Where the Hand of Man Has Never Set Foot

In a world of the comprehensivist as manager and in which the population is actor the new roles are again those of the hunter. The TV eye is not a convergent focusing eye but an environmental scanner that works at speeds which reveal the hidden patterns that demand programming. The same speed-up of technology creates ecological configurations that end the old classifications of knowledge. The shift is from concept to percept. THE MANAGER MOVES HIS ACTION FROM THE MANIPULATION OF THINGS TO THE ANTICIPATION OF PROCESSES BY UNDERSTANDING THEIR CAUSES.

Chapter 1

Postures and Impostures
of Managers Past

Maneggiare (Italian)—to handle, especially to manage or train horses.
Ménager (French)—to use carefully, to husband, to spare.
Diehard—His *not* to reason why; breakdown by keeping uptight.
Dropout—His *but* to reason why; breakthrough by keeping in touch.

Politics and morals are divorced. Each of the two has its own ends, each its own means. They are not reconcilable. There is no middle position of compromise. Niccolò Machiavelli, *The Prince*

I put no ceiling on progress.
 Alfred P. Sloan, Jr.

History is bunk.
 Henry Ford

 History has many cunning passages, contrived corridors
 And issues, deceives with whispering ambitions,
 Guides us by vanities.
 T. S. Eliot, "Gerontion"

History is not a compilation of facts, but an insight into a moving process of life. S. Giedion, *Space, Time and Architecture*

History as Observatory of Change

Today the cultural historian can reveal the hidden factors in the cultures of the past, just as the programmers of innovational processes have the means of seeing the effects of any action before it begins. The approach is that of the instantaneous testing of processes under controlled conditions. *When we push our paradigms back, we get "history"; when we push them forward, we get "science."* The historian, such as Eric Havelock in his *Preface to Plato*, has now the same power to recall ancient events. History offers the controlled conditions of a laboratory for observing patterns of change, much as primitive societies living in prehistory (preliteracy) give postliterate man the means of observing the action of the latest technologies.

Such instant retrieval joins prehistory and posthistory in an inclusive NOW of all traditions.

> The providence that's in a watchful state
> Knows almost every grain of Plutus' gold,
> Finds bottom in the uncomprehensive deeps,
> Keeps place with thought, and almost, like the gods,
> Does thoughts unveil in their dumb cradles.
>
> Shakespeare, *Troilus and Cressida*

The American executive now experiences the European "existential" anguish in the clash between job and role. The more responsible he is, the less power he has—the more involved, the less freedom.

With the acceleration of change, management now takes on entirely new functions. While navigation amidst the unknown is becoming the normal role of the executive, the new need is not merely to navigate but to anticipate effects with their causes. At instant speeds in our resonant Echoland, it is fatal to "wait and see." "Feedback" relying on experience is now too slow. We must know in advance of action. The "feedforward" of knowledge based on pattern recognition of process is essential for reprogramming beyond ideologies. What had always appeared inevitable can thus be bypassed.

THERE IS NO LONGER ANY NEED TO BACK INTO A PROPHYLACTIC FUTURE WITH MILDEWED HINDSIGHT.

1

Role Becomes Job

The academic historians of Ford's time strove to make history into a science by a *matching* process. Henry Ford turned to *making* history by scrapping the agrarian world around him. He was one of the greatest creators of new social clothing and service environments. While altering every pattern of the contemporary world and of history, he resolutely averted his gaze from the past and present alike. It was in a spirit of somnambulistic compensation that he built Greenfield Village in the eye of the industrial maelstrom.

Henry Ford, one of the most antiquated and tribalistic of all industrial managers, was "*The* President." There were no other members of the hierarchy. In dispensing with the conventional organizational hierarchy, Ford naturally resorted to the tribal form of government by Mafia methods. He was ahead of his time. He could afford to junk history, since he *was* history.

At the other extreme in the motor industry was Alfred P. Sloan, Jr., of General Motors, whose very conventional hierarchical organization is portrayed in detail by Peter Drucker in *Concept of the Corporation*. With his archaic dream of decentralization for General Motors, Sloan involuntarily restored the baronial pattern of managerial bosses and autonomous groupings in his empire. This pattern readily enabled his representatives to see themselves as "knights in shining armor." This "Court of King Arthur" sort of world was seen by Henry Ford, through the spectacles of Mark Twain, as pure bunkum.

The Rear-View Mirror

Henry Ford teamed up with Thomas Edison to build Greenfield Village, a nostalgic RVM evocation of the agrarian world that they had junked by their innovations. Daniel J. Boorstin, in *The Image: Or, What Happened to the American Dream*, need have gone no further than Greenfield Village to reconstruct the stages of slaughter, interment, and monumentality, by which Bonanzaland became a universal parking lot. The extreme forms of urban decentralism created by the car led swiftly to extreme forms of managerial centralism. Ford and Sloan split apart over this. Ford saw it as a means of strengthening centralist control, while Sloan chose the strategy of decentralism as in accord with the mobility of the car.

Having already stated the contrast between oral and written patterns of social and legal procedures of the past, it is possible to see these traditionally opposed forms of order once more in the center of the management dramas of our present world.

Mini-Mafia

> Oozing charm from every pore
> He oiled his way across the floor
> *My Fair Lady*

The effect of satellites is the conversion of the planet into a global theater that demands spectacular programming beyond anything conceived by the old Hollywood. The global theater demands the world population not only as audience but as a cast of participants.

In *Fortune* Magazine, July, 1969, Tom Alexander wrote on "The Unexpected Payoff of Project Apollo." He describes, on the one hand, the extreme fragmented hierarchical and specialized organization that went into the project, and, on the other hand, the emergence of an integral "musical" organization of all these components into an unexpected kind of "NASA Mafia."

Horse Collar and Stirrup as Extensions of Man

Machiavelli is now as obsolete as Gutenberg from whom he stems. "Old Nick" was among the first to observe the psychic and social fracturing that resulted from the alphabet ("alforabit") when speeded by the new press. Let us ask what sort of a pamphlet might have been written by an equally sharp observer when the stirrup and the horse collar were new. Lynn White has detailed the political and urban revolutions that proceeded from those medieval innovations in *Medieval Technology and Social Change*. The stirrup created the feudal system, revolutionizing landholding and all the structures of social power. The knight became the invincible tank.

With the horse collar came "horsepower" and the agricultural and transportation revolutions. New cities, new markets, Gutenberg, and gunpowder shot these structures to pieces by sheer speed-up and specialism. From the most ancient times the perfections of natural beauty had been the supreme focus of intellectual contemplation by those in power. The sudden break from regarding nature as beauty to exploiting nature as a source of power and wealth came suddenly. It gathered momentum in the sixteenth century with the press and was dominant until the turn of the nineteenth century.

Humpty Dumpty: China Egg on the Magazine Wall

. . . a break-through after a long accumulation of tension, as a
swollen river breaks through its dikes, or in the manner of a cloud-
burst . . . Applied to human conditions, it refers to the time when
inferior people gradually begin to disappear. Their influence is on the
wane; as a result of resolute action, a change in conditions occurs, a
break-through. . . .   *I Ching*

The story of the fall of Humpty Dumpty, as it were, is recorded in all the
classics of the sixteenth century, from More's *Utopia,* and *Don Quixote* to
Shakespeare. The entire works of Shakespeare are concerned with the unhappy dissolution of personal faith and loyalty and the rise of the Machiavellian Iagos, Edmunds, and Macbeths. Calculating adventurers, usurpers,
and opportunists seemed to Shakespeare to have succeeded an age of harmony and music:

> O! when degree is
>   shak'd,
> Which is the ladder to all high designs,
> The enterprise is sick. How could communities,
> Degrees in schools, and brotherhoods in cities,
> Peaceful commerce from dividable shores,
> The primogenitive and due of birth,
> Prerogative of age, crowns, sceptres, laurels,
> But by degree, stand in authentic place?
> Take but degree away, untune that string,
> And hark! what discord follows; each thing meets
> In mere oppugnancy.
>
> Shakespeare, *Troilus and Cressida*

*The pre-Gutenberg world assumed resonance and music as the physical
basis of social order.* The shift to individual self-interest and private goals
instead of corporate role playing was a sixteenth-century drama that is being
played backward today. The return to resonance as the physical basis of
being itself is now asserted by science and implemented by instant electric
circuitry.

The timeless appeal of Prince Hamlet as a chief of state lies in his being
torn between his corporate princely role and the new private-power politics
of the strong-arm Fortinbras types. "Moreness" went with the divide-and-
rule tactics of the new print age of mass production. Machiavelli saw that
the uniform repetitive products of the press created the universal market of
uniform pricing. He saw that the principle would also extend to ambitious
people engaged in specialist activities created by the Gutenberg technology:
"Every man has his price." This was not a cynical observation under the
circumstances.

Lear's Dilemma

King Lear is like Hamlet, trying to play it both ways, the pathetic case of a man seeking to be "with it" but lacking awareness of the Machiavellian consequences of the new forms of delegated authority.

"L'esprit de Quantité"

The villain Edmund is the Machiavelli of the play. He is imbued with the new idea of *moreness* as power goal (*l'esprit de quantité*), which became the basis of the new idea of "sovereign states." Whereas the medieval monarch had "put on" his subjects as his "corporate mask," the Renaissance prince saw his people contained within visual and geographic boundaries.

KING LEAR IS A WORKING MODEL OF THE PROCESS
OF DENUDATION BY WHICH MEN TRANSLATED THEMSELVES
FROM A WORLD OF ROLES TO A WORLD OF JOBS.

King Lear is a kind of elaborate case history of people translating themselves out of a world of roles into the new world of jobs. This is a process of denudation which does not occur instantly except in artistic vision. But Shakespeare saw that it had happened in his time. He was not talking about the future. However, the older world of roles had lingered on as a ghost just as after a century of electricity the West still feels the presence of the older values of literacy and privacy and separateness.   Marshall McLuhan, *The Gutenberg Galaxy*

The State as a Work of Art

As the old medieval world of organic coherence fell open, many, like Machiavelli, saw the possibility of dealing with the state as a work of art. Jacob Burckhardt spent a volume on this theme without knowing that any old structure automatically becomes a work of art. In a word, the Machiavellis were looking back to the medieval times through Renaissance glasses. All utopias are images of the immediately preceding society projected into the future. Such is More's *Utopia* as much as Orwell's anti-utopia *1984*. Samuel Butler saw the dilemma in his title *Erewhon* by spelling his utopia backward. All power became a masquerade of fakes and fictions. Loss of the traditional forms of identity and loyalty freed everybody to become an isolated person in somebody's game. The popular name for these new adventurers was "honest men." Shakespeare has typified them in "honest Iago," the "honest engine" of power and intrigue, the fabricator of "ocular proof."

OFF-Again—ON-Again—FINN-Again

There are only two basic extreme forms of human organization. They have innumerable variants or "parti-colored" forms. The extreme forms are the *civilized* and the *tribal* (eye and ear): the Cromwellian specialist and the Celtic involved. Only the civilized form is fragmented in action, whether in business or in politics or in entertainment. Hence the anarchy of the contemporary world where all these forms coexist.

Dependent upon the materials and hence the technologies available to mankind, the pattern of social organization and management swings violently from stress on the entrepreneur and the virtues of the lonely individualist to the close-knit and emotionally involved group. In the diversified scope of modern business structures, these extremes can express themselves at different levels of the same organization. Tribal cliques can grow in the shade of the old organization tree. The telephone can foster such groups, especially when the "bugging" of the phones is on a large scale. The oral substructure *ground* quickly undermines the organization "tree."

> By the law of change, whatever has reached its extreme must turn back.   *I Ching*

It is explained in the same context of this 4,000-year-old management manual that innovation "does indeed guide all happenings, but it never behaves outwardly as the leader. Thus true strength is that strength which, mobile as it is hidden, concentrates on the work without being outwardly visible." What is actually visible in new situations is the ghost of old ones. It is the movie that *appears* on TV. It is the old written word that *appears* on Telex. The hidden force of change is the new speed that alters all configurations of power. The new speed creates a new hidden *ground* against which the old *ground* becomes the *figure* of the dropout. The function of the dropout is to reveal the new hidden *ground* or environment. This development can occur either as individual or corporate. The role of the typical "drop-in" or consultant is to prop up the collapsing foundations. Freud arrived too late to save the nuclear family. He was dumped by the nuclear age.

THE HIDDEN PERSUADERS AND THE FRUSTRATED RADICALS

All management theories and political ideologies follow an involuntary procedure. The idealists share with the experienced and practical men of their time the infirmity of substituting concepts for percepts. Both concentrate on a clash between past experience and future goals that black out the actual but hidden processes of the present. Both ignore the fact that *dialogue* as a process of creating the new came before, and goes beyond, the *exchange* of "equivalents" that merely reflect or repeat the old.

2

New Resumes Old

The A-Stone-Aged Manager

Having scrapped the medieval world, the Gutenberg technology extended man's powers of retrieval by speed-up. The medieval scriptorium had no means of coping with the whole of antiquity, but the Gutenberg press dumped all the ancient classics into the Renaissance lap. There was an orgy of paganism and miming of ancient styles of prose and dress and art.

Pope, in *The Dunciad*, records the ultimate development of Gutenberg as a kind of supermarket abundance of books, which swamped the human intelligence and befogged the wits of men in clouds of ink. The seventeenth-century "balance" between "hardware" and "software" yielded quickly to the eighteenth-century triumph of "hardware," familiar to every schoolboy who reads Goldsmith's *Deserted Village*. William Blake, however, took an even grimmer view of the change than that expressed in the pastoral lament of the genial Irishman.

U.S.A. as Laboratory for Social Experiments, Past and Present

is the theme of Peter Farb's *Man's Rise to Civilization as Shown by the Indians of North America from Primeval Times to the Coming of the Industrial State*:

> North America is the place in the world most nearly ideal to observe the evolution of human societies and customs, institutions and beliefs, for these are revealed there with all the clarity of a scientific experiment. The story of the Indians in North America provides modern man with a living test tube, in which the major ingredients that went into the experiment, the intermediate reactions that took place, and the final results are largely known.

The electrotechnic age, having rendered obsolete the age of industrial "hardware" and its organization chart, has unexpectedly retrieved the most primitive and archaic cultures of many times and places. We now are swamped by a new environment of preliterate forms. This brings us full circle on our tour with

Pastimes Are Past Times

The new expert, along with the old executive, has been swept away in a flood of comedies. New environments of information and enterprise have revealed the contours of these obsolescent types, even as the satellite has created a sudden and universal awareness of "pollution."

MEN OF EXTINCTION UNITE; WITH HARDENING OF THE CATEGORIES YOU'VE NOTHING TO LOSE BUT THE CHANGE.

Lost Interface

The French revolutionaries were determined to abolish the *ancien régime* that had become a rococo masquerade long before 1789. The old feudal hierarchy of costumes and roles had to be scrapped at any cost. *Le grand monarque,* with his surround of china shepherdesses, was swept aside to make way for *l'empereur,* whose enormous centralist power was derived, not from the feudal pennies of the peasantry, but from the cannon and "hardware" of the new middle-class manufacturers. The puny and slow-moving bureaucracy of the Bourbons was replaced by the speed of production and road movement of Napoleon's legions. Napoleon introduced a semaphore telegraph system that gave him four-hour intervals of intercom with Rome. He ran the army and the country as a centralized industrial corporation. He invented the rule of using the right-hand side of the road to create traffic speed and conformity. He introduced the fragmented uniformity of the "metric" system and the speedy Code Napoleon. The old common law disappeared under a monumental catafalque of classical solemnity and senatorial dignity. The egalitarian dreams of the Jacobins were gaily sacrificed, to *la gloire et l'honneur de la patrie.* The idealists had fought for liberty and equality, and they got a military state with careers open to talents. Napoleon anticipated the later organization chart with "staff and line," proclaiming the right of every private to envisage a marshal's baton in his old kit bag.

These were the visible developments that reversed the dreams of the *avant-garde.* A far more insidious force was inherent in the entire speed-up of the new industrial "hardware" complex.

3

"Ground" Remakes "Figure"

Hidden Environments Reshape Their Makers

In Europe and in England alike the extreme specialism of the industrial revolution created a massive retrieval of medieval sensibility in the arts and crafts, and in religion. This was the new hidden *ground* that entered into abrasive interface with the pronounced *figure* of the dominant new industrialisms. This hidden action in the later nineteenth century has its parallel at present in the retribalizing process of electrotechniques. While detribalizing is assigned top priority for civilized advance in all backward areas, regardless of geography or ideology, there is also occurring a complementary and hidden process of retribalization that is independent of either plotters or planners, ideology or geography. The most archaic societies now begin with our latest electric technology. They by-pass the civilized phase that occupied Western energies for thousands of years and plunge even deeper into their own tribal traditions.

The Renaissance or the rebirth of pagan antiquity was the unexpected consequence of demolishing the feudal system. The return of the pagan gods and pagan humanism had not been the objective of any of the reformers. The Luthers and Calvins had sought to purge the church of its accretion of political impurities. Driving toward primal simplicity, they encountered innumerable schisms and doctrinal specialisms as the dominant *figure* of their actions. The hidden *ground* was the overwhelming new retrieval of pagan antiquity via print technology. The very technological instrument of individual "inner light" and liberation immersed them in a new environment of merely utilitarian objectives.

> The hateful siege of contraries.
> Milton, *Paradise Lost*

In our own century the same siege of hateful contraries and dramatic reversals was played out in the Eastern medieval theater of the Romanoffs. The Russians sloughed off the feudal hegemony of the Romanoffs and grasped the latest means of Western organization of industrial production. The slogan was:

CATCH UP AND SURPASS!

Just when the West was plunging Eastward, and when the enlightened spirits had either booked a passage to India or, like Yeats, were already on

the iconic route to Byzantium, cultural anthropologists like Sir James Fra-
zer set out to retrieve the Great Mother and the mythic figures of archaic
consciousness. But the anthropologists failed to note that these forms of
awareness had become totally pervasive even before the jazz age of the
1920's. The instant telegraph had established modes of social order that
radio broadcasting pushed all the way to Hitler's ovens.

The same cruel paradox involves the American Negro, whose jazz
rhythms integrated the cultures of the entire world for the first time in
history or before. The same Negro is now expected to "integrate" with the
subculture of literacy after having created a universal culture of tribal
jazz.

James Joyce put it all in a phrase about the heroine of *Finnegans Wake*.
She is Anna Livia Plurabelle, musical mother of all forms, the hidden
ground of being:

> Sheshell ebb music wayriver she flows.

The hidden *ground* and force of the anthropological enterprise, as much
as the business world of the consumer-producer, lay in the power of instant
electric communication to restore all things to an inclusive present. By involving all men in all men, by the electric extension of their own nervous
systems, the new technology turns the *figure* of the primitive society into a
universal *ground* that buries all previous *figures*. The naïveté of the anthropologists, "secure" in a civilized literate stockade, is matched again and
again by would-be innovators who head for specific goals:

ERLE STANLEY GARDNER
WORLD'S BIGGEST SELLING WRITER DEAD
Toronto *Star*, March 12, 1970

The author of Perry Mason often felt the irony of his situation. Having
set out to write, that he might have leisure for hunting and fishing, he spent
his life dictating to a team of secretaries. The hidden *ground* of his plight
was precisely hunting and fishing. His hero, Perry Mason, is a full-time
hunter and fisher of men and clues. The sleuth, the undercover man, is a
major posture of the hunter against the new electric *ground* of the telephone and TV.

Man Hunter and Sleuth: Posture and Imposture

In one of Sherlock Holmes's adventures his quarry demurs when Holmes
declares that he had seen him at a particular spot. The quarry retorts that
"I saw nobody following me there." And Holmes comments, "That is
what you may expect to see when I follow you."

Half the world today is engaged in keeping the other half "under surveillance." This, in fact, is the hang-up of the age of "software" and information. In the preceding "hardware" age the "haves" of the world had kept the

"have-nots" under "surveillance." This old beat for flatfoots has now been relegated to the world of popular entertainment. *The police state is now a work of art, a bureaucratic ballet of undulating sirens.* That is a way of saying that the espionage activities of our multitudinous man hunters and "crediting" agencies are not only archaic, but redundant and irrelevant.

GALLUPING ESPIONAGE CREATES THE UNPERSON:
THE MAN THAT NEVER WAS

POSTURE AND IMPOSTURE AS WAYS OF LIFE
NOW MERGE IN THE GLOBAL THEATER

Chapter 2
Tribal Community to Magnetic City:
Irresistible Force By-passes
Immovable Object

1
Evolving

Jane Jacobs, in *The Economy of Cities*, stresses that cities at any time and no matter when, how, or why, create adjacent agriculture. She explains how cities foster many service activities in ever-proliferating patterns. The general public has been piqued by this reversal, much as if they suddenly discovered that the egg had decided to invent the chicken in order to get more eggs. Today we live in an age of simultaneity rather than of sequence. We start with the effects before the product. The consumer becomes producer.

"HARDWARE" CITY

When Le Corbusier first glimpsed the Manhattan skyline he said, *"C'est le jazz hot en pierre!"* (It's hot jazz in stone!) When jazz, with its involving intervals, was new, and the syncopation of space by skyscrapers was new, the excitement of city lights, the great Broadway of Jimmy Walker were thrills that lured the farm boys and girls into the "asphalt jungle." Canada, being a backward country, is still full of such naïve rural types for whom the big town remains the big thrill. Belatedly, these people seek in the electric age (when the "urb orbs" and the jet creates the circulating "jet city") to create the massive "hardware" bricks and mortar effects that formerly enthralled the newly industrialized populations of the world. Meanwhile, the jet set gaily slides down the razor blade of life.

2

Developing

Big Squeeze for the Quick Buck

The mayor of Toronto dreams of congregating 27 million residents in a colossal "carsophagus," or high-density dump. The practical advantage of this congestion is, of course, *ease of taxation*. The paw of the tax man can scarcely reach to the farmer's overalls. Great wealth departs to "offshore" havens, where by simply purchasing small governments it enjoys total tax immunity. Congestion is the ready way to easy taxation and accelerated "development."

Hick-town Hang-up

Metro must expand or be strangled.
            Toronto *Star*, October 11, 1969

When Landlords Walk Away

. . . in many of the nation's troubled central cities, the most visible housing difficulty is . . . a lack, not of buildings, but of neighborhoods deemed fit to live in, even by the poor. As a consequence, acres of houses and apartment buildings have been abandoned by their owners and tenants to decay.   *Time*, March 16, 1970

From Piles of Refuse to Monolithic Slums

When "order" is pushed to extremes by complementarity, law becomes ordure. Ordure, pushed to the extreme, results in new order, or society as art form. The engulfing of the human scale in providing living accommodation by high-rise creates the hardware monolith where *figure* and *ground* grind each other to numerical bits.

GUILTY IN KILLING OF 400,000, STANGL IS JAILED

Throughout the seven-month trial, he stubbornly insisted that he had only done his *duty*. The court president, Dr. Heinz Meven, said in delivering the verdict that the accused had "silenced his own conscience."   Toronto *Globe and Mail*, December 23, 1970

This assembly-line functionary "silenced his conscience" by the usual process of fragmentation and specialism. The sheer method and vastness of the operation motivated this perfectly typical somnambulist. Today, the utmost degree of social fragmentation achieved by the vertical city streets of high-rise units makes it obvious that the entire social strategy is ready for reversal. When the housing unit itself becomes the environment, *i.e.*, when *figure* becomes *ground,* there is no more interplay to create community. This is *the antisocial monster.* The slum is the reverse, but more tolerable. Multiple families crowded in single dwellings turn the environmental *ground* into *figure.* This is *the social monster.* The social monster of the swarming slum has many values of diversity and great powers of endurance. Its antisocial opposite, the high-rise "slum," has no power of survival save as archaeology. YOU TAKE THE HIGH SLUM, AND I'LL TAKE THE LOW SLUM.

The powerful dynamism of transformation inherent in all intensive interfaces of urban life manages to be concealed even from the most astute planners. Nineteenth-century Toronto, instead of seeking entry into the twentieth century by vigorous programs of extreme decentralism, is proceeding on the assumption of

MORENESS OF SAMENESS AS ROAD TO PROGRESS

The Metro planners of Toronto take for granted that "it is, and will continue to be, impossible to limit significantly the growing volume of traffic" (*Globe and Mail,* March 27, 1970). The proposal of public transit as a solvent for private congestion fatally ignores the deepest American grain: AMERICANS ARE UNIQUE IN THE WORLD IN THEIR DEMAND FOR PRIVACY WHEN THEY GO OUT AND FOR COMMUNITY WHEN THEY COME HOME.

Not to Be Outdone, Let's Copy Others' Mistakes, Not Learn from Them!

In Los Angeles, the automobile town par excellence, Barbara Ward found that 60 to 70 per cent of the space is devoted to cars (streets, parking, and freeways). . . . Parks, sidewalks, everything goes to the automobile. E. T. Hall, *The Hidden Dimension*

The decision to abandon the lower Manhattan throughway on August 22, 1969, came after eight or nine years of fervid obstruction by citizens concerned to preserve human scale in a superhuman environment. It was the same with the killing of the Spadina Expressway in Toronto. The city is a place for the heightening of human awareness by providing the greatest possible range and diversity of space for dialogue. A large real estate operator in Toronto recently abandoned an empire built up during a lifetime of exploiting city spaces by increasing density. The turning point came for him when a group of hippies began to camp and sprawl in a parking lot that belonged to him. They explained, "We can find no place to sit in Toronto." It struck him that everything going on in the "exciting city," to which he had contributed much impetus, was in direct conflict with any

possibility of ordinary human community or enjoyment. From that moment, he began a program of spreading enlightened alarm with the hope of
retaining some of the residual qualities of a modest nineteenth-century provincial capital.

3

Petrifying

Petrified Forest of High-rise Homogenization

The technocrats persist in their strategy of homogenization, which fosters a filling-in of all the older "spaces" of the city with massive structures, obliterating all intervals of human scale and their Victorian vestiges. It kills community.

Car-apace Wedded to Wired City Creates Police State as Work of Art

Each human being creates a kind of "space bubble" that he carries with him as his osmic mask. This BO as a hidden chemical vesture is enormously enhanced by the private motorcar. It turns each of us into a kind of beetle with a steel carapace, or cover. Our attachment to this armor may well become more intense with crowding and noise, and may be one of the reasons for the common abhorrence of public transit.

Those who saw the movie Z will have noticed how a quite ordinary bureaucracy of elected functionaries is transformed into a police state through the speeding-up of old bureaucratic functions by telephone and intercom.

One of the prices we pay for our coexistence with the motorcar in large cities is the increasing need for an ever-larger police force to maintain traffic mobility. The same process of electric speed of the new environment, felt in our schools, causes them to appear to the young as intolerable "police states," in which everybody is kept "under surveillance" and everything is kept moving by the specialized packaging and the universal presence of functionaries. *The mere existence of the "police state" anywhere is the sure sign of old arrangements being propped up by newer forms that have already rendered the older forms irrevelant.*

4

Fragmenting

Gottmann's megalopolis extends the "asphalt jungle" to an urban strip. As an alternative, the pseudoquality of the Garden City of Ebenezer Howard is that it is all *figure* minus *ground*. In neither is there the proportion of town and country to create the effect of either one. The Garden City is low-level homogenization of space and sensory life. The megalopolis is the high-rise level of homogenization and intense specialism of sensory life. Both kinds of homogenized space drive young and old on inner trips of flat despair. William Empson's sonnet opening: "Law makes long spokes of the short stakes of men" reminds that the wild-cat speculator can claim new ground even in the old urban settlement.

INsight and UNsight

The ultimate in inability to approach city problems is illustrated by an article in *The Economist* titled "The Cities That Came Too Soon" (December 6, 1969). The reader is encouraged to hasten into the depths of editorial analysis by this intriguing title, but may be a bit dashed to find that the writers mean that we have built the cities before we knew what we were doing. The citizens are thus like people who are stupid enough to get cancer or bubonic plague before the cure has been discovered. William Cobbett, at the beginning of the nineteenth century, saw wee London as the "Great Wen," or cancer. Now, in 1969, *The Economist* belatedly concedes the case to Cobbett: URBAN GROWTH HAS BECOME PATHOLOGICAL.

What hope is there for controlling really terrifying innovations like TV and the extensions of our nervous systems if it takes centuries to notice the discommodity of mere bricks and mortar and the internal combustion engine? *The Economist* displays a fatal disproportion between *cognition* and *recognition*. Colonel Blimp joins hands across the sea with Al Capp's General Bullmoose in this incisive observation: "One would not confidently offer Tokyo or New York or even London as models of urbanity." This resonates with the anguished diffidence of the Elizabethan courtier, who, upon breaking wind in the presence of the Queen, uttered, "*Sic transit gloria mundi*," and retired to a Trappist monastery for life.

Survival of the Unfitted as Center of Urbanity

Toronto has advantages that are becoming appreciated in the twentieth century, especially in those metropolitan areas of the United States that destroyed their similar assets decades since. Cleveland, Detroit, Philadelphia, Los Angeles, Pittsburgh, Chicago, Newark, St. Louis, and many others scrapped in the railway age what in Toronto had survived into the electric age.

Don't Expedite: Impede

(A formula for ending auto intoxication)

Douglas Fullerton has the imagination to spot the solution *in* the problem of "Monoxide Manor" itself:

> The man appointed by Prime Minister Pierre Elliott Trudeau last year to make Ottawa a capital to be proud of has declared war on the automobile.
>
> Douglas Fullerton, an angry economist who is chairman of the National Capital Commission, is leading his forces into battle with cries of "impede traffic, don't expedite it."
>
> Fullerton says old streets should be blocked off from the main thoroughfares—creating a maze of cul de sacs which would discourage motorists.   Toronto *Star*, February 2, 1970

City planners seem to be incapable of understanding *figure-ground* relationships. They want uniformity. Everything must become *figure*, or everything must become *ground*. The interface or interplay of *figure* and *ground* necessary to community, or social dialogue and diversity, are alien to their uniform concepts and blueprints. They are *motivated somnambulists* for whom transit is a way of life and for whom our servants, the car and truck, are left to do our "living" for us.

These planners are in effect designers of "cement kimonos," or a mob of morticians. In the information age the planners have managed to achieve a monopoly of misallocated misinformation.

The huge advantage of Canada in general is its backwardness—its inadvertent retention of human scale in its urban environments. In the nineteenth century it did not commit very much of its space or working life to the fragmented assembly-line processes that were frantically pursued in more advanced areas in England and in the United States.

5

~~✦~~

Diversifying

Enrichment Through Diversity

While the TV generation feels alienated from the "hardware" cities built
on the centralist patterns of steamboats and steam railways, the most "advanced" planners remain locked into these forms. The recent pronounce-
ments of Lewis Mumford (*The Urban Prospect*) show that he still sees
core cities surrounded by satellites as an ideal regional pattern.

Today, in the jet age, every "city" in the world is a suburban "satellite"
to every other city. The only possible regional environment for existing or
prospective cities, large or small, is the planet itself.

Global Caravansary

The suburban or satellite city created by the decentralizing power of that
private "space bubble," the *auto*mobile, now must yield to "instant" mobile cities such as the Woodstock and Mariposa festivals or the "disposable" cities we associate with World's Fairs since 1851. Airports and trailer
parks are faint intimations of the return of nomadic communities. Business
is conducted in restaurants and recreation spots around the world. In the
information age of the "magnetic city" all "hardware" city forms are obsolescent and tend toward the status of tourist attractions and museums. The
old "hardware" form is made vivid by the new "software" frame, or information surround. What had been *ground* becomes *figure* in a new *figure-
ground* relationship.

Hollywood's Lesson for Town Planners: The Disposable City

Disneyland or Paramount Studios or Universal City in Hollywood are
only precursors of a new type of "disposable city" made by technology. The
movie as art form comprehended all times and cultures. Since the jet has
given swift access to the entire planet as city, the movie has also shifted to
the globe as movie set. In a word, cities can survive new technological innovations only as centers of nostalgia and *tourisme*. Hollywood revealed the
city as an Arabian Nights entertainment. Le Corbusier saw the house as a
"machine for living in," and we now experience the city as a kind of flying
machine for living in. The city can be tailored to the size and needs of any
kind of group. It can be donned or doffed like clothing. Hollywood taught
us how to make disposable cities to order.

FALLACIES OF MISPLACED CONCRETENESS

Hollywood's High-rise Cemeteries: Going Halfway to Meet Your Maker!

WELFARE REPORT SAYS CANADA LACKS FACILITIES
FOR YOUNG WANDERERS

Seventeen-year-old Mary had been travelling for three months, and expected to stay on the road for another two years because she enjoys it.   Toronto *Globe and Mail*, March 9, 1970

The twentieth-century TV generation has no interest in nineteenth-century "hardware" cities at all. The kids are not beguiled by the fallacy of "misplaced concreteness" or high-rise. They prefer the instant cities of sound-light shows or large-scale imagery. As far as the old industrial establishment in general is concerned, they see it merely as a jumping-off place. So do many top executives. They are dropouts.

Mile-high Sky-rise: Technical Solution Escalates Land-Rent-Tax "Viscous Circul" into Dead End

New bricks and mortar high-rise, relics of the nineteenth century, and "Elijah" Otis, produce "instant slums," a new dimension of disservice environment on the very edge of a new frontier, the end of "real" estate. With computers we reach again toward "urbanity" through the end of "steel" by plunging into Echoland and ecology.

Planners of the Future: Short-order Chefs for Every Taste

The housing and city styles of the immediate future will be as flexible and as programmed to taste as cassettes. This trend became visible with the great World Exposition of 1851 and its Crystal Palace. These "instant" festival cities were programmed in every respect. Today, as work becomes play through depth involvement in knowledge, only festival cities will be meaningful to the new citizen of the global theater. Spaceship Earth will demand a perpetual renewal of repertory for its Phoenix Playhouse.

The magnetic city is our own nervous system put outside as an environment of information. This gesture of self-awareness scoffs at all the previous dimensions of "hardware" planning and "hardware" scale. When a child in a playpen can have access to universal knowledge and experience, the scale of the largest city or building in the world is puny and meaningless. The TV set is a kind of restoration of the reading carrel of the ancient scholar, a little Echoland in which all dimensions of word and being resonate. Under instant conditions, megalopolis is a bad joke, a garbage dump that is useful only as a resource for designing magnetic cities.

6

Retrieving

Outermost Sub-urbia Reserved for "Muddle Crass" While Artist Retrieves Slum as "La Bohème"

We do not allow people to walk; we "transport" them.
C. A. Doxiadis, *Science*, October 18, 1968

In early movie days we created "mob scenes" by running a dozen people in a figure 8.   Gilbert Seldes in a remark to Marshall McLuhan

What will threaten us in advance of overpopulation is crowding. . . . Scientists believe it lies at the root of sickness, crime and violence. . . .
Bernard Asbell, *THINK*, July-August, 1969

The population of the world could all stand together on the Isle of Wight.   Denis B. Jackson, *The Exam Secret*

DONE IN BY HIGH-RISE

The exclusive module of mini-art for the many.

The end of urbanity and horizontal neighborhood, by courtesy of "ELIJAH" OTIS Space Chariot

High-rise as vestibule for new Cave Man.

The laundromats are the residual quest for community.

The Peregrine Pickle of twentieth-century man: from castle to coffin and from mansion to mews, to ultimate goal—hotel hermit.

Why should discarnate man go to work when work can come to him?

RETURN TO STONEAGE

Chapter 3

Households to World Shopping Centers:
The Real McCoy and Genuine Fakes

Start with the other man's ignorance if you would acquire his knowledge swiftly.   Samuel Taylor Coleridge

I have never yet been afraid of any men, who have a set place in the middle of their city, where they come together to cheat each other and to forswear themselves.   Cyrus the Great, King of Kings

While visiting Babylon during the years 470–460 B.C., Herodotus noted the absence in Babylonia of the troublesome food market of his native Greece. The Babylonians practiced risk-free forms of trading, directly controlled by the palace bureaucracy. Cyrus tolerated the market as a political sideshow to placate the foreigners who crossed back and forth between the Eastern and Western worlds, between his Asian territory and Greece. When markets were cutting a new *figure* in the communal scene, Aristotle discovered the *ground* rules of the economy.

Peter Drucker is quite prepared to grant a quantitative priority to the new knowledge industries of our time without pursuing any of the significance or consequences of these industries as they have reshaped the goals of the Establishment of the Western world. Drucker is aware that we live in an *Age of Discontinuity*, but he does not look into the *effects* of electric speed in substituting resonant intervals for the continual hang-ups and the hierarchies of power, both in the economy and Western civilization at large. He does not see, even quantitatively, that as the hidden *ground* has shifted from "hardware" markets to "software" information flow, it has reversed the old assumptions of order and power. For if knowledge is power, consider the invincible weapon of organized ignorance resulting therefrom. THE IGNORANCE OF HOW TO USE NEW KNOWLEDGE STOCKPILES EXPONENTIALLY.

1

Make-for-All

PRODUCTION FOR USE AND EXCHANGE

Karl Polanyi devotes Chapter 5 of *Primitive, Archaic, and Modern Economies* to "Aristotle's Discovery of the Economy." Aristotle's nineteenth-century editor, Benjamin Jowett, "with the full-blown specimen before him, overlooked its existence." Amidst the new tribal features of the twentieth century, Karl Polanyi could recognize the genius of Aristotle in first discerning the structure and dynamics of an economy before it had got under way. It needed the clash of *two* worlds to see one. Even today, some archaeologists and Orientalists assume that markets existed in archaic societies, *i.e.*, production for exchange rather than for use. In another work, *The Great Transformation*, Polanyi proceeds this way:

> Aristotle insists on production for use as against production for gain as the essence of householding proper; yet accessory production for the market need not, he argues, destroy the self-sufficiency of the household as long as the cash crop would also otherwise be raised on the farm for sustenance, as cattle or grain; the sale of the surpluses need not destroy the basis of householding.

Aristotle also stood on the frontier between two worlds. The one was oriented toward production for the use of a complex household or clan; the other was newly ready to accept production for a market conducted by those outside the household group.

Aristotle saw the fragmenting threat to household unity and the common good in the readiness for exchange that did not serve community needs:

> The rate of exchange must be such as to maintain the community. Again, not the interests of the individuals, but those of the community were the governing principle. The skills of persons of different status had to be exchanged at a rate proportionate to the status of each; the builder's performance exchanged against many times the cobbler's performance; unless this was so, reciprocity was infringed and the community would not hold.
>
> Karl Polanyi, *Primitive, Archaic, and Modern Economies*

Polanyi makes clear why Aristotle adhered rigorously to the communal vision of tribal society even on the threshold of the crack-up into civilized specialism of goals.

In Money and Currency, Ornament Preceded Use

The magical and talismanic functions of ornamental and magical medals long preceded their specialist functions in exchange. "The pearl of great price" was "priceless" because unmatchable in its direct efficacy in the world of ESP-rit. It seemed natural during the innovational period of currency to give all your treasures for the *one*. The qualitative effect remained superior to the quantitative heap of treasure. In our own time, the bizarre phrase "Diamonds are a girl's best friend" still resonates with some of the primitive magic.

The old *Britannica* (eleventh edition) leads off on the matter of coins ("Numismatics") by indicating that the Greeks of the seventh century B.C. were the instigators of repeatable uniform coinage for exchange purposes. Nobody has tried to assess the ways in which this breakthrough, created by the market pressures, may have prepared the ground for the unique form of the Greek phonetic alphabet.

If gunpowder and printing undermined the medieval world of troubadours and chivalry, coinage and alphabet subverted the Greek quest for the Good and the Beautiful.

Like All Utopias, the Vision of Plato's "Republic" Mirrors a Departed World

As the Greeks entered on the individualist quest for the *kala kai agatha* (the beautiful and the good), they isolated the existence of the scarcity principle, both psychic and economic, both the inner and the outer, both "software" and "hardware." It was a discovery that could only have occurred at the time that Eric Havelock has carefully designated in his *Preface to Plato*.

How Did the Greeks Ever Wake Up?

While all other societies persisted in the tribal or communal dream of corporate unity, the Greeks took a second look. Havelock notes: "The fundamental answer must lie in the changing technology of communication." The unique innovation of the phonetic alphabet released the Greeks from the universal acoustic spell of tribal societies. Visual detachment via the written page also gave the power of the second look—the moment of recognition. This broke people out of the bondage of the uncritical and emotionally involved life. It also fostered the cult of private competition and individual emulation in sports and politics. The quest for private power came quickly.

Once the Greeks transcended barter, as they had transcended tribalism, "money" became an indispensable commodity for the measurement of values. This generated the demand for a uniform and repeatable coinage to accelerate transactions. The phonetic alphabet of the Greeks was the only instrument of writing by which *any* oral language could be translated into visual Greek. Inherent in this instrument of cultural exchange lay the great Greco-Roman ground for an imperial economy with a uniform bureaucracy and coinage. The process got mythic capsule form:

King Cadmus Sowed the Dragon's Teeth
and They Sprang Up Armed Men

The letters of the alphabet are an extremely aggressive extension of the body. Only teeth, in their uniformity and lineality, are comparable to the nature of alphabetic letters. These uniform letters, when committed to parchment or paper, permitted the organization of force at a distance, namely mobile, military bureaucracies. These mobile structures by-passed the old priestly bureaucracies of the great temples of Egypt and Babylon.

It is significant that the uniform and repeatable coinage created for the new markets predated the rise of the military bureaucracies with power to levy tribute on subject populations. Trade preceded literacy.

2

Money-for-All

Money and Writing as In-vestment

One of the major modes of clothing that Joyce assigns to his Second Thunder in *Finnegans Wake* includes money and writing. No commercial empire has a proper base without these means of organizing human transactions. Money for the market and writing for the record. Money as a universal and uniform measure of human services enormously accelerates "production" for exchange, generating still more money. Nothing comparable to a uniform currency had occurred in social clothing or public-service vesture until Gutenberg. By translating the handicraft of the scribe into the uniform, repeatable character of movable types, Gutenberg was able to speed up written transaction and information retrieval in the same degree that a uniform currency had been able to do for the commercial world earlier. That is, the social garment of a uniform currency represents uniform, marketable, and portable packages of information. These are the indispensable building blocks of a market economy.

"Usura" the Booby Trap of the Ancient and Medieval Worlds

"From tribal brotherhood to universal otherhood."
Benjamin Nelson, *Idea of Usury*

Money, like literacy, created huge, hidden service environments that speeded wealth making far beyond the agrarian processes of nature. Looking only at the visible "hardware" of money, all could agree with Aristotle that "money does not breed." Ironically, the *average* man who got hung up in this catch phrase refers to the *averagium*—"the day's work which was done by tenant with beasts of burden." As always, men see the *figure* more readily than its *ground*, just as they hear tunes more clearly than background music.

Jews Get Boot While Christians Grab Loot

While *usura*, or money interest, was ig-noble, the *averagium* of compulsory toil was enforced as the NOB's due. Anybody could observe the sweating of men and animals as productive and *natural*. The much greater productivity of the total new service environments created by the human artifacts of money and writing remained unacknowledged.

Royal Fisc-for-All Before Queensberry's Ground Rules

All environmental services represent social clothing: the King's English, and the King's purse (or "fisc"). In Cyril Tourneur's *The Revenger's Tragedy*, Vendice, the "revenger" dropout type of the Elizabethan age, meditates with the skull of his murdered mistress in hand:

> The very same.
> And now methinks I could e'en chide myself
> For doating on her beauty, though her death
> Shall be revenged after no common action.
> Does the silkworm expend her yellow labours
> For thee? For thee does she undo herself?
> Are lordships sold to maintain ladyships,
> For the poor benefit of a bewildering minute?
> Why does yon fellow falsify highways,
> And put his life between the judge's lips,
> To refine such a thing—keeps horse and men
> To beat their valours for her?
> Surely we are all mad people, and they
> Whom we think are, are not: we mistake those;
> 'Tis we are mad in sense, they but in clothes.

The playwright here alludes to the various public services of the kingdom as perverted by lust "for the poor benefit of a bewildering minute." "Yon fellow" is the lust-driven villain and intriguer who corrupts every phase of the community. Vendice, staring at the painted skull, starts with the silkworm as the center of the luxury textile industries. The silkworm undoes itself in order to clothe women to their undoing. Next, the feudal lordship, with its palatial "clothing," is destroyed to create a lady of the highest fashion, who sells her body at a very high price for a moment of lust. Next, the villain is observed "falsifying highways" in order to achieve his ends. This alludes to the abuse of both money and public roads to enforce his private purpose. This violence leads to a perversion of justice, since it puts his life in jeopardy of the law, which must be twisted to accommodate his immoralities—all to "refine" or glamorize a wench. The monetary play of words between "falsify" (coinage) and "refine" (metals were commonly debased, as with the mistress) leads to the final corruption of the entire chivalric order: "Keeps horse and men to beat their valours for her." "Beat," pronounced *bate* or *bait*, links both the lures and the abating of honor.

In a word, it was natural for Elizabethans and Jacobeans to regard their society as a web of interwoven patterns and textures. Once more today, in the simultaneous awareness of the citizens of Echoland, nothing is irrelevant and nothing can be ignored. A totally new kind of social harmony becomes a universal demand, beyond the dreams of the age of chivalry.

"Hardware" Repetition as the First Power Binge Harbinger

The primitive economy is one in which the service environment generates wealth at the seasonal cyclic rhythm. When major human inventions are brought into play, the natural "rim spin" of change and wealth making is speeded up. We have discovered how markets are formed by new aids such as coinage and writing, which both store and exchange services much more rapidly than direct barter can do. The same technologies can accelerate or retard economic action.

Technical innovations, like coinage, can intrude suddenly into cultures where they are unknown. This is a pattern of change in which a technological figure appears in a radically new ground. When tribal folk first see several printed copies of the same book they are astonished to discover that each is a duplicate of the other. It is this kind of shock that sent the Japanese on their first duplication binges decades ago. Duplication yields sudden quantitative power.

Stoned Money
Sterling Character

W. Furness tells the story of a man who had traded all his personal treasures for a single "money stone" at some faraway island. Returning home, he ran into a storm. His boat sank, and the "stone" went with it. He was rescued by fellow islanders, who afterward treated him as a wealthy man, for they knew where the stone was. It became his credit.

Brazen Character

In the days of the Great Depression, Ivar Kruger, the "Swedish Match King," bolstered his tottering conglomerate empire by displaying his collateral of "gold bricks" as security for loans. When it became his discredit, there was no one to save him.

To Every Man a Penny

It is uniformity that creates the means of measuring human services as well as the means of storing and retrieving human services. No merely tribal society could conceive the scale of such arrangements. Even the scriptural parable of the workers in the vineyard threatened the whole plan of the early money economy, when those who had worked for only an hour in the vineyard received the same pay as those who had worked all day. As in "primitive communism," money ceases to be a measure in this parable. Money has here made a claim on realms other than the economic one.

In today's vast superfluity, niggardly Malthusian measurement and calculation are becoming inadequate. The American colonies introduced the latest European technology into a vast natural environment. The Gutenberg technique of mechanizing handicrafts by minute fragmentation of "time and motion" became the ground plan of the entire American "experiment in democracy." Exactly repeatable tasks enabled the least skilled workers to get jobs at once. The Gutenberg principle of mechanization by fragmentation and specialism was extended as much to the Constitution as the ballot box and the box office. This principle was introduced equally into education and into the market place.*

BENJAMIN FRANKLIN'S INFALLIBLE TECHNIQUE FOR ACHIEVING MORAL PERFECTION WAS TO COUNT YOUR VICES AND ELIMINATE THEM ONE AT A TIME TILL SANCTITY WAS ACHIEVED.

Gutenberg created a major frontier in America by setting up a continental interface between the preliterate and the civilized or visually specialized man. The celebrated study (1890) of Frederick J. Turner concerns

THE SIGNIFICANCE OF THE FRONTIER IN AMERICAN HISTORY.

His theme is that the interfaces and frontiers of European culture are as innumerable as historic, set up among dense populations with fortified boundary lines. In America, on the contrary, the most advanced technology was set against the edges of free or open land with a population density of two or three to the square mile. The historical and legal commitments were nonexistent. There was no backlog of traditional ways and means to stall the instant application of the latest technologies of Europe. Just as ancient Europe had been oblivious to the interplay between the old agrarian technologies and the hidden service environments of the new coinage and literacy, Turner was unaware of the hidden power of the Gutenberg technology to process the wilderness at high speed. Tocqueville, an outsider, was better able to observe this unique process.

The Virginian by Owen Wister is one of the first Westerns. It has a romantic theme perpetuated today by the tourist industry, by horse operas and their numerous offspring: the wilderness masters the colonist; it finds him a European in dress, industries, tools, modes of travel, and thought; it takes him from the railroad car and puts him in the birch canoe.

The Image: Or, What Happened to the American Dream by Daniel J. Boorstin bemoans the contemporary reversal of the Turner frontier theme. At high speeds of communication, frontiers disappear along with the distant horizon and the open road. The movie *True Grit*, with John Wayne in a parody of his "rugged-individual" role, presents the collapse of the frontier as a way of life. The continuing appeal of the Western and the frontier in pictures like *Midnight Cowboy*, *Easy Rider*, and *Alice's Restaurant* has varied roots. The frontier, with its stark interface of contrasted ways of life,

* In his classic *Empire and Communications*, Harold Innis traces the effects of communciation media on human organization.

the simple and the complex, the virtuous and the corrupt, urban and rural —such a frontier, its image borrowed from nineteenth-century America, now portrays a world situation. Today, movies in backward countries create "cargo cults" of natives dreaming of floods of consumer goods. Radio moves directly into tribal territories of the Middle East or the Pacific Islands. "The Forsyte Saga" from the BBC studios stops work in factories of the U.S.S.R. The "Saga" image of the acme of these nineteenth-century literati stirs great Russia with the stylized elegance of a departed bourgeosie. The Russians, who now aspire to appear like Yankees of yesteryear, secretly yearn for the fleshpots and culture of Bloomsbury.

The Planet Has Become a Single Household with Many Monitors and Conflicting Programs

The rigid boundaries of sovereign states created by the Gutenberg hardware remain as archaeological relics.

Harold Innis noted that Canada had gone from colony to nation to colony in a decade. It had become a DEW line for the United States instead of being a flying buttress of the British Empire. What Innis failed to note was that the United States itself had gone from archaic wilderness to literate centralized nation to neotribalism in a century.

The TV generation has voted unanimously for a return to archaic tribalism. The hippie dreams are being realized in the reawakening of the ethnic memories and masks of energy organization in the North American Indian. For masks and costumes, like names, are vortices of power.

Tickling Commodity the Bias of the World

When markets were new, Cyrus, King of Kings, cynically and shrewdly noted that the money game was one of the most diverting and harmless ways of using up human energies and malice. In the Renaissance the Gutenberg technology had produced the first uniform and repeatable product matching money itself. The resulting impetus to trade was great. Trade became a new "hardware" frontier in direct conflict with the old social structure of the intangible human loyalties of the feudal system. Most of Shakespeare's dramas take place on this frontier between the Machiavellian figure of the individual careerist and the traditional ground of corporate loyalties. The interface of the two worlds is quite explicit in his early play *King John*.

> Bartering his soul for more than it's worth.
>> Jonathan Swift

Shakespeare's *King John* has a natural subplot of St. Joan. There is a parallel relation of *figure* and *ground* in riches and beggary and war and peace. Commodity, "the bias of the world," is counterpointed against religion: "Gain, be my lord, for I will worship Thee!"

That broker, that still breaks the pate of faith,
That daily break-vow, he that wins of all,
Of kings, of beggars, old men, young men, maids,
Who having no external thing to lose
But the word "maid," cheats the poor maid of that,
That smooth-fac'd gentleman, tickling Commodity,
Commodity, the bias of the world;
The world, who of itself is peized well,
Made to run even upon even ground,
Till this advantage, this vile-drawing bias,
This sway of motion, this Commodity,
Makes it take head from all indifferency,
From all direction, purpose, course, intent:
And this same bias, this Commodity,
This bawd, this broker, this all-changing word,
Clapp'd on the outward eye of fickle France,
Hath drawn him from his own determin'd aid,
From a resolv'd and honourable war,
To a most base and vile-concluded peace.
And why rail I on this Commodity?
But for because he hath not woo'd me yet.
Not that I have the power to clutch my hand
When his fair angels would salute my palm;
But for my hand, as unattempted yet,
Like a poor beggar, raileth on the rich.
Well, whiles I am a beggar, I will rail,
And say there is no sin but to be rich;
And being rich, my virtue then shall be
To say there is no vice but beggary.
Since kings break faith upon Commodity,
Gain, be my lord, for I will worship thee!

Coin and cash had been *figure*. With Gutenberg scale and speed-up, money underwent a metamorphosis from mere medium to "capital." A new environmental *ground* processes everything in its own image while remaining hidden. "The Emperor's New Clothes" are always invisible.

MARKET HOMOGENIZATION AS NINETEENTH-CENTURY NOVELTY

Many people in the computer age are still inclined to consider the nineteenth-century industrial world as a "normal economy," just as they tend to regard the "nuclear family" of mom, pop, and the kids as the "normal family." In fact, both these modes of production and reproduction were the great innovations of the nineteenth century. On the one hand, the new factories, with their wide range of uniform and repeatable commodities, depended on new transportation systems for both supplying the raw materials and dispersing the finished products. On the other hand, these industrial novelties transformed every facet of the domestic, educational, and political establishments. Free education, universal suffrage, and the rise of a vast consumer public provided the uniform *ground* for industrial entrepreneurs. Thomas Carlyle's *Past and Present* (1843) marks the new frontier by a utopian retrospect of the organization and household management of a medieval monastery. On the frontier of a world of extreme individualism Carlyle studied the communal values and the satisfactions derived from the exercise of craft skills. His work marks a social watershed as clearly as Shakespeare had in *King John*.

Chafing at the Bit to Get Back to the Eighteenth Century

Elaborate filing systems are made possible by writing and secretaries. The Pentagon is the biggest filing cabinet in the world.

The service environments of technological clothing created by the written word in the area of social legislation and jurisprudence constitute the biggest of all hidden environments. These vast empires of services and disservices generate massive "back spins" to slow down the opportunist energies of entrepreneurs and confidence men. When this structure of massive inertia encounters a driving entrepreneurial force, the rending of social attire and the stripping of social garments is called "revolution." One gets an inkling of this process in the current encounter between the tribal hang-up of the mini-skirt, and the countervailing pull on the hemline by the panicky textile industries and their detainers, the fashionmongers. Totally concealed from this darkling clash of ignorant armies are the TV causes that drive skirts on high.

Equally in the dark about the filing cabinets in the political sky is the legal establishment. The laws for the "separation of powers," by which eighteenth-century wisdom contrived to contain the surviving progeny of the feudal system, were soon set to work to curtail the rampaging energies of the robber barons born of steam and steel.

Incongruously, the pattern adopted by the new technological imperialism was that of hard paternalism. New technological environments are commonly cast in the molds of the preceding technology out of the sheer unawareness of their designers. In the case of the unprecedented power and speed of steel and steam there was no relevant managerial model to offset the sudden retrieval of medieval and Oriental forms. Nothing was less foreseen than the upsurge of feudalism in art and society in the wake of mechanical industry. This event was classified as "reactionary" and "escapist" and "aesthetish" and "decadent" and "pre-Raphaelite." This pattern of incongruity had occurred with Gutenberg revival of antiquity, as it is now occurring with the electric revival of primitive occultism.*

* The process is the subject of *From Cliché to Archetype* by Marshall McLuhan and Wilfred Watson.

3

Free-for-All

THE UNDERTAKER RETRIEVED: THE GRASS ALWAYS LOOKS GREENER ON THE OTHER GUY!

Historically, two essentially different forms of market organization had proceeded from the diverse technologies of money and writing. Both are now being scrapped by the speed-up of credit and "data-banking" services. The type of management favored by the accelerated "spin" of money is entrepreneurial. The money economy is venture-oriented. It demands quick turnover. It created the "South Sea Bubble" of the eighteenth-century. At that time, the word "undertaker" was a term applied to entrepreneurs who began and contracted for large enterprises. Building contractors were the men who possessed the horses and wagons and materials needed for human burial. The term "undertaker" is a late derivative of this entrepreneurial service. It reached its natural conclusion by becoming a "fun thing" in the popular radio show of some years ago: "Digby O'Dell the Cheerful Undertaker."

For the connoisseur of pop macabre, there is the great trade journal *Casket and Sunnyside*, with its ads:

UNLESS YOU'VE USED OUR EMBALMING FLUID YOU AIN'T LIVED
DRIVE CAREFULLY—WE CAN WAIT

In contrast to the ebullience and euphoria of the mortician is the funereal dead pan of "the spirit of enterprise" in a book like *The American Business Creed*, prepared for the Harvard University Press by Seymour Harris and others. Page 1 opens with slogans of the American business community:

WHY YOU CANNOT GET AHEAD LIKE YOUR FATHER DID
SURE AMERICA'S GOING AHEAD IF WE ALL PULL TOGETHER
WE CAN'T LEGISLATE HAPPINESS

Marxism provides the ideal counterenvironment for the business world, bringing out its patterns and contours in strong relief: "First, it is a 'foreign ideology' . . . a polar ideology to the business creed . . . but the part it assigns to the businessman . . . is diametrically opposed."

A Dialectical Punching Bag

Provided with this ideal means for the daily workout, the capitalist toiler in his lonely penthouse can keep in trim for cracking all eggheads. The "egghead" type of intellectual authority is frequently challenged in the business creed, where it is claimed that "the businessman's practical wisdom is superior to the academician's unworldly theorizing." And so it went until the computer reversed the priorities of experience and knowledge.

The great advantage that the perceptive businessman enjoys over the conventional academic is his recognition of at least some consequences of innovation. The business climate changes at once when you step into the worlds of John Kenneth Galbraith and Peter Drucker. In *The New Industrial State* Galbraith's formula for the new entrepreneurship is the security of the government contract. Gone is the primacy of the buyer and the entrepreneurial producer, guided by the "invisible hand" of "supply and demand": ". . . the great producing organization which reaches forward to control the markets that it is presumed to serve and, beyond, to bend the customer to its needs.

The Mafia Goes Soft: I Can Get It for You Wholesale Have Paid Off Government; My Conscience Is Clear

Time was when the Las Vegas roulette defaulter who was short a few grand might expect a visit from the strong-arm boys. Today, as gambling props up the Establishment, it is the collection agency that calls on the delinquent. No arms are broken, but the prospect of the immediate "rub-out" of his credit image is more effective. At today's tempo, information replaces the big bank roll. Our time of transition from the old industrial "hardware" through the age of "software" image merchantry is bridged by the "organization of crime." As the old order goes under, only an unlicensed group of pirates can exploit the innovational technologies that have undermined the Establishment. As literate, legal, civilized codes crack under the strain of instant, oral, and electric speeds of transaction, enter the usurpers. Such is the theme of Donald R. Cressey's *Theft of a Nation*.

Cressey hasn't a clue about *why* this "Mafia" take-over is occurring on a global scale. The very title of his book, in stressing "Nation," indicates his failure to recognize the scale and causes of this technological revolution. The paradox presented by Cressey, *i.e.*, that *organized* crime ceases to be criminal because it creates new order, is another example of the solution always lurking in the heart of the problem.

The Nineteenth-Century Crowd of Notable Nobodies

The ground has changed drastically at present. The computer is a portent of the return to Carlyle's medieval ideal of the cottage economy, when large enterprises can be run from a kitchen, as it were.

The Piranhas Swallow the Whales: When the Bark Is Gone and the Dentures Remain

By living electrically and doing everything at home, the Babes in the Woodwork terminate Big Business.

Homage to homogeneity is fading fast. Just when mass production reaches its peak in the Western world, the marriage of the computer with automation promises the reproduction of anything that can be specified.

Levity the Hidden Hand
Gravity: A Mysterious Carriage of the Body to Conceal the Defects of the Mind

Just as Newton's gravity was the invisible or "hidden hand" that guided the stars in their courses, so for the new economists the invisible and all-grasping hand of "self-interest" ensured a firm basis of order amidst the anarchy of human whims and passions.

> We all bear the misfortunes of others with Christian fortitude.
> Jonathan Swift

Adam Smith's optimism was rooted in his preference for the new mechanical speed-up that seemed to end all former social and natural barriers. Thomas Malthus (1766–1834), who has been called "the classical pessimist," was obsessed with the grim theme that population growth always exceeded the power of Nature to feed hungry mouths. His dismal economics may well have created a moral beachhead for Darwinian and Spencerian "Nature red in tooth and claw." The struggle for survival produced a new elite of top dogs whose energies entitled them to the fruits of survival.

Dead Reckoning or the Laws of Inhuman Nature

David Ricardo's "iron law of wages" is an echo of Malthus to the effect that "real wages" could not rise above the level of subsistence. Such a rise would disrupt the natural "law of supply and demand" that governed the market place. An increase in real wages would create a population explosion, resulting in the depression of wages below the subsistence level. Death would restore the balance of Nature.

Clearly, the new market as "natural" social ground had transformed the traditional spiritual courts of natural law into marketable commodities.

Unassailable Harmonies of the Natural Order

The equilibrium economics of Adam Smith (1723–1790), like the Nature theories of the physiocrats, sprang from the Newtonian clockwork of the cosmos. Adam Smith's idea of free trade brought the mechanisms of the market place into rapport with the unassailable harmonies of the natural order.

The political theories of the division of powers as a means of equilibrium, via checks and balances, was in some minds confused with the *laissez-faire* doctrines of the physiocrats.

Ring In the Old and Wring Out the New

"Gresham's law" (discovered by Oresme and Copernicus) that bad money drives good money out of circulation gets its plenary statement in Shakespeare's passage on the all-transforming power of *commodity*, already cited from *King John*.

Old Nonconformists Discover Power of New Conformity: "Le Grand Prix Unique"

Until Gutenberg created the first form of uniform commodity, all marketing was horse trading and haggling. The buying and selling of manuscript books, like modern art dealing, relied on the unique product pattern. Uniform prices could only be imposed by royal fiat until the Quakers discovered the economic advantage of "the just or uniform price." The effect of uniformity is over-all acceleration of "turnover," which revealed a new source of wealth. Complementary to this process of pricing is competition that drives people and things alike toward uniformity. This created "the world of fashion" in consumer goods. As a recent ad put it:

IMITATION: THE SINCEREST FORM OF BATTERY.

High speed of turnover replaced high markup of prices as a new source of wealth. It was the first economic process to involve everybody on the same basis.

Mass Production Produced the Masses

Commodity as the basis of the new market, with its innovation of repeatable products and uniform prices, was a hidden cultural environment in the sixteenth century. It remained hidden until the nineteenth century applied steam power to speed up the process. Adam Smith, in his narrative about the division of labor leading to the speed-up of the production of pins, was the first to make people aware of the means of applying the Gutenberg process to all manufacture whatever. Machiavelli had been two centuries ahead of Smith in noting the application of the Gutenberg process of divisibility to the manipulation of political power.

Reverberations of "Usura" in the Gutenberg Milieu: Discredit and Credit

Gresham's insight into fiscal dynamics was a faint anticipation of the apocalypse of public credit in the eighteenth century. Gresham retained a residue of the traditional doctrine of *usury*, which reigned from Aristotle to Gutenberg. The concept of usury was a fiscal dynamic rooted in the seasonal turnover of nature. With windmills and water wheels and horsepower augmenting man power, the West went on a rampage of applied knowledge and the acceleration of natural processes. The whole development ends with cybernation and instant electric circuits, just as Xerox and *reprography* end the reign of movable types and uniformity.

The hidden process, both in the usury hang-up and in Gresham's law, is the action of new service environments in eroding or diminishing the power of their predecessors. As the service environments "etherealize," in Toynbee's sense of doing more and more with less and less, money moved from hard cash to paper promises. As service environments become entirely man-made, Gresham's law vanishes. Good and bad coins alike become museum pieces. All old technologies become "art" forms. Even nature itself begins to become *found art* as early as the eighteenth-century cult of the picturesque. The popular romantic pastime of looking at the outer world as if it were a gallery of paintings has today become the acceptance of the planetary frame and surfaces, as architecture without architects. In the economic sphere cash becomes credit: Money becomes the poor man's credit card.

The Meek Take a Look at the Earth

Sitting in coal and surrounded by fish, otherwise ill-provided.
Anonymous eighteenth-century estimate of British prospects

Ricardo, contemplating the British predicament at the outset of the industrial revolution, would have been fascinated by the not dissimilar condition of the Japanese in the twentieth century. The Japanese, by knowledge and fish (though lacking minerals), were able to leap over much of the nineteenth century into the electric age.

The dichotomy between knowledge and experience, between "software" and "hardware," had earlier got pushed into high relief by the Gutenberg technology for mechanizing handicrafts through fragmentation and repetition. This split between mental and manual labor by intense specialism of both pushed economic and political organizations into new configurations.

Seven Pillows of Was-dom

Both economic and political power become matters for intense study and manipulation. As always, these innovations were accompanied by a passionate regard and esteem for a new class of "antiquities." The antiquary is always a prominent snob figure in every period of innovation. Today, horoscopes and heraldry and the occult in the West, and the I Ching and ancient therapies in the East, go with the advent of the computer. This is a "lock-in" process which insures that every new technological surround will translate or process all inputs (including the preceding environments) into the same kind of output. Thus in the nineteenth century all existing forms were processed mechanically, and Samuel Butler, the biologist, recognized the steam engine as the latest creation of the evolutionary process. On the other hand, the engineers of the Crystal Palace found their solutions for mechanical problems in the work of the landscape gardener Joseph Paxton.

Grit in the Gears

Adam Smith, the child of Newtonian cosmic mechanism, stressed "the invisible hand" as the economic equivalent of the hidden gravitational bond of the solar system. For the perfect working of such a system, "perfect competition" is essential. In the words of Paul A. Samuelson in *Economics*: "As soon as we have imperfect competition in the real world, we have left the Garden of Eden. . . ." It was one thing to speak of "perfect competition" in terms of Newtonian absolutes. But as soon as the workaday world came under economic scrutiny, economists were happy to settle for "active competition" and relatively "free markets."

The polluter of the purity of all classical economies is government interference. There is no question about why the business world feels enthusiasm for classical economics. We find in *The American Business Creed*: "Government, as it is seen in the business creed, is inherently evil." The sand in the oil turns out to be the serpent in the Garden of Eden, the destroyer of the best of all possible worlds.

Giants Before the Flood

(Recent sticker on small car: HELP STAMP OUT TALL DOGS)

Whenever one dips into Adam Smith, the reader feels he has touched the core of his theory. Smith observes that when an entrepreneur organizes his operation for maximum profit,

> he intends only his own gain, and he is in this, as in many other cases, led by an invisible hand to promote an end which is no part of his intention. . . . By pursuing his own interest, he frequently promotes that of society more effectually than when he really intends to promote it.

In this quotation from *The Wealth of Nations* (1776) Smith is paraphrasing Bernard Mandeville's *Fable of the Bees, or Private Vices, Publick*

Benefits (1714). It was fitting that the professor of moral philosophy at the University of Glasgow should have heeded Mandeville's moral paradox about the transformation of social disservices into unexpected services to mankind.

The Hidden Environment Behind the "Invisible Hand"

Whereas the age of Gutenberg had reeled backward in horror at the ruthless self-seeking egotism of the calculating careerist, by the eighteenth century these entrepreneurial success *figures* had become the base *ground* of the new social order. Moralists now lay waiting to transform these unprincipled individualists into social benefactors. Shakespeare's preference for the corporate medieval harmony, or social music, often led him to describe the new social types, as in *Troilus and Cressida*:

> Take the instant way;
> For honour travels in a strait so narrow,
> Where one but goes abreast: keep then the path;
> For emulation hath a thousand sons
> That one by one pursue: if you give way,
> Or hedge aside from the direct forthright,
> Like to an enter'd tide, they all rush by,
> And leave you hindmost;
> Or, like a gallant horse fall'n in first rank,
> Lie there for pavement to the abject rear,
> O'er-run and trampled on. . . .

As indicated by "take the instant way," Shakespeare saw these "upstart courtiers" as men out for "the fast buck" and devil take the hindmost. It was no mean accomplishment for Adam Smith to transform Mandeville's scornful satire about "private vices, publick benefits" into the all-encompassing and automatic care of the beneficent "invisible hand." That is, Smith saw that though

Hell Is Paved with Good Intentions, the Utopia of Natural Liberty Is Made by Bad Intentions

To defend a paradox was the highest endeavor of the classical orator, since it called for the fullest range of learning. Adam Smith, a *doctus orator*, or encyclopedic mind, enchanted and awed the massive intellect of Edmund Burke, who declared that *The Wealth of Nations* was "probably the most important book that has ever been written."

The classical orator applied knowledge to the acquisition of political wisdom and power. Smith turned his knowledge to the study of how wealth could be increased by the application of knowledge to industry. The great exemplar had been Gutenberg, who in turn had diverted the attention of subsequent centuries to the same question: "How can knowledge be made to increase man's power over Nature?" From Galileo and Leonardo da Vinci to Adam Smith and his friend James Watt, there is a mounting interest in the basic means by which wealth is increased.

When Pins Came High

Smith lived in an age when "pin money" meant no small change. Pins were expensive feminine ornaments. Smith was fascinated by the new *division of labor* with its introduction of machinery, by which pins could be produced swiftly and cheaply. This speed-up created moreness of product and market.

Smith's "Bad Connection"

Smith, unlike Aristotle, never had an opportunity to observe the origins of the market economy. As George Soule writes in *Ideas of the Great Economists:*

> Unlike Plato, he did not think that diversity of occupation arose from differing talents, but rather that differing talents resulted from diversity of occupation. The real cause of the tendency to specialize in production, he held, was man's innate propensity to barter and trade, which he alone among the animals exhibits. "Nobody ever saw a dog make a fair and deliberate exchange of one bone for another with another dog."

Smith is clearly a "behaviorist" ahead of his time, just as J. B. Watson (author of *Behaviorism*, 1925) was long behind his time. Smith saw human "talents" as "intrinsic" and determined by the opportunities and by the habitual actions of the past. This outwardness of his orientation naturally inclined him to ignore the inner psychic effects of the new environment of mechanical industry. The employees in this new world had all come from the older handicraft environment, just as today all employees in the new electric environment carry the "talents" and irrelevant habits of the preceding mechanical environment, which render the new and *actually determining* environment invisible. What Smith assumed to be innate in man, Aristotle had actually observed as developing from the interface of two worlds: from household to market. By Smith's time this agrarian and paternalistic process had been overlaid by the new environment of industrial England.

Where Wealth accumulates and Men Decay.
Oliver Goldsmith, *The Deserted Village*

Time Is Money.

What's the *use* of worrying,
It never was worth while.
"Pack Up Your Troubles," World War I song

Smith, like all "classical economists," thought that the real or "natural value" of anything was "measured by the labor which would have to be devoted to making it. Nobody would take the trouble to make anything unless he thought it worth while" (George Soule, *Ideas of the Great Economists*).

Where Ignorance Is Blitz: Harmony by Collision Unltd.

Where every prospect pleases and only man is vile.
Oliver Goldsmith, *The Deserted Village*

In *Leviathan* (1651), Thomas Hobbes had reaffirmed in the seventeenth century Shakespeare's vision of merely competitive social existence with his phrase that the natural life of man is "nasty, brutish, and short." He regarded a "social contract" as indispensable for survival. What Hobbes saw as necessary to prop up a collapsing society, Rousseau and Jefferson saw as a revolutionary means to attain "life, liberty, and the pursuit of happiness." Hobbes parallels his contemporary Leibniz (whose *Monadology* presents the war dance of inner-directed modules) as he marches straight toward the mechanist idea of a self-regulating cosmos. Long before Adam Smith, Alexander Pope had stated the blessings of noninterference with the "external" laws of the "social machine" in *An Essay on Man* (1732–34). Its theme is summarized in the familiar lines:

> All nature is but art unknown to thee,
> All chance, direction which thou canst not see;
> All discord, harmony not understood;
> All partial evil, universal good;
> And, spite of pride, in erring reason's spite,
> One truth is clear, Whatever is, is right.

Pope here asserts the equilibrium principle that later reappears as the basis of Norbert Wiener's homeostasis and cybernetics. Economists, historians, and social climbers alike are released from all moral hang-ups in this "best of all possible worlds," based on visual order by *matching*.

The Millionaire Dropout Behind the Iron Mask
As Intellectual Drop-in Didn't Know the Trap Was Set

Having made a fortune as a man of affairs, David Ricardo (1772–1823) took a fresh look at the economic slopes he had navigated. He indulged in the study of political economy, guided by the "iron law" that wages could never be far from the minimum level of subsistence because of the action of demand and supply in the labor market. The exchange of goods and services became the central figure of his contemplation of

The Mysteries of Value, Price, Profit, and Rent

Actually, he lived far above this process. The interface between this pattern of exchange and the new environment of public services created by this same process had accelerated the wealth-making functions of the economy to a high degree. Meanwhile, the exchange process itself continued to monopolize the attention of economists then as now. The vast and growing surround of services generated by a speeding economy escapes the economic categorist.

In the nineteenth century, the nature of the action of the new environments created by industrial technology appeared mainly as disservices. So it had been when the invisible service environments of writing and money had created the visible distress of USURA. Aristotle had seen production for exchange as a threat to the integrity of the household. By the mid-nineteenth century in England this separation of market and household, of work and residence, was felt acutely. With artistic prescience Wordsworth caught the mood fifty years before:

> The world is too much with us; late and soon,
> Getting and spending, we lay waste our powers
> Little we see in Nature that is ours;
> We have given our hearts away, a sordid boon!

The Speenhamland Law as English G.A.S. to By-pass French Revolution

G. K. Chesterton once pointed out that the most important event in British history was a historical "missing link," namely, an English revolution to match the French Revolution. The reason for this gap in the historical chain of iron necessity was the desperate ploy of the squires. When the break came between work and residence, there was starvation in the deserted villages and violence in the new manufacturing centers. The country gentlemen and fox hunters rallied to produce a law in 1795 to prevent society from falling into the iron trap of the "pure" market place.

4

All-for-Money

Karl Polanyi noted in *The Great Transformation* that "the market for labor was, in effect, the last of the markets to be organized. . . ." The reason was that "to establish such a market, especially in England's rural civilization, implied no less than the wholesale destruction of the traditional fabric of society." An acceleration of this same process occurred almost a century later, as noted by E. R. Leach, the anthropologist:

> In the old days, bonds of neighbourhood, kinship and occupation tended to coincide; most people spent their whole lives close to the place where they were born, so they were always surrounded by kinsfolk, not just brothers and sisters, but uncles, and aunts, cousins, nephews and nieces, grandparents.   A *Runaway World*

Such patterns still exist in pockets of Britain today, but most of them disappeared with the railways:

> The effect of this change is as much psychological as social. In the past, kinsfolk and neighbours gave the individual continuous moral support throughout his life. Today the domestic household is isolated. The family looks inward upon itself. . . .   A *Runaway World*

The Iron Law of Charity

The Speenhamland G.A.S. concocted by the British, who were threatened by the industrial technology, was nothing less than a *guaranteed annual subsistence*. The new law provided subsidies to wages in relation to the price of bread. A minimum income was assured to all. But the process of extending this total service to all resulted in a tyrannical bureaucracy with a paradoxical gain for employers and a loss for the industrious workman, which Polanyi summed up as the conversion of "a charitable law into a bond of iron."

At the time Karl Polanyi was writing about Speenhamland another gap had opened in the economy. There had been the crisis of labor reduced to a market commodity in the early nineteenth century, accompanied by the splitting of work and residence. The resulting collapse of social values that came with this new specialism and speed-up in the wealth-making process led to further fragmenting of the entire social structure.

Parallel to the "daring" of the English gentry in 1795 was the action of F.D.R. in the 1930's, when the United States faced the paradox of

POVERTY IN THE MIDST OF PLENTY:
THE MARKET AT ANY PRICE.

The English squires were prepared to save the English way of life by a leap into seeming socialism. F.D.R. was prepared to save the structure of the market economy by subsidizing nonproduction and by destroying what could not be transferred or processed through the market. His Speenhamland law began with the N.R.A. and petered out in the multitudinous pot-holes of the W.P.A.

What *appeared* as the welfare problem was actually the need for distributing the abundance of mechanized agriculture and the speedy assembly lines. The hidden environment of new electric technology, of radio and movies, went with a general speed-up of transportation, both of "hardware" and of information. The existing bureaucratic processes, in business and government alike, were not able to relate to this new social "rim spin" of innovation. Whenever the social speed exceeds the power of social and psychic assimilation, there is a sudden decline of satisfactions, which is the formula for DEPRESSION:

The Law of Civilization and Decay

Brooks Adams in 1896 produced his classic study of the effect of acceleration on social institutions:

> Nothing so portentous overhangs humanity as this mysterious and relentless acceleration of movement, which changes methods of competition and alters paths of trade; for by it countless millions of men and women are foredoomed to happiness or misery, as certainly as the beasts and trees, which have flourished in the wilderness, are destined to vanish when the soil is subdued by man.
>
> *The Law of Civilization and Decay*

Adams made an analysis that is in harmony with the self-regulating systems of the classical economists from Adam Smith to Karl Marx. What the classical group of economists—Smith, Malthus, and Ricardo—had not studied or even observed, was the effect of new products in creating new environments. So far, no economist has discussed this action of products in creating their *own* environments. It has always seemed natural to assume that products of any kind will insert themselves into the existing environments of any time or place. The spin-off from new products is always an invisible new suit of clothes for the entire society.

What Is New in Any Innovation Is Not the Product But Its Effects

During periods of rapid innovation and the consequent interplay of new and old services there is a complementary flood of disruption and disservice. We have seen how the well-intentioned Speenhamlanders with their program of universal charity produced a new breed of rigorous tyrants. It was precisely the greatly improved communications of their time (press, post, and travel) that made these tyrants so much more formidable than their predecessors.

"Chuck" the Giant Killer Spots Chink in Armor

Charlie, you're my darwing.
James Joyce, *Finnegans Wake*

> O yet we trust that somehow good
> Will be the final goal of ill. . . .
> Tennyson, *In Memoriam*

The single word "darwing" indicates the end of the ironclad system of clanging mechanisms that had satisfied the ideas of order in the classical "age of reason." "Charlie" Darwin's evolutionary approach opened the closed, self-regulating systems to a cosmic process of innovation that was totally environmental. This new approach had lurked in the Romantic idea of all-presiding time spirit or *Zeitgeist*. It echoed in Swedenborg and Blake and Hegel, and came forth fully clad in Carlyle's *Sartor Resartus* with its theme of "the world in clothes." Carlyle's doctrine of the hero in history provided the time spirit with a vocal vortex and a specific image or mask of personal power.

The wistful Tennyson whimper that "we trust that somehow good" will result from the blind bludgeonings of chance betrays the new note of uncertainty that accompanied the collapse of the Newtonian clockwork cosmos. Newton had provided the centennial garments of the rigid decorum of the eighteenth century. His hidden clockwork environment had shaped every modality of the age of reason with its classical morals and sociology. From Laplace and Diderot to Ben Franklin and Thomas Jefferson there was a complete confidence in the rigorous laws of Nature.

The Gaps in Nature

Charles Darwin's "missing link" opened up the closed system that had stood adamant for centuries. His "gap in Nature" began a new interface of rapid change and breakthroughs that still resonates. That *the gap is where the action is* is now acknowledged as the basis of chemical and physical change. At first, however, the gap spurred the archaeologists and anthropologists to world-wide explorations.

Whereas Darwin (1809–1882) had flawed the mechanisms of the scientists, "Chuck" Marx (1818–1883) found the same chink in the "iron law of wages." Coming from another culture with a medieval setting, Marx had the advantage of starting with the ignorance of his predecessors. English thinkers enveloped in the new industrial environment were not as conscious of its dynamics as Marx, the immigrant observer. Marx had the benefit of an antienvironment such as Tocqueville had enjoyed earlier.

The Great Expectations Gap

"Charlie" Dickens had his own antienvironment of absolute poverty amidst the new industrial affluence. He had learned how to "whitewash the world" as a child in a blacking factory. When he went to America as an eager social radical visiting a republican utopia, he came to a "democratic, kingless country freed from the shackles of class rule." Like Marx, experiencing the new industrial society of England, Dickens was shocked by the disservices proliferating amidst the new service environment of the United States. In 1842, during a six-month visit to the United States, Dickens wrote his friend William C. Macready: "I believe the heaviest blow ever dealt at liberty's head will be dealt by this nation with ultimate failure of its example to the earth."

The Chink in Ricardo's Armor

Since Ricardo is still a giant ghost of economic theory, it is important to know how Marx brought him low. When Marx published Part I of his *A Contribution to the Critique of Political Economy*, he fired point blank at Ricardo. This occurred in 1859, but he had noted much earlier: "If the exchange value of a product is equal to the labour time which it contains, the exchange value of a labour day is equal to its product. Or the wage must be equal to the product of labour. But the contrary is the case."

Ricardo had insisted on the *matching* of work and product, leaving the worker at the subsistence level of Malthus. Marx noted that there was a *making* of profit out of the work process. His procedure had been to seek the origins of *value, price, profit,* and *rent* in the market process itself. To this end, he undertook extensive historical studies of exchanges under varying market conditions. Like Darwin, Marx sought the causes of the effects he had noted in developmental terms. By the time he had settled in England, after the 1848 political upheavals in Europe, the English market had perfected the means of translating end products of all human action into monetary terms.

The Dropout Kings of Cotton

Like the communist utopian, Robert Owen (1771–1858), the textile millionaire Frederick Engels, patron and friend of Marx, was also a King of Cotton.

What Machiavelli had noted as a moral aberration in the sixteenth century ("every man has his price") had been generalized by the market into a social climate in the nineteenth century. What had been slowly squeezed from Gutenberg's "wine press" had been spun speedily from the steam-powered spindles of the cotton mills.

Marx-Magic-Money

What Machiavelli had spotted as the moral metamorphosis of his age, namely, the translation of honor into cash, Marx studied as the primary magic of his century:

> It is not money that renders commodities commensurable. The very opposite is true. Because all commodities, in so far as they are values, are embodied human labour, and are therefore commensurable, their values can all be measured in one and the same specific commodity; and this latter can therefore be transformed into the common measure of their values, into money. Money as the measure of value is the necessary phenomenal form of the immanent measure of the value of commodities, namely labour time.　　　　*Capital*

In other words, Marx saw money as the magical transformer of all things whatever to money prices. As a member of the literati, he sought the matching principle, or the common denominator of "socially necessary labor," as the underlying drama of the nineteenth century.

As the eighteenth century had hit upon the principle of mass production via *exactly repeated* acts of human labor, so the nineteenth century intensified and extended the process of uniformity and repetition of commensurable prices and commodities. The process of wealth making thus moved steadily from "hardware" to "software."

Marxmanship—the Big Mist: Buried in "Figures"
Never Broke "Ground"

By concentrating on the new dehumanizing and specializing market of the industrial age, Marx mistook the new service environments as mere crumbs for the poor from the tables of the rich. These "crumbs" soon became the new staple diet of rich and poor alike. Marx missed the entire body of human services that provided the "ground" for the industrial market. In this much more complex time he repeated the error of Aristotle's attack on the new *usura*. Aristotle had ignored the invisible new service environments of writing and currency as extensions of man, speeding the wealth-making process over and beyond nature. Marx ignored the hidden environmental effects of the fantastic speed-up of work via steam, which had transformed during the period of his historical studies all the components or situations that he analyzed.

Marx shared with economists then and since the inability to make his concepts include innovational processes. It is one thing to spot a new product but quite another to observe the invisible new environments generated by the action of the product on a variety of pre-existing social grounds.

THE MESS-AGE IN THE DIALECTICAL MASS-AGE: CONCEPTS RUB OUT PERCEPTS

Marx saw that social change differed from human intentions. In *A Contribution to the Critique of Political Economy*, he notes

THE BASIS FOR THE CLASS STRUGGLE BETWEEN OWNERS AND WORKERS

In the social production which men carry on they enter into definite relations that are indispensable [to production] and independent of their will; these *relations of production* correspond to a definite stage of development of their *material powers of production*. The sum total of these relations of production constitutes the economic structure of society—the real foundation, on which rise legal and political superstructures and to which correspond definite forms of social consciousness. The mode of production in material life determines the general character of the social, political, and spiritual processes of life. It is not the consciousness of men that determines their existences, but, on the contrary, their social existence determines their consciousness.

The appearance of complementarity in this statement is in fact a mirror reflection of correspondence and *matching*. The dynamic interface among the environments as such is lacking.

Steam as Medium Reduced the Labor Content Necessary for Industrial Production

The new service environment created by the increased *speed and power* of steam, as the new extension of man, was hidden from Marx, and all economists then and since. Like Marx, they saw the "content" of the process in the form of "hardware" *products* pouring out at ever greater speed. The "message" of steam as a new "medium" was not the products, but the acceleration of all the functions in the social surround, *i.e.*, the new "rim spin."

Steam as Message Increased the Physical-Psychic-Social Rim Spin

> Her life was turning, turning,
> In mazes of heat and sound,
> But for peace her soul was yearning,
> And now peace laps her round.
> Matthew Arnold, "Requiescat"

As the Gutenberg speed-up scrapped scribe and scholasticism, it transformed the scribal *role* into the type-setting *job*. As steam scrapped craftsmen and community, it created the jobs of the mechanics and the assembly-line workers. These jobs lingered on into the nineteenth century. But it is the much greater speed of electric technology that makes manifest the new patterns produced by the Gutenberg and steam-power innovations, when seen from the plateau of the electric age, constituting a kind of "feedback" of dramatic merging of causes and effects in "double ends joined." Norbert Wiener borrowed the very word "cybernetics" (*cybernetes*: Greek for Latin *gubernator*, or governor) from the steam engine. It was a young lad yanking a string on the steam cock of an engine who had the wit to tie the string to the flywheel, thus creating a "steam governor" and reinventing "feedback control." Otto Mayr, in "The Origins of Feedback Control" (*Scientific American*, October, 1970), traces the evolution of "feedback" from the Alexandrian water clock of Ktesibios (circa 300 B.C.) to the early nineteenth century. The much greater electric speed-up of today enables us to shift from information overload to pattern recognition, from experience to knowledge, and from reaction to anticipation:

> And we are here as on a darkling plain
> Swept with confused alarms of struggle and flight,
> Where ignorant armies clash by night.
> Matthew Arnold, "Dover Beach"

From Finn Asleep to Finn A-wake

Steam speeded the market process toward standardization and homogenization, toward more bucks and war bucks. At the same time, the main activity of the market was transformed from producing commodities to satisfying the psychic need for "moreness." The new exchange speeds caused money to "spin off" from the total process into

CAPITAL: BUCKS in "Vacuo ad Infinitum"

Every new service environment not only scraps its immediate predecessor but retrieves or evokes a much earlier form of human activity. Gutenberg, while scrapping scribe and "schoolmen," retrieved the whole corpus of classical antiquity—the Greek and Roman heritage that manuscript culture could not cope with.

The new service environment of steam as the enlargement and speed-up of human work retrieved the ancient idea of

Laborare Est Orare

The idea of work as a sacramental bond between man and Nature had begun to echo in the work of Blake, the prophetic poet, painter, and engraver. At the very moment when toil had lost all dignity through speed and fragmentation of the labor process, there came from Thomas Carlyle (in *Past and Present*, 1843) a major manifesto of the Gospel of Work. *Retrieval is not reaction, but a part of the systole-diastole of a pulsating society:*

> On the whole, we do entirely agree with those old Monks, *Laborare est Orare*. In a thousand senses, from one end of it to the other, true Work *is* Worship. He that works, whatsoever be his work, he bodies forth the form of Things Unseen; a small Poet every Worker is.

Machina ex Deo

Lynn White, Jr., in *Machina ex Deo: Essays in the Dynamism of Western Culture*, goes much further in demonstrating the broad pattern of Christian influence: "Although to labor is to pray, the goal of labor is to end labor."

Labor Power as the Unique Commodity That Can Generate More Exchange Value than It Consumes

In Gestalt terms of *figure* and *ground* Marx designated the social process of production for market as *ground*. The *figure* over or against this *ground* on which he concentrated was the new commodity of hourly labor, or the salable fragment of some ability to work—what Marx called "labor power." The market had newly "alienated" or separated the "labor power" from the man in the mechanical age. Under preindustrial conditions "labor power" had, as it were, remained embodied in the whole man. This man was not an independent worker but dependent on a man-master relationship. The market broke this personal bondage and freed "labor power" to sink or swim on the competitive market waves, along with its possessor.

In his historical analysis, Marx clearly separated the labor process from the forms it may assume "under particular social conditions." For him the labor process had now broken away from the agrarian household, with its tribal bonds of kinship and personal subordination. The labor process for Marx comes to include all commodity exchange. It does not include consumer satisfactions, since these are to be assumed as a necessary condition or motive for exchange. For those unfamiliar with the Marxian analysis, the following passage will illustrate his approach:

THE LABOUR PROCESS CHANGES HUMAN NATURE

The use of labour power, is *labour*. The buyer of labour power consumes it by setting the seller of labour power to work. Thereby the latter becomes what he was before potentially, labour power in action, a *worker*. In order that his labour may be embodied in commodities, he must, above all, embody it in use-values, in articles capable of satisfying wants of one kind or another. Hence what the capitalist sets the worker to produce is some particular use-value, some specified article. The production of use-values, of goods, is not affected in respect of its general nature by the fact that it is undertaken for a capitalist and under his control. In the first instance, therefore, we must consider the labour process apart from the particular form it may assume under particular social conditions.

Primarily, labour is a process going on between man and nature, a process in which man, through his own activity, initiates, regulates, and controls the material reactions between himself and nature. He confronts nature as one of her own forces, setting in motion arms and legs, head and hands, in order to appropriate nature's productions in a form suitable to his own wants. By thus acting on the external world and changing it, he at the same time changes his own nature.

Capital

As a traditional humanist, devoted to establishing a "science of history," Marx shunned the evolutionary drift of his time. He felt the Samuel Butlers were too ready to reduce historical process to that of biological evolution:

**MAN IS AN EXTENSION OF NATURE THAT REMAKES
THE NATURE THAT REMAKES MAN**

In terms of Hegelian orchestration, which Marx assumes, the music is worse than it sounds.

History Makes Man While Man Makes History:
The Music of the Vibes

In earlier times this process had been unconscious, but in the socialist age, when man assumes control of his production processes, Marx saw man as becoming master of his own history. His tools were developed in the rearview historical mirror. He never abandoned concepts in order to go "through the looking glass" into the world of percept. Marx did not join the existentialist struggle of the Kierkegaards and the Rimbauds to discard the conceptual apparatus in favor of direct perceptual confrontation. Marx preferred the nineteenth-century version of "freedom is the recognition of necessity."

The approach to this "freedom" for Marx had to be through "changing" historical concepts that are inevitably one stage behind "where it's at." Meantime, the existentialists and artists had begun the conscious probing to determine "where it is at." At this point the audience became actor rather than puppet in the historical drama. But Marx uses "history" as a plenary category for current developments. *There is no such thing as past history, since it is always a fiction fabricated by the preferences of the present.* Therefore, Marx's desire to get with the historical process was as whimsical and hopeful as "getting with the market."

THROUGHOUT MODERN TIMES THE INTELLECTUALS OF THE WEST HAVE BEEN COMMITTED TO TRANSLATING ALL PROCESSES INTO MATCHING CATEGORIES AND CLASSIFICATIONS.

5

All-for-Free

What Marx Didn't Know: Low Marks for Charlie

Immersed in the free-information resources of the British Museum, Marx paid no heed to the new service environments created by the products of the work process. He began by ignoring the inner satisfactions in production and consumption. He went on to ignore the stages by which public services available to the worker had by his time far exceeded the services that private wealth alone could buy. In his determination of "exchange value" Marx lumps all communal service environments as "socially necessary." These services include the gestation of the mother and the skill of the midwife, the access to the natural environments of air and earth and fire and water. They also include all man-made services of languages, traditions of culture—everything long related to the King's English, the King's highway, the King's justice, and the King's purse or currency.

Socially Unnecessary Labor as Fruit of the Organization Tree

In the industrial and postindustrial speed-up of innovation the new man-made services rapidly surpassed the traditional service environments.

> It is only in the working of the total system that the working of the social process is clearly seen.　　　　　　　　　　Karl Marx

When Marx speaks in this manner he means something much less than "total." Like contemporary "general systems scientists," he has a rigid set of classifications, of systems and subsystems.

Loved Labels Lost

Marxists never cease to polish the rear-view mirror, now that they have, in effect, control of the means of production in major sections of the world. In the electric-information environment the old categories of "class" and "economics" and "history" are meaningless. For fifty years the West has provided the same multibillion-dollar environmental services for rich and poor. "Charlie, you're my Darwing" now has the nostalgic ring of an old favorite.

At the Speenhamland moment when labor had already become a marketable commodity, a strange reversal occurred. The creation of a labor market involved a wide range of rapid innovations and speed-up of specialized transactions. The "market" was a complex giant of integrated information and transport services, extending far and wide.

The Gutenberg speed-up by fragmentation of a major handicraft had scrapped the scribes and the feudal system while retrieving antiquity. The new industrial market, many times greater than Gutenberg, scrapped the world of the craftsman and retrieved a primitive awareness of work as sacramental.

Whither History and Whether Science?

From the interaction of all environments in transforming physical, psychic, and social perceptions, the Marxists select the "class struggle." The age-old struggles between "owners" and "workers" are abstracted from all the service environments created by human innovation and extensions of human powers. What remains is what they call "the science of history." Science, by definition, is an extreme abstraction from the total complex of human affairs. In 1850 science looked like the bandwagon of progress that had replaced the anarchy of humanist history. The Marxists' ambition to explain the whole course of history was both noble and feasible, but not on economic terms. Their concern was with the struggle between the "forces of production" as the "material basis" and the "relations of production" reflected as the social and legal "superstructure" required for actual production.

On the Wrong Side of the Looking Glass

Not only is Marxist analysis concerned mainly with the new specialist "hardware" but it uses, unconsciously, only visual models of classification as explanation.

It is this naïve obsession with "hardware" and visual models that makes Marxism easy for the literati to comprehend. Once science went through the vanishing point into acoustic or resonant space, both scientists and economists were left on the wrong side of the looking glass, because they were mostly unable to make what Bertrand Russell cited (on the first page of his *ABC of Relativity*) as the indispensable preliminary act needed for grasping Einstein: "What is demanded is a change in our imaginative picture of the world. . . ."

Sink Deep or Touch Not the Cartesian Spring

Russell himself never eluded the Cartesian grid. He avoided the acoustic sense of the "auditory imagination," as is plain from the very words he uses—"imaginative picture of the world." It is not strange that a century earlier Marx and Engels should have been unaware of new hidden environments that frustrated their intents. It was natural for a non-Euclidean mathematician like Lewis Carroll to fight his way out of the visual trap contrived by the preceding ages of Western culture. Marx and Engels were Western literati, uncritical of the sensory assumptions embedded in Western literacy. At every turn they express their merely visual assumptions and goal orientation:

> We will not, then, oppose the world like doctrinarians with a new principle. *Here is truth, kneel down here!* We expose new principles to the world out of the world itself. . . . We explain to it [the world] only the real object for which it struggles, and consciousness is a thing it *must* acquire even if it objects to it.
>
> *Karl Marx and Friedrich Engels Correspondence*

What is obvious here is the visual reliance on the *inner light* of private interpretation, dear to the literati of all ages. That the revolution should not have come in a highly literate and industrialized society was therefore a surprise to the disciples of Marx. As the world moved into the electrotechnical phase it retrieved primitivism in many forms. All "backward" or nonliterate countries were the first to respond to the resonance of the electric message, since they already lived in acoustic space.

At the time when the age of reason and enlightenment was at its peak of literacy and decorum, there came that sudden flip into romantic and mythic imagination that coincided with the recovery of the sacramental doctrine of work.

Mystic and Gravitational Bond Between Man and Nature

The poet is the unacknowledged legislator of the world.
                    Dr. Johnson's *Rasselas* via Shelley

The new romantic doctrines of art and nature and society quickly asserted the priority of the artist as the social navigator. In the very midst of industrial mammonism, Walter Pater, John Ruskin, and the poet and millionaire manufacturer William Morris concurred in assigning the role of social leadership to artistic invention. The poet and artist became the vehicles and voices of the "time spirit" as art aspired once more to the condition of music and social programming. As Joyce's Stephen Dedalus (suggesting Dead-all-us, and recalling Daedalus the inventor of flight) sums it up on the last page of the *Portrait of the Artist*:

> I go to encounter for the millionth time the reality of experience and
> to forge in the smithy of my soul the uncreated conscience of my race.

The industrial age of steel generated its own antithesis by sheer speed-up. The new frontier at "the end of steel" was not the Wild West at the rail end, but the telegraph that ran beside the railway. As late as 1854, a reporter for the London *Quarterly Review* could write that "the telegraph is rarely seen in America running beside the railway." The telegraph, which was of primary concern to the newspaper world, in effect created a new instant-information environment that boded the end of steel:

"Tout Seul et Toute Suite"

The unexpected result of treating the two systems of rail and wire to a marriage of convenience was the new frontier of the twentieth-century information world. Marx ignored this event, but in 1844, in his *Concept of Dread*, Sören Kierkegaard responded to the first telegraph service with an outpouring of gloom and dread. Kierkegaard foresaw the scrapping of Western literate technologies, but he did not realize that the electric environment would soon scrap nature as such.

Marx, while ridiculing utopian socialism, used a utopian rear-view mirror to advocate the take-over of all technologies for an over-all social programming "to *make* history." He was not prepared for the take-over of nature and history alike by the instant information environment. Like the activist kids of today, he was inclined to take over the old bureaucracies or the "state apparatus."

The Chink in the Ointment

Today ideological Communism has taken up its uneasy abode in China and in Russia. These ancient and immense bureaucracies had been built on totally different grounds and assumptions. The Chinese world, which gave its civil-service expertise, via India, to the British ruling elite in the eighteenth century, was clan to the core.

> Wearing number nine in Yangste hats.
> James Joyce, *Finnegans Wake*

The cultural base of the Chinese world was and is the iconic ideogram with its elegant compression and economy and uniformity for the whole of China. China is a world of visual unity and acoustic anarchy, where the advent of radio and electricity has ended the visual unity and enhanced the acoustic anarchy.

The Chinese mandarinate had built a hierarchy of musical components. Their feudal loyalties were protected against the Western literate fragmentation by the indestructible coherence of their audile-tactile ideograms. Having withstood the visual onslaught of Western lineality and "connected logic," they were caught off guard by the new electric resonance that was transforming the West and the world.

For the Chinese, Marx can be only another Western philosopher with a system of visually connected concepts. Whereas the Western mind seeks to reduce differences to common denominators, the Chinese seeks to give salience to uniqueness and difference. This he does by symbolic juxtaposition or carefully calculated intervals. Our "connections" he sees as mere hangups, surpassed only by the abstract inhumanity of our organization charts and blueprints.

THE JAPANESE SANDMAN
and
THE MOTH AND THE FLAME

The delicacy of Chinese perception is now tormented by the passion to have a nineteenth century of "hardware" moreness and industrial power. The Japanese, through shortage of raw materials, were compelled to by-pass most of this nineteenth-century world, and to seize the twentieth-century proffer of electric circuitry and "software" design.

Mao is torn between East and West in the age when the West is going East. Russia did not have to resolve this conflict, since its tribal feudalism was of Western structure and yielded belatedly to newer Western technologies. WHAT HAS DERAILED EAST AND WEST ALIKE IS THE ADVENT OF ELECTRIC CIRCUITRY AND INFORMATION FLOW THAT KNOWS NO BOUNDS.

The Grumbling Industrial Hive: Public Benefits Private Vices Lazy Fairies in Bunny Clubs

What Marx called "the process of producing surplus value" is the nineteenth-century version of usury. Whereas Aristotle saw Nature as the *ground* against which appeared the gargoyle of usury, Marx saw the market as the *ground* from which stared the Gorgon of surplus value.

Let an entrepreneur buy materials and "labor power" on the market and combine them in a production process to create a buggy. Let him next sell the buggy in a free market. The difference between his investment and his take is his profit or loss. Marx assumes a continuing operation backed by a whole social superstructure of services. He would define as "accident" a single transaction. "Surplus value" results from the private use of the entire superstructure of social services. The basic *figure* is the material "production process" looked at against the *ground* of the social "superstructure." Access to this corporate superstructure is via the new fragmentation of the market process. The ancient political principle of "divide and rule" had now permeated the entire social fabric. All the human institutions that had been built to serve the common good could now be channeled into private pockets.

Private Rents and Public Taxes

From folk-land to book-land.
F. W. Maitland

The result of rending or tearing apart; a separation of parts produced by tearing or similar violence. . . .
Oxford English Dictionary on "Rent"

I have torn my Petticoat with your odious Romping; my Rents are coming in.
Jonathan Swift, *Polite Conversation*

Centuries before labor had been partitioned into marketable packages, the rending of land for hire or purchase was regarded as violence against nature.

In his classic *Domesday Book and Beyond* (1897) F. W. Maitland revealed 1086 as the traumatic date of English history. It was then that Duke William the Conqueror, who had taken over in 1066, decided to convert the old Dane geld tribute into a regular tax. The "folk-land" of the tribal population was translated into "book-land" by the law of 1086. The Doom or judgment on the folk took them from the tribal-oral to the written jurisdiction of the Roman law. The Doomsday book converted the old *immunities* of the "Anglo-Saxon land-book" into new increased tax *liabilities*. Those taxed were "renders in kind, in service and in money." By consensus "there had been a catastrophe . . . Domesday Book is full of evidence that the tillers of the soil are being depressed."

Duke William the Conqueror instituted a vast new system of service environments that transformed England into a police state. Superimposed on the old oral and tribal communities was the efficient and rigorous administration of specialist or civilized Roman laws and culture.

A man's a man for a' that.

The best things in life are free.

Taxes are for group services or public benefits. Access to public benefits or new social environment at first tends to be easier for the top dogs. In those Norman days it was easier for the sheriff of Nottingham to enjoy the new services than for the displaced Saxon Earl of Huntington, known to us as Robin Hood.

The underdog of the oral culture cuts a better figure in popular tradition than the earnest "pig" of Nottingham. Robin Hood and his Merry Men took to the woods and left behind the environments of privilege. Their cult resonates in human hearts like the songs of Bobbie Burns from another oral tradition.

Beyond Price and Without Price

The air we breathe and the sun we share are at once priceless and without price. Adam Smith had seen land as a scarce monopoly and designated rent as the price exacted for the use of such monopolies. Ricardo pushed further, pointing out that if land were as abundant as air it would not be rentable or taxable. He lived when new service environments, far beyond the scope of private landholding, were being created by new knowledge and technology. Today the electric-information environments have realized his hypothesis of "free goods" that are universally available and relatively rent-free. More and more programming of the highways and the air waves creates "software" environments more ethereal and pervasive than the air we no longer dare to breathe.

> "I want to join the few."
> "Sorry, there are already too many."
> *Beyond the Fringe*

G. B. Shaw and the Fabian socialists were conscious of the vastness of these new service environments, but they failed to note that private wealth could not achieve such services on its own. In a word, the private privilege of enjoying major service environments ceased in the nineteenth century. When private CLUBS were the only TRUMPS left, the wealthy took to global tramping and trotting. Slumming incognito became the thing for sophisticates and the blasé:

> Let us go, through certain half-deserted streets
> The muttering retreats
> Of restless nights in one-night cheap hotels
> And sawdust restaurants with oyster shells. . . .
> T. S. Eliot, "The Love Song of J. Alfred Prufrock"

John Stuart Mill: Publicist of Politically Programmed Distribution

> What a blow that phantom gave me!
> Don Quixote

Mill rebelled against the long tradition of "natural" equilibrium economies. He intuited that the man-made environments of services were now in excess of the natural sources for satisfying human needs. The new corporate organization of industry had provided environmental services that surpassed the limits of both household and natural economies. Mill proposed that government take over from "the hidden hand" that had been squeezing the new industrial society. He was a precursor of Echoland and ecology, but knowledge had not yet reached the level necessary to supersede experience.

The Steak Line and the Soup Line:
The Ballad of Double Ends Joined, Or Turning Turtle

The specter that was "haunting Europe" in the *Communist Manifesto* of 1848 has become our familiar bedfellow. While Marx was scripting melodramas based on past revolutions and "the fool-fury of Seine," the actuality of Communism in the industrial West had been achieved before Marx was born. Utopians and antiutopians are always obsessed with a period preceding their own. Orwell's *1984* happened in 1930. Bellamy's *Looking Backward* as if from A.D. 2000 is merely a retrospect of the Robert Owen community of 1810. Marx presented nineteenth-century science as a basis for future social programming.

Marx was an enthusiast for the work of anthropologist Lewis Henry Morgan (1818–1881), whose report of the social organization of the Iroquois in 1851 had great European vogue. It was regarded as the first scientific account of an Indian tribe ever given to the world. He was always concerned with the evolution of intelligence via inventions, with the stages of government growth, the idea of the family, and the emergence of the idea of property. The achievement of his maturity in 1868 was

THE AMERICAN BEAVER AND HIS WORKS.

Those ignorant of the extent of the fur trade between America and Europe may be inclined to smile at this beaver item. The War of Independence had been fought to eject the fur traders from America in order that they might have free access to the Wild West.

The Line from Linnaeus to Darwin

"So sing they sequent the assent of man.
James Joyce, *Finnegans Wake*

Lineal classification as a basis for science and historical evolution had been pushed to its limit and now performed the flip or reversal that is incidental to ultimate development. Marx went all the way to the boundaries of scientific classification seeking an outlet into a "field theory" via Hegelian dialectic. He was certain that "everything is *interconnected*." He was unprepared for *interplay*, the resonant interval where the new action is. The old action had been in the cosmic connections of "the great chain of being," whose common denominator was "matter-in-motion." He was also unprepared for the sudden *nowness of the past* in the speed-up of the electric age. The new electric speed-up had created the interval that was classified by the old-line scientists as

The Missing Link

The resonant gap in nature, reverberating with greater intensity, by-passed the Hegelian process of interconnectedness, restoring the structure of acoustic space to Western experience:

> It will remember itself from every sides with all gestures, in each our
> word.   James Joyce, *Finnegans Wake*

Acoustic space is, like a pun, a resonant sphere whose center is everywhere and whose boundaries are nowhere. To the visual man, the effort to define and to visualize this space is unnerving. Even contemporary scientists persist in making visual models to explain and confuse their publics concerning nonvisual processes. Marx eventually repudiated the Marxist expositors of his perception of social process, but he remained meshed in his own paradigm trap.

Ideologies Always Retrieve Old Solutions for New Problems

Samuel Gompers, long-time president of the American Federation of Labor, became what he fought—a man with one goal: MORE!

The major economists after Marx hastened back to the secure basis of the old visual solutions of classification. Alfred Marshall (1842–1924) did a recap of his classical predecessors, coming to rest on the concept of "the marginal theory of utility." The center-margin theme is an entirely visual concept of quantified preference, by which available products are chosen by the "average man" on a basis of incremental calculation.

In the affluence of the later nineteenth century, Marshall turned his discussion from the precarious Malthusian subsistence to the assurance of "a standard of comfort." An inveterate quantifier, he turned to analyzing national income "in a climate of judicious universalism where one could find a place for almost every idea and an exception to almost every rule" (George Soule, *Ideas of the Great Economists*).

From Content Analysis to Media Magic

Alfred Marshall's successor at Cambridge University was A. C. Pigou, who extended Marshall's idea of the total "national dividend" and the "hardware" "standard of comfort" to the concept of *The Economics of Welfare* in 1920. As the Speenhamlanders of 1795 countered the French Revolution with a minimum-income policy, the postwar world of the 1920's turned aside the hex of the Russian Revolution with welfare policies, concentrated on "hardware" products.

In this radio decade of tribal jazz and Western transformation there suddenly appeared an economist who turned from consumer concerns and

moral anxiety to the effects and processes of the monetary medium of exchange as such. It was already deep in the new age of electric information
that John Maynard Keynes split off the economic *content* from the *medium* of the production-for-exchange process.

The Keynesian Mutiny or the Hindsight Saga

Keynes demonstrated how to control the economic process by manipulating the monetary environment. He saw how to manage the climate of the
monetary environment by managing the interest levels. By programmed
interplay between "savers" and "spenders," he sought to ensure maximum
employment. He took the existing established production processes for
granted, ignoring the new stress on the information components.

Keynes overlooked the rapid change of the monetary medium from "hardware" (bullion) to "software" (credit and promises). He had no means of
determining the quantity or speed of money in circulation. He also missed
the shift in the very nature of the main volume of commodity exchange
from products to services.

PRODUCTION! PRODUCTION! PRODUCTION!

In the time before the "crash" the prototypical social model was Sinclair
Lewis's George Follansbee Babbitt: "It was big—and Babbitt respected
bigness in anything; in mountains, jewels, muscles, wealth, or words." The
very name "Babbitt" proclaimed the new "bearings" in American society.
Sinclair Lewis was giving the "back of his hand" to the genteel Harvard
humanism of the Boston Brahmin Babbitt. It was already the new PR age
of "other-direction" and the new knowledge industries. The 1920's brought
in the telephone, the car, the gramophone, the talkies, and the radio. The
"information age" with its intense and all-involving "rim spin" had begun
in World War I with its universal reliance on espionage and the appraisal
of industrial war potential around the world. The speed-up of innovation
had become the crux of warfare and business competition alike.

In the midst of the accelerating concern with innovation and novelties
for use and diversion, there arose the censorious voice of a formidable de-
tractor. Thorstein Veblen (1857–1929) in his *Theory of the Leisure Class*
(1899) brought the entire Western economy under the scrutiny of a sternly
abstemious peasant morality.

All the classical economists had stressed moral as well as economic deter-
minism while ignoring the technological effects of the new products as creators of new environments. Veblen captivated the vast Puritan sentiment of
guilt that accompanied the new affluence. He spurned the fatuity of the
vulgar new "captains of industry" promoting "conspicuous waste" and
"conspicuous consumption." It was easy for him to overlook the really massive consumer activity of the Big Berthas and the fabulously expensive

"sets" of Kaiser Bill's military grand opera. War is the industrial economy in high gear, in both production and consumption. But war is also the heyday of the moralist. Thus it was a sort of unclouding of the economic and social sphere when John Maynard Keynes brushed aside the besetting concern with morals as a substitute for understanding the actual processes released by money.

Making Money Is Making News

In the new information age, the forms of money and credit proliferated multitudes of new dimensions. The phrase "making money" came in at the beginning of the twentieth century and assumed co-status with "making news." Both activities were aspects of the new electric communication.

Marx had noted in his analysis of "the accumulation of capital" the tendency of the market of his time to push products from "hardware" status into the "software" state. Actual products tended to get translated into a store of money. Products were ceasing to have a primary consumer character and began to take on the aspect of money power or capital. To the extent that this pattern was recognized by the big operators, they accentuated it, even to the detriment of consumer needs.

Marx, like his fellow economists, was unaware of the electric communications speed-up that enhanced the wealth-making process quite independently of social welfare. Keynes, freed from mere moral distress about these inequities by his aristocratic abstracting power, concentrated on the techniques of the money medium. Keynes was the first conventional economist to *imply* that the medium was the message.

Cursers and Pre-cursors

Mankind crucified upon a cross of gold.
William Jennings Bryan

Lord Keynes saw the old medium of money against the familiar *ground* of the market process. Like his precursors, he failed to take into account the new hidden *ground* of enormously accelerated information transactions. At very high speeds the environmental involvement of world populations is inevitable. More and more of the productive effort *etherealizes*, in Toynbee's term, becoming image and information making. Design services and promotion render the "hardware" secondary.

Cars Are Not Made to Last but to Turnover

Just as the first marketeers, in the age of Aristotle, discovered that money could make Nature cycle faster, so at the complementary extreme in the twentieth century has come the discovery that by making money circulate at high speed, Nature is expendable. *Money as such has become a pseudo-event—information only.*

6

Fake-for-All

THE GENUINE FAKE BECOMES THE REAL MC COY

In the nineteenth century, when mass production was new, the process of the "fake" was done by matching and by mirrors. The Japanese got this message in their first phase of copying. Then, like us, they went beyond art into making the genuine fake: "I always paint fakes" (Picasso). The true artist knows that he must go beyond nature, if his making is to aid man in his evolution:

> Yet Nature is made better by no mean
> But Nature makes that mean: So, over that art,
> Which you say adds to Nature, is an art
> That Nature makes.
>
> Shakespeare, *The Winter's Tale*

Keynes conks out when money as legal tender becomes a very small part of the information transactions in an age of electric communications. Credit ratings based on the new data banking supersede conventional banking. Such "banking" is based on corporate and private

PROMISES PROMISES PROMISES

People of promise, and promising enterprises, like promissory notes, have become inseparable from the promises of promotion and advertising itself. Money in turn is a promise to pay promises, and the plausible con man has returned as the stand-in for the traditional gentleman.

Inflation Is Pollution: The Dilution of Promises

Inflation is a tribute levied by those who know on those who don't. As W. C. Fields saw it, "Never give a sucker an even break." In a world of promises and con men only the sucker will take valuable time to acquire socially useful skills, such as carpentry or plumbing or "keeping" the books.

They Had the Looks When Cooking the Books

Ask any international manager operating under conditions of rapid monetary inflation how he plans and how he keeps his accounts. He will explain why he has one set of books for the local tax authorities (based on "historical values"), another set in "soft" currency to satisfy other local accounting conventions, and still another batch in "hard" currency to enable head office to estimate profits, or the real McCoy. These monies of account are soggy "software."

THE POOH PERPLEX

Money Freaks Out: Information, the New Currency of Business

Accountants themselves are increasingly perplexed about procedures and assumptions underlying accounting practice. What constitutes suitable yardsticks for private business "performance"? With the shift from manufacturing to service industries, the market value of people's knowledge in a "going concern" more and more exceeds the value of its plant. The resale value of a past-perfect or a "gone concern" tends to vanish completely. Business profit is no longer *counted* as cash, either in the till or in the bank. It has become an *estimate* of "potential cash": the difference between what you might sell your operation for now and this time last year. It also assumes buyers. The selling price of a business depends on its *promise* of continuing profits, which are also *promises* of cash, that is, of "legal tender" or government I O U's.

Hijack Country Where Host Is Hostage

As a financial colleague puts it:

> The whole business picture today is a field of hijackers. One of the most outstanding examples of this is the recent bankruptcy of Penn-Central Railroad, when a corporation with eight billion dollars of assets went bankrupt because management had tied up its assets in ventures in which the management had special personal interest. . . .

It is a balancing act with other people's money.

The Larger the Operation the Less the Control

Our colleague continues:

> The biggest and most prominent organizations are the ones which are going under or are in the greatest difficulty and where the worst abuses are taking place. . . . The fine art of accounting has been used to a great extent to mislead the investors in such a way that the transactions which they believe are taking place are quite different from reality.

Whereas hijackers used to rob "hootch" from other "bootleggers" for delivery to their own customers, today the hijacker says in effect: "You run your show, but I'll tell you where to land and deliver." He avoids interference in the operating process, whether of aircraft, business, or country, as he renames the game. Now hijacking has shifted from "hardware" to "software," and that has changed the nature of the game.

PLUGGING THE GAP AS LEARNED IGNORANCE

Keynes had built a superstructure of hypotheses based on old "hardware" production-for-exchange and the assumptions of an industrial economy. His concepts derived from the same matrix. His embalming fluid has lost its rejuvenating powers. The mere acceptance of Keynes by the academic and bureaucratic establishments was evidence that his theory had predeceased its application. But John Maynard's doctrine, embalmed in economic legislation, goes marching round in ever-decreasing government circles.

"Fax" and "Grafs": Reason Without Rhyme

What the "practical man" doesn't know is that facts are something *made,* as the word tells us (*facio*). Moreover, a fact cannot be *connected* without "seizing up." The interval or gap is necessary to any practical action. The gap is where the action is. "Ask the man who owns one." The artist and engineer exist to create the right gaps and to avoid unfunny connections.

> *Calling Spiro Agnew: "Now Hear This:*
> *the Media Are Bigger-than-youse—*
> *Bigger-than-news"*

All facts and graphs are artifacts contrived by man.
All facts are composites of *figure-ground* relationships.
All graphs are obsolete curves to be enjoyed in the rear-view mirror.

AT HIGH SPEEDS ART REPLACES NATURE, AND NATURE GOES TO SCHOOL,
TO THE ARTIST ON PLANET ECO-POLLUTO.

NOTHING EXCEEDS LIKE EXCESS

Writing on the "Failures and Successes of Economics" (*THINK,* May-June, 1965), Kenneth E. Boulding cites "Phillips Curve" to the effect that beyond a certain point "the more employment the more inflation." Boulding, in *The Image,* was one of the first to note that the gist of economic life had moved into the information or "software" orbit. Political economy had, in fact, become economic politics. The trend to what he calls

THE GRANTS ECONOMY

is a reversal of an age-old and opposite trend of the separation of work and residence. The increase of "software" and information as industries become knowledge-oriented can have only one terminal, namely, the restoration of the decentralized "cottage economy." So far this development has been called "moonlighting" and "starlighting."

"Do-it-yourself" now permits use of the total environment as a private resource. Earlier, it had been an elite that exploited the "public benefits for private vices." Now it is everybody who gets in on the act. This, naturally, via Hertz Law of Complementarity brings the flip or reversal of effect. In Boulding's words, "grants may be made out of fear rather than out of love." The grant as tribute, levied on a puzzled public, becomes a feature of the "threat system," as in Speenhamland.

Everybody becomes a bureaucrat in some branch of civil service, and this constitutes a police state, in which "the economics of fear" can have no rival. After increasing beyond some point, any service becomes a disservice. School kids and postdoctoral researchers alike now wait anxiously for the renewal of their annual grants. For example, the top researcher knows he must not rock the academic boat or knock a great hole in the hull by some ill-advised discovery. Louis Pasteur made that mistake and never got aboard again.

COOL DEALS BY HOT TIPS

The Hella-ments of Heca-gnomics: A Hex on All Your Houses

As oral resonance erodes the boundaries of the old economies, turning the planet intð a single Echoland, a word now makes the market. The sequential causality of classical economics is meaningless and fatal in a world that "will remember itself from every sides, with all gestures in each our word" (*Finnegans Wake*).

It is an insult to carry an order book in the American South or in any oral society where

A Man's Word Is Better than His Bond

In the new world of resonance the stock market has become the Western cargo cult.

Expectation and waiting have become our greatest products.
Scarcity causes hardship, but affluence creates poverty.
Is your face or your frame your game?
Spock's spooks speak in Twiggy and Tiny Tim.
Put on the whole world as your mask of power, says the electrotechnical switch.

Money Profit as the Criterion for "Performance" Is Now Passé for Running a Complex Business Organization

Some management consultants imply that executive "performance" may soon be measured by computer with as many separate criteria as there are separately defined corporate "goals." It is also becoming clear that the simple arithmetic which now serves to express the exchange of one "hardware" commodity for another is inadequate, where each party merely gains what the other loses. The process of exchanging "software" information is one where neither party loses and both may gain through *dialogue*. Old measures of both "performance" and "profit" thus fail to meet new management needs:

> It is no longer resources that limit decisions. It is the decision that makes the resources. This is the fundamental revolutionary change.
> U Thant

APOLLO AS DESTROYER AND PRESERVER

> Wild Spirit, which art moving everywhere;
> Destroyer and Preserver; hear, oh, hear!
> Percy Bysshe Shelley, "Ode to the West Wind"

This dual aspect of the pagan god of wisdom and order now appears where government and business merge through space programs as surrogates for war. The *Report from Iron Mountain on the Possibility and Desirability of Peace* notes:

> The lack of fundamental organized social conflict inherent in space work, however, would rule it out as an adequate motivational substitute for war when applied to "pure" science. But it could no doubt sustain the broad range of technological activity that a space budget of military dimensions would require.

The GNP (gross national product) reduces all inputs, whether for destruction or preservation, to the common denominator of money.

Economics—Education—Entertainment Merge in the Global Fee-nix Theater

Apollo 11 included the entire population of the world as its cast. The occupants of the space capsule were the directors of a world theater. Operation Apollo was the biggest educational TV program ever devised to date (1969). More people learned more in a shorter time than ever before in the history of mankind. The audience was world-wide and totally participant in the operation. This is the inevitable dimension and structure of the "magnetic city"—the term that Wyndham Lewis uses in *The Human Age* for electronic man.

Myth Is Today's Reality

James Joyce simply noticed "the urb orbs even as the orb urbs." These are not mere figures of speech or word play. At instant speeds of information, these are literally true accounts of current processes. What has been called "mythic" in the past merely means *an instant vision of a complex process* or a capsulated statement of such processes. At electric speeds we cannot avoid being mythic in our every gesture. What has happened with electric speed-up is that *the now* contains all pasts whatever, including the most primal and primitive modes. Wyndham Lewis said: "The artist is older than the fish." Electronic man is older than the fish. His magnetic city comprises and includes the most painful conditions of Paleolithic hunter, as well as the most luxurious "dreams that money can buy." For example, the astronaut undergoes psychic hazards and physical hardships beyond the dreams of the Paleolithic hunter, while at the same time living in the most "advanced" conditions of probing and research.

DOMINION OF MARKET PUSHED TO EXTREME RESUMES KINGDOM OF MAN

Whirled at electric speeds, the old market-pricing process, whether MINI, MAXI, or MIDI, fails to provide new compensations for the old forgone satisfactions. What emerges is awareness of pattern and dramatic action, which offers the possibility of total audience participation in social programming through dialogue. The nineteenth-century market melodrama of "haves" and "have-nots," of "thud and blunder," was a form of audience participation based merely on "hardware" and consumer goods. Regardless of any theoretic formulation, there is the physical fact today of the world enveloped with a service environment of electric information. The main drama of our time thus shifts from the market and "exchange of equivalents" to the fecundating of the entire social matrix by knowledge and information. The new drama of cognition and recognition ensures unlimited diversity of satisfactions, which obsolesces the uniformity of market compensations. Again, at electric speeds, the calculating seesaw game of "what are you getting?" and "what am I getting?" out of this as of now vanishes in an ecstatic blur.

"Back to the market" is becoming as nostalgic as "back to the land." In the age of the "military-industrial complex" the market place has already become an art form that no longer measures or motivates the main "economic" activity. Nor do health, education, and welfare embody the main bulk of the wealth-making process. Rather, the bulk is to be found in the "consumption" of sheer information, whether in entertainment or its opposite. We have finally reached awareness of the unconscious itself as the major hidden resource, since we have learned the role of sleep and dreaming as "social work and purgation" in the psychotherapeutic age. What had been the scandal of idleness, ignorance, and sleeping-on-the-job will be available to spin the new vortex of social action in the electric age.

Households Are Now World Shopping Centers

To include in a single capsulated space the totality of planetary ecology is characteristic of electronic man in every phase of his activity. What Peter Drucker calls the "world shopping center" is identical with the scope of Apollo 11. The world shopping center does not have to be big enough to include the world population or all the "hardware" packages in the world. On the contrary, it has to be a capsule *structurally* inclusive of all possible forms. The amount of any one component that is present is unimportant. If Apollo 11 had been a half-mile in diameter it would have had no more ecological features than it had. That is, it had to be a complete model of space capsule Earth. In the same way, the world shopping center has to be viable in a planetary, *structural* sense, not in the sense of *moreness*. It is an inclusive service environment of information and images that is indicated by the phrase and concept "world shopping center."

A world shopping center is precisely what we now have at home. Any catalogue of the Sears-Roebuck variety is itself a world shopping guide. Some will remember the fate of the African chief who became a convert to the catalogue. He filled his hut with folding furniture. Then he decided to dispense with his large throne chair and placed it in the attic. Soon his hut collapsed.

THOSE WHO LIVE IN GRASS HOUSES "SHOULD"
NOT STOW THRONES

The Etherealization of "Hardware" by "Software": From Wired Connections to Resonant Interfaces

The human body is the magazine of inventions. . . . All the tools and engines on earth are only extensions of its limbs and senses.
Ralph Waldo Emerson

There were the poets . . . who told anyone who would listen that a wish is more important than a fortune, and a dream can weigh more than iron or steel. Jacques Lusseyran, *And There Was Light*

Stand up to hardware and step into style.
James Joyce, *Finnegans Wake*

New uses of the words "hardware" and "software" have come in with computer technology. It is a typical case of using the old media and terminology in new specialist ways. "Interface" is another instance of inept appropriation of an ordinary word to express "the connexion between any two units" of computer systems (see Anthony Chandor, *Dictionary of Computers*). There are, in fact, no connections in the material universe. Einstein, Heisenberg, and Linus Pauling have baffled the old mechanical and visual culture of the nineteenth century by reminding scientists in general that the only physical bond in Nature is the resonating interval or "interface." Our language, as much as our mental set forbids us to regard the world in this way. It is hard for the conventional and uncritical mind to grasp the fact that *"the meaning of meaning" is a relationship: a figure-ground process of perpetual change.* The input of data must enter a *ground* or field or surround of relations that are transformed by the intruder, even as the input is also transformed. Knowledge, old or new, is always a figure that is undergoing perpetual change by "interface" with new environments. Thus it is never easy to divorce knowledge and experience. In the same way that knowledge and experience are continuously modifying each other, the relation between "hardware" and "software" is not fixed but is in a perpetual state of metamorphosis.

1

Designing

"Software" Is Not Just Data but the Organization of Information

There is no information in a telephone book—just DATA.

The computer unit or equipment as new "hardware" has a major component of "design," which is "software." Further, this "hardware" unit can be used only by a program of "software" instructions that is also "software" style or design. Yet this "software" program may execute a series of orders of the most antiquated "hardware" type. For example, a computer can be programmed to simulate all the old assembly-line scheduling and execution patterns.

> B. J. Muller-Thym was historically among the first to note that the form intrinsic in automation ultimately is not standardization but variety, because all mechanical processes with variable dimensions can be programmed by tape to manufacture a customized product, where every changeable item can be tailored precisely to the buyer's specifications. Muller-Thym's favorite example is the single machine that can "make up to eighty different kinds of automotive tailpipe as rapidly and cheaply as you can make eighty of the same one," and he notes that most extras and other variables on automobiles are nowadays assembled precisely to the individual customer's order.
>
> Richard Kostelanetz, *Master Minds*

It is in this new dimension of "software" design that the difference between the old mechanical industry and the new electric circuitry becomes manifest. It is a difference not only of speed and diversity but also of knowledge and of the programming for special, personal needs.

The potential of the computer has been used no more than that of TV. Any new form is always used for the old job, because those in control are the servants of past experience rather than the masters of present fact.

THE IRON LAW OF "SOFTWARE":

The Complementarity of Host Medium and Guest Product

Every product as *figure* seeks a host medium as *ground*. Every product has the power of imposing its own "assumptions" or ground rules on the entire social context. The disc jockey who appears to be manipulating a record player is, in fact, applying this technology to the hidden service *ground* of radio. The disc as product, when crossed with the radio *ground*, activates a vast new world of musicians and consumers of music. The radio-created *ground* provides instant access to a new public diversified in age and condition. The LP disc creates new needs and new markets by assuming the hidden *ground* of radio. The service environment of radio is almost coextensive with the entire consumer market. And the disc jockey has direct access to this vast world, which is potentially in the disc itself as product. It does not follow that the same disc jockey could create a similar market either for audio or video "cassettes." The *figure-ground* or host-medium relations undergo far-reaching change with the slightest modification of design or service.

Going Groovy

The disc jockeys and their new music packages created a new kind of audience involvement in the music-making process. Millions of youngsters went "groovy" and began to enjoy the exact nuance that characterized each band and each performer.

If anyone were to try to guide the disc jockeys and their audiences into a new pattern where a "cassette" would replace the LP disc, they would discover at once that the conditions of both recording and playing would be different. The kinds of participation and skill demanded of musicians, disc jockeys, and audience alike would change. One of the effects of the disc-jockey world was to create a large number of musical performers of rudimentary skills. The "hardware" world often requires a high degree of technical skill on the part of the performer. The pianoforte is more demanding than the "guitar" or ukulele. As the radio and TV age created new dimensions of audience participation, the levels of skill were shifted from the performer to the service designer. The electric light demands an easy switch in order to be a universal service. *To the degree that anything becomes an environmental service, it must be simple in use.*

If the radio cassette reduced the radio public by increased demand in "hardware" skill, the proposed video cassettes could not possibly become a service as extensive as radio or TV. The reason is not just in the "hardware" complexity of a cassette that could be played on a TV set as if it were an LP disc. Rather, there is the fact that the immense involvement of the TV public in this medium demands a completely new type of nonspecialist programming. For example, everybody is acquainted with the popularity of the new "talk" shows on TV. The use of "guests" as a major program device is a recognition of the fact that the TV medium is a social one. In contrast, there is the solitary character of both radio and movie. The movie viewer tends to be "alone," even in a crowded theater.

MAN IS THE CONTENT

The TV "talk" show reveals the need not only for a studio audience but for a new type of dialogue that crosses many fields. Anybody who thinks that an effective TV cassette could consist of a lecture or a solitary performance would soon discover that he misunderstood the TV medium. The audience would simply not present itself for such fare.

"Include me out, pal!"

This quip of the 1920's is useful to any student of media, since most programs for any new medium are merely taken over from earlier media. They tend to "include out" the new potential public. Video cassettes will "include out" their own new uses simply by being designed to capture earlier publics created by earlier media. The makers of video cassettes will gradually discover that their real public does not want to share a consumer process but a process of discovery and invention. It is therefore the "software" design of the program that demands the major effort from this new "universal" medium. The top shows needed for video cassettes cannot be the mere encounter of casual acquaintance or "names" in a studio. Paradoxically, as the TV medium embraces everybody as its *content*, it has to dramatize the learning process itself—the process we all share as sentient, conscious beings. Video-cassette dialogue will have to present the *play*, not so much of words as of thoughts. "The thoughts that rise" in us as we encounter our world are the *effect* that things have upon us. They are not the things. It is the distinction of the "artist" in any field that he commands this power to convey the *effects* of things when the ordinary person is merely numbed or robotized by things. The fascination of child behavior and child art is the same.

For the Small Child, the Thing and Its Effect Are One

Child to father on its first air flight: "Daddy, when do we start to get smaller?"

The child, who experienced space as undergoing change in the outer world, expects space in the cabin of a plane also to be dynamic. One of the mysteries of visual perception is the static character of enclosed space. Lewis Carroll in *Alice Through the Looking Glass* provided a mathematical demonstration of the nonstatic character of space. TV is what Joyce calls a "collideoscope."

All Publics Are in the Public Domain

The abrasive interplay and collision of perceptions in the TV medium fostered new kinds of dialogue and awareness on the part of the TV users.

The TV user is the *content* of TV. Everybody who exists within any man-made service environment experiences all the effects that he would undergo in any environment as such. Environments work us over and remake us. It is man who is the *content* of and the *message* of the *media*, which are extensions of himself. Electronic man must know the *effects* of the world he has made above all things.

No More Stops at End of Steel

> Where the deer and the antelope play.
> "Home on the Range"

With the "end of steel," paradoxically, services include everybody. The electric light far surpasses the motorcar in scope and use. The railway, relative to the motorcar, was an elite service with specialist "engineers" and "conductors" and "dispatchers" and "stationmasters." On the principle that as services are maximized, skills are minimized, the motorcar is an obvious illustration. Anybody can drive one, and, one hopes, any teen-ager can "fix" one.

Spaceship Earth is still operated by railway conductors, just as NASA is managed by men with Newtonian goals. In the nineteenth century the end of steel made a very visible "frontier" for the man who had gone West. Owen Wister's *The Virginian* reveals the new awareness of the prairie man: "With him now the East-bound departed slowly into that distance whence I had come. I stared after it as it went its way to the far shores of civilization."

Computer Supplants Locomotive God

> The computer is the first machine that consumes and produces the
> same material—information.   William Jovanovich

Today the end of steel is no mere metaphor, since the "hardware" now disappears inside the computer by design; but the new frontier is as invisible as a radio wave. There are no tracks to identify or to locate the new frontiersman, even nostalgically. He has neither retrospect nor prospect in his instant space-time field. It is all pasts and all futures in an eternal present.

> The loud lament of the disconsolate chimera.
> T. S. Eliot, *Four Quartets*

The American dream of the open road has been abandoned to "Easy Riders" ready to blow their minds. The new frontier is pure opacity, but our conductors still look for Ye Olde Station Stop, which haunts them like a Gegenschein of a galloping poltergeist.

The Crusader and the Stainless Steel Chastity Belt

When the foul paynim had to be routed from the Holy City, the traveling knight put on his "hardware" and used more of the same to lock up the "software" treasure of his lady's chastity. Today the urge to go into the breach is even greater, but the possibility of preserving the treasure grows less. In medieval times a chastity belt was a formidable obstacle. Today it is the key to the problem. The age-old rivalry between the safe maker and the safecracker has resulted in a gradual reduction of the period of immunity from penetration. "Hardware" thinking persists in a "software" world, driving secrecy and security measures to comic lengths:

TOO HOT TO HANDLE

BURN BEFORE READING

TOP SECRET. WHEN YOU GET THIS, DESTROY YOURSELF.

2

Secreting

He Leaned His Ear in Many a Secret Place

The forms of management that are fostered by writing as a means of control at a distance are well illustrated by the famous Fugger newsletter service of the Renaissance. The need for close intercom and secrecy in the early stages of private enterprise led to family banks, such as those of the Rothschilds and the Wallenbergs. The only people who could be trusted to receive confidential communications at a distance were members of a single family. This is a paradox. That is to say, the very form of communication which later became the model of delegated authority and the organization-chart structure at first favored family tribalism as a business pattern.

The clannish household that had been the origin of trade in the ancient world helped the Phoenicians to maintain monopolies of navigational lore. The same pattern reappears with the Fuggers in the Middle Ages and with Henry the Navigator in Renaissance Portugal. Secret knowledge of trade routes or "software" made possible monopolies of "hardware" treasures.

SECRECY IS A FUNCTION OF SLOW INFORMATION MOVEMENT
MONOPOLIES OF KNOWLEDGE DISAPPEAR IN RATIO TO SPEED-UP

In the "software" world of instant information secrecy is either of brief duration or easy to by-pass by direct research.

It is not possession of the solution, but the recognition of the problem itself that provides a resource and the answers. *Only puny secrets need protection. Big discoveries are protected by public incredulity.* The atom could not be split until it was regarded as a problem.

For the "hardware" mind, somebody has to do something before it will admit that there is a problem to be solved. Once one atom bomb had been made, anybody could make one without stealing anybody else's know-how.

Secrecy is for the birds.
Little bird saying

No military secrets can be kept under bed covers.
The Secretary's Manual

The need for clannish protection of information grew out of the extreme slowness of movement of such information. The diplomatic pouch has never been in a hurry.

George Washington: "Let's Write to Our Ambassador, Benjamin Franklin, in Paris; We Haven't Heard from Him for a Year"

With speed-up, the same written form created an entirely different pattern of administration. It also created secret writing and codes (such as da Vinci's). The cult of coding in the seventeenth century had reached the point where it was an aesthetic game.

Sam Pepys, founding bureaucrat of the British Navy, kept a detailed personal diary in a code known only to himself. He mimed in private life the hidden pattern of his public life. Like the cave painters, his work was never intended for any audience whatever. Let us suggest that he was his own audience in a game of solitaire. As a repeat or playback of his outer life, the diary helped to keep his psychic house in order. It was a catharsis, or a private repetition of what he was doing in another set of public situations.

Espionage Fun Books Proclaim the End of Secrecy in the New Spin Age

Man hunting ever since Sherlock Holmes has been a major entertainment industry. The popularity of these *passé* activities has not deterred governments from massive competition with the thriller packages.

If You Take the Bull by the Horns You'll Get a Lot of Bull

Bureaucratic virtuosity in these measures and countermeasures has enabled countless bored agents and officers and undercover operatives to lead lives as exciting as any kid ever enjoyed playing cowboys and Indians. In China, Confucian courtesy is applied to unscrewing the inscrutable West by the members of *the social affairs department*.

The British are more ascetic and antiseptic in using both numbers and letters: M.I. 5, M.I. 6. The U.S.S.R. is less playful and sporty than the British. The successors to the CHEKA and the OGPU are the KGB and the GRU with few overtones of playfulness. The United States is alone in stressing "I spy with my little eye": FBI and CIA. The Canadian Mounties are a horse of another color.

Plots for All: Any Rumor May Apply

Man and information hunting and exchanging have become the largest business in the world. As surveillance takes over the whole of society, it reverses its functions and characteristics. For a tiny fraction of the commercial and military espionage budgets, genuinely creative research can be carried on. It is now possible to "invent" anything that is needed, and quicker than stealing it from a rival.

The New Role of the Patent Is to Be a Blueprint for Its Successor

The old role of the patent was to provide the pause that enriches—slowdown.

The new role of the patent is the reverse, *i.e.*, to provide a blueprint for its successor—speed-up.

Legislation and law enforcement have normally been used to put brakes on social changes that had occurred previous to the legislation. Leviathan does not fly on angel wings. *Whereas convictions depend on speed-up, justice requires delay.*

Today, however, law enforcement is also directed toward expediting current events, *e.g.*, traffic flow. The police state has thus an interest in accelerating convictions. When written legal forms impede transactions, the oral "fixers" move in. So do the T-men.

In Ratio to Speed-up the Mafias Take Over

The Mafia is no more extralegal or extraconstitutional than political parties and their machines. The hidden "rim spin" of information speed-up by-passes written legislation and restores the oral tradition in all transactions.

Caesar never did wrong without just cause.
Shakespeare, *Julius Caesar*

The oral tradition easily penetrates the innumerable loopholes inherent in any written code. However, the "gap" between the old legislation and the new "fixers" creates a world of ever more rapid change. The natural result of pushing this process is, first, the reign of "organized crime." Then comes the retrieval of the ancient cliché of "common" or oral law: "Where there is no remedy there is no crime."

From Age of Gold to Age of Steal and Return?

Taking the goose from the common
and
Taking the common from the goose

Rodger Wildness, in a recent project proposal, "N.E.T. Proposal for a Fundable Project," notes:

Because man is a creature capable of unbounded action amplified through the technology he has created, the manner in which he communicates, understands, and invests his psychic energies is today our greatest concern.

There was no need for law until man had created ordure by transmuting the age of gold into the age of iron through technology. Now, in the electric age, it is law that creates ordure. But, pushed to the extreme, ordure results in new order—society as art form.

3

Innovating

**THE ARTIST AND INVENTOR ARE THE ULTIMATE ENEMIES
OF THE ESTABLISHMENT**

The artist makes new perception that changes all the social *ground* rules.
The inventor creates products and processes that transform environments.

An instance of invention is the nose cone for the space capsule. It is a
new design with new materials for a new job, for which neither design,
need, nor materials previously existed. The nose cone that had been created
for a single use thus proliferated a number of other materials and processes
that quickly evoked new service/disservice environments. *Every new conquest of speed moves toward the minimizing of "hardware" and the maximizing of "software" or structural design.*

As the West approached this awareness in the nineteenth century, biologists began to ask, "Why is there so much unused beauty in Nature?" The
answer came later, from the mathematicians in the world of "software." "If
an equation is symmetrically beautiful, it is almost certain to be true."
What the artist has always known, namely, that the greatest effects result
from the utmost economy of means, has now become a truism of the material sciences.

**THE UNEXPECTED EFFECT OF "HARDWARE" SPEED-UP HAS BEEN TO RE-
STORE THE WORLD AS WORK OF ART OR OBJECT OF CONTEMPLATION.**

As a work of art, the world impels the viewer to *Make It New*, to cite the
Chinese injunction to the artist concerning his role. Man becomes both
explorer and maker of beauty as "hardware" and "software" merge. The
"hardware-software" complementarity is a new version of the old form-and-
content relation. The old hang-up about "form" and "content" had arisen
under the regime of merely visual culture, where "content" had to be contained *in* something. With the *figure-ground* relation of Gestalt psychology, the "content" was continuously created in the *gap* between *figure* and
ground. The new physics carried this relation even further, citing *resonance*
as the very stuff of "hardware."

The Movie Fakirs of Reel Magic

The mere visualizer wants to *see* what's resonating. No greater fulfillment of the visual man's preference has occurred than the faking of the real world in the "software" world of "celluloid" and the silver screen. In this "reel world" a vast simulation of the outer realities was provided as a fantasia of the semiconscious movie patrons.

The whole world was translated and transformed by the film medium into a genuine fake. On the one hand, the movie provided a consumer package of "dream girls" and "dreamboats" for the affluent West. When the same movies appeared in preindustrial societies, however, they were not additions to the "hardware" goods but substitutes that intensified the craving for the imagined riches of the West. *Cargo cults* sprang up around the world. Natives stood on the shores waiting for Uncle Sam's big boat of goodies and iceboxes.

The Emperor of Ice Cream Took Over the East as Well

On the eve of affluence by mass production, Wordsworth and the Romantics took a final stand on nature. Just as the man-made service environments were beginning to take over from the agrarian economy, Wordsworth proclaimed the "filial and gravitational bond" that related man to his mother earth, by stating, "The child is father to the man." This seemed a wild proposition in his day, but it has since been accepted as obvious: the child's environment shapes adult perception and preference. Man-made environments replaced nature, and these new environments became the mother of the man. *The Medium Is the Message* concurs with Wordsworth in stating that our service environments of new media shape the new physical, psychic, and social attitudes of world populations. The psychic and social "software" is effectively programmed by the new "hardware."

Inevitably, as the total human social matrix shifts from the natural to the man-made, the fact of art as a substitute for nature creates a world of confusions.

Should Old Aquinas Be Forgot?

Aquinas reminds us that "all sensible qualities are related" by a power which had long been called "common sense." This intellectual power is that by which every sense experience is simultaneously translated into all the other senses, presenting us with a unified sensory experience, which is consciousness. Consciousness is thus the act of *making sense*, and "the material change affects the sensible quality as well as the one sensing" (Vernon Bourke). T. S. Eliot expressed it simply:

> . . . for the roses
> Had the look of flowers that are looked at.

Aquinas and Eliot share the classical idea of the "magical" interplay of mutual transformation that occurs between man and his world. There is no question of a mere matching or mirror correspondence between man and things even in the older world of nature. Today, when the entire environment is directly created by man himself, the bond between man and things takes on a much greater scope and intensity of resonance.

Discovery and Suspended Judgment

It has been said by A. N. Whitehead that the greatest discovery of the nineteenth century was the discovery of the technique of discovery. That technique consists in the retracing of any process of generation or cognition. Bertrand Russell noted as complementarity that the greatest discovery of the twentieth century was the technique of "the suspended judgement" —not single but multiple models of experimental exploration. The need to suspend points of view and private value judgments is indispensable to the programming of total environments.

T. S. Eliot, in "Tradition and the Individual Talent," gave classic statement to the theme of strategy of "the suspended judgement." Citing the role of platinum as catalyst in effecting new chemical combination, Eliot observed:

> The mind of the poet is the shred of platinum. It may partly or exclusively operate upon the experience of the man himself; but, the more perfect the artist, the more completely separate in him will be the man who suffers and the mind which creates; the more perfectly will the mind digest and transmute the passions which are its material.

WHAT NEITHER WHITEHEAD NOR RUSSELL SAW WAS THE IMMINENCE OF SUBSTITUTING ART FOR NATURE BY THE ANTICIPATION OF EFFECTS WITH CAUSES THROUGH PATTERN RECOGNITION OF THE RELEVANT PROCESSES.

The Genuine Fake as a New Service Industry
Trash and Treasures: New-found Art

> I have painted almost 1,200 pictures. More than 2,500 of them are in the U.S.A.   Henri Matisse

If the function of art is the training and programming of *new* perception, what is the role of the "genuine" fake? Fakes of Picasso, Vermeer, or Klee? If the experts are baffled by such artifacts, does it follow that the public is being cheated of its art experience when looking at a genuine fake such as a van Meegeren "Vermeer"?

If a great pianist hams Bach or Chopin, is he *putting on* his audience rather than his composer? Shakespeare was branded by his better-educated contemporary Robert Greene as "an upstart crow beautified with our feathers."

If anyone today were to fabricate a fake Shakespeare play that surpassed the powers of the critics to invalidate it, would it be a "good or bad thing"?

In the age of massive reproduction in raving colors, in the age of hi-fi recordings and the retrieval and reconstruction of art from all past cultures, what are the functions of contemporary art and invention? When nature has been enveloped and swamped in man's artifacts, what is the role of the artist? He can no longer appeal to nature as *norm*. After Sputnik, art became norm. Nature was supplanted.

IMPERIAL FAKES FOR ALL

> In the room the women come and go
> Talking of Michaelangelo.
> > T. S. Eliot, "The Love Song of J. Alfred Prufrock"

When asked whether he might substitute "the Masters of Siena" for "Michaelangelo," Eliot replied to the would-be French translator of his "Prufrock": "These Boston culture snobs had never heard of the Sienese painters. They knew Michaelangelo in popular postcards."

The genuine inventor raids his predecessors fearlessly and just as contemptuously casts aside his discoveries when they are accepted by the undiscriminating. The role of the artist-inventor is to create new fields of perception. As soon as the squatters move in, he moves on to a new world. William Butler Yeats explains the sterility of acceptance in his "A Coat":

> I made my song a coat
> Covered with embroideries
> Out of old mythologies
> From heel to throat;
> But the fools caught it,
> Wore it in the world's eyes
> As though they'd wrought it.
> Song, let them take it,
> For there's more enterprise
> In walking naked.

Yeats confesses his rifling of old mythologies to *make* a great peacock costume for the pride and joy of his eye. The moment it became fashionable and marketable, he flung it aside:

> For there's more enterprise
> In walking naked.

As poet-emperor, the maker of new environments for his subjects, the entrepreneur-maker will appear naked to those whose eyes are shielded by cliché and "good taste." Joyce and Eliot were called "drunken helots" or riffraff pirates when they first appeared. But in art, as in the biggest business innovations (*e.g.*, Xerox), the explorers appear naked even in the act of *putting on* the whole world as their costume. What appears as "nudity" to the common-or-garden sensation seeker is the artistic strategy for taking over the public as a resource or power vortex.

Cheaper and Quicker to Rediscover than to Retrieve in Big Business

The reason that "mission-oriented" research and development drowns in the superabundance of available data is very simply by-passed by the artist. He asks: "What precise *effect* do I want to have on my public? What precise emotion do I wish to evoke and define?" The artist starts with the *effect,* since the *means* to such an effect are everywhere. The "mission" men with their teams cannot get clear of the irrelevant data. Their vision is dimmed by an excess of *means.*

We Didn't Know Exactly What Questions to Ask

Typical of the bewildered manager is the comment of General Howell M. Estes in *Armed Forces Management* (December, 1966) in reply to an Air Force Request for Proposal:

> . . . the total weight of the paper submitted was 35 tons—the maximum payload of today's C-141. It took more than 400 Air Force experts five months to read and evaluate that mass of data. This, to me, hardly represents progress in the management of management information. One reason is that we didn't know exactly what questions to ask—so we asked far too many in our RFP.

It may seem incongruous that the masters of the air should be interred in a mass of information of their own making:

> In fact, it has been estimated that it is cheaper to re-do a technical project—if the cost is less than $100,000—than to go through the process of trying to learn if someone has already solved the problem.

Industrial giants on all fronts are belatedly engaged in producing "old-hat" "hardware."

Project Hindsight in the Mini-splendored World

There is even pathos in the recognition of futility in the most advanced efforts that money can buy. Herbert Hollomon, Assistant Secretary of Commerce for Science and Technology in the United States, was cited at a conference on "Technology Transfer and Innovation":

> Hollomon, referring to Project HINDSIGHT, explains that today's innovations are based largely on 30-year-old science because most engineers—those who actually utilize research outputs—learned their science from textbooks in school.

Among the numerous hindsights retrieved by the members of the conference was the ancient discovery that for the most part, information users—both cosmopolites and locals—get the word by ear rather than by eye. Reading seems to play a relatively small part in the process of transfer; conversing is far more important.

Growth as Rumor

GALBRAITH DISPUTES LEADING ROLES OF GROWTH, PROFIT,
AND GNP AS MEASURES OF SECURITY

I'm not talking about a world in which people work less and consume more—that's still impossible. I'm talking about a world in which, above a certain level, people are not driven like lemmings to work more because they are persuaded they must consume more. And more. And more. And more. That world is possible. The goal in this world is not consumption, but the use and enjoyment of life.

Frances Cairncross, London *Observer* Service, December, 1970

The tribal outlook of the young TV kids is as anti-innovation and anti-growth as in any tribal society of the past. Those who "play it by ear" are instantly aware of the *effects* of change. The same electric technology that has retrieved ESP and the occult for many levels and areas of American life has turned the kids away from "moreness," from glossy consuming to homespun and "camp" and "found" art. They are finished with both job goals and market values. This change of outlook is not ideological but psychological. These children are very much their own "fathers," in that their early man-made environment programmed their sensory and perceptual lives for a totally different range of satisfactions than those of their parents and teachers.

TIME MARCHES DOWN

"Avant-Garde" as Camp Followers

As an ever-probing *avant-garde* organ, *Time* turns with the times, like the Vicar of Bray or the old Duke of York, who marched his troops right up the hill and marched them down again. It senses a new climate of opinion forming and hastily changes into an appropriate costume. Its "Business" section for March 2, 1970, plays both sides of "the street" with bigger and better on one side and noble poverty on the other: "More and more critics argue that obsession with economic growth has tended to blind men to the depredations that it leaves in its wake."

Here is the specter of Pandora's Box and the recognition that all services are paid for with disservices. *Time* senses a sudden yen for human scale amidst the palaces and pleasures:

Urbanologists fret about cities swollen to dinosaur dimensions that defy efficient management and create immense social costs through crime, congestion and drug addiction. Ecologists raise the specter of a planet made uninhabitable by the pressures of a rising population. Some environmentalists go so far as to advocate a no-growth society; they call upon rich nations to welcome declines in their gross national products.

Typically hindsighted, the ZPG kids imagine their problem to be population control and its solution: Zero Population Growth. In fact, the crunch has become the enormous speed-up of physical and information movement that has scrubbed and reduced community satisfactions by allowing people no time or peace to relate to one another.

The Effluent Society: Pollution of Human Satisfactions

In market terms, *inflation* and *depression* are "hardware" correlatives of "outer tripping." In social terms, inflation and depression are "software" correlatives of "inner tripping." The older generation experienced the bitterness of broken economic promises and ambitions. The inner-oriented TV kids have experienced in the old "hardware" world "the bitter tastelessness of shadow fruit" as the old environment begins to fall away.

The new impulse to exploration in an all-at-once world is not so much novelty of impression as depth of commitment:

Organized Ignorance

> My poems—I should suppose everybody's poems—are set to trip the reader head foremost into the boundless. Ever since infancy I have had the habit of leaving my blocks, carts, chairs, and such like ordinaries where people would be pretty sure to fall forward over them in the dark. Forward, you understand, *and* in the dark.   Robert Frost

One of the breakthroughs of World War II was Operations Research, which began as "brain storming" and soon dried up as *expertise*. The play element was professionalized. At first, however, the *ground* rule was to "clear out the experts." These men always vetoed a suggestion on any subject, since they knew "it couldn't be done." They were unaware of the great "metaphysical" insight of Coleridge that the entrée to anyone's knowledge was through the back door of his ignorance. Since then, we have learned that it is the refuse heap of discarded theses and unsolved problems that is the greatest resource available to man. The expert doesn't know the right questions, so he rejects the right answers. Hence the need for a playful and spontaneous approach to real problems.

Dislocating the Mind into Perception

All people have "mental sets" or habits of perception that conceal the real game from their eyes. "Serendipity" is now a popular word for the game of random by-passing of ingrained habits and concepts. The word was coined by Horace Walpole in 1754. He explains that "he had formed it upon the title of the fairy tale *The Three Princes of Serendip,* the heroes of which were always making discoveries, by accidents and sagacity, of things they were not in quest of."

Most discoveries are unexpected by-products of activities quite unconnected to them. Every artist makes breakthroughs as soon as he meets a difficulty. Today the need for problem solving is so great that techniques for this purpose have had to be developed.*

Brain storming, which looks wildly chaotic to the analytic mind, is in fact the only way of swarming all over a complex situation. It is an intuitive, all-at-once method of intellectual grasp. Playfulness and creativity and invention are inseparable. Even before these playful approaches, "value engineering" had been the name used by General Electric for techniques of meeting new competition in "hardware" products. The "cheaper mouse trap" had to be conjured up in a form requiring less material and labor.

The Challenge to Spring the Rivals' Trap

Gradually the uptight managers of the most responsible business operations conceded the necessity of sinking into the most undignified forms of mental horseplay in order to cope with their need for innovation.

The Penman and the Punman: Invention Is Found in Acoustic Not in Visual Configurations

Discoveries issue from "the resonant interval" of quantum mechanics rather than the visual connection of rational systems. Many people of professional demeanor "shun the punman," having been warned that verbal play is the lowest form of wit. These people have to bite their lips a good deal in order to repress their enjoyment of the most natural feature of all language, namely its inexhaustible richness of incompatible meanings.

James Joyce knew that any word was a storehouse of innumerable human perceptions that could be released by abrasive interplay with other words. Given any two words, he could invent a verbal universe. The following fugue or dance of tones and gestures, if read aloud, provides a dramatic account of organized ignorance.

* One of these techniques has recently appeared in the DEW line card deck. The cards can be dealt out to any group. The mélange of wacky aphorisms puts any group or committee into a relaxed and confident posture. If the members are then invited to relate the aphorisms to their top problems, new answers appear from every direction.

The Past-Present-Future of Invention

In the ignorance that implies impression that knits knowledge that finds the nameform that whets the wits that convey contacts that sweeten sensation that drives desire that adheres to attachment that dogs death that bitches birth that entails the ensuance of existentiality.

Finnegans Wake

Starting with the gap of ignorance that generates many-layered perception, Joyce moves to the interweaving of new patterns of knowledge. The "nameform" must be the exact word or formula for a specific *effect*—a major means of "tuning in." His repeated use of "that" is demonstrative stress, not mere linking. The *exact* name whets or sharpens the wits or senses, and sets up new contacts or echoing intervals that enrich sensation. The inventor is the man abounding in sensational vigor and fresh energies derived from sharp contacts. He is ruthless in his quest and his pertinacity as he reaches for his natural prey. He is like the unleashed retriever pursuing to the death, or the bitch in heat who will replace the lost generation and ensure the continuity of the living and the existent.

Joyce here encapsulates the mental and physical drama of social man beleaguered by innumerable problems. All solutions are in the very words by which people confuse and hide their problems until the *punman* releases the secret of the magical word: the service itself reverberates with the labels that will ensue. In the same way, the more pains taken to protect a process or product, the more clues and opportunities are provided for those who wish to appropriate or to emulate the same:

Patent System as Chastity Belt

Admittedly some form of protection against technological competition is provided by the patent system, but it is often more nominal than real. The development of synthetic leather provides a recent example. Du Pont spent £10 million over fifteen years to develop *Corfam* and at the same time built a sizeable patent barrier around it. However, when the Chloride Electrical Storage Company came up against these patents, far from being a hindrance they provided the stimulus and the guidance necessary for producing an allegedly superior product.   J. S. Metcalfe, *Metals and Materials*, February, 1970

Big Business uses market responses as guides to the selection of new products and services. The fact that the "market" is a corporate donkey, which is never given a nibble at more than one out of every two hundred "new carrots," is only a meager index to the waste and ignorance exercised by bureaucratic idea sifters.

"The rape of the lock" is mandatory and inevitable. Anybody who provides a "public" for a new service has robbed himself, since all "publics" are in the public domain. As soon as a taste for Coca-Cola is created, a rival is provided as part of the process. Hitherto, products have been studied at the "expense" of publics. Thus there are endless histories of literature but little study of reading publics. A "public" is structured by conflicting layers of taste and satisfaction, which swiftly erode each other. At any time a totally new "public" may envelop any old public. The new TV public may go around the old movie or radio public, creating unexpected new products and satisfactions. The same happens with every form of transportation, each one engendering diverse satisfactions and needs that modify all earlier ones. TODAY, THE BUSINESS OF BUSINESS IS BECOMING THE CONSTANT INVEN-TION OF NEW BUSINESS.

As We Do More with Less We Invent by Design

Just as decision creates resources, the X-ray vision of all processes renders invention an easy consequence of perceiving causes in action. Surrounded by "activists" and obstreperous interventionists, the managers of our society seem unaware that all the monopolies of knowledge have vanished via the electric environment; illumination has become X ray.

Nothing Now Is IN CAMERA: Everything Is ON CAMERA

Human motives now stand out as starkly as factory chimneys did form-erly. The "tapped wire" is programmed to mislead the secret observer. All actions are now "transparencies," featuring and filtering and infiltrating each other as diaphanous webs.

At this stage of interpenetration of goals and values, experts and monop-olies of information sustain each other like a vocal refrain. Private monopo-lies yield to corporate involvement, and experts in the professions are obso-lete before completing their training. In school and business and laboratory alike, the specialist cannot get into action in time to have relevance. The *ground* changes faster than the *figure*.

> "Have you heard the latest?"
> "It isn't out yet."

The reason why the specialist has lost capacity for relevant action is that the very novelties he has been invested with invariably revive a world of ancient forces and preferences in his society. It is the flood and speed of innovation that send most people reeling backward in a quest for simpler and more "primitive" satisfactions. When change itself becomes the staple or *ground* of our lives, the central *figure* will be an antique.

Every Plan Better than the Next

The principle that every new technology retrieves a much older one, just as every new mode of "software" or knowledge retrieves some older "hardware," demonstrates the fact that we live in worlds that burrow on each other. We burrow and borrow and barrow (or dump) our trash and treasures in an endless ballet of making and unmaking and remaking. The speed of this process is now such that a child can see it.

Zombies of the Old "Hardware"

While all attention is directed toward the fantastic transformations of library and information storage services, the main verb in the new process is the recovery of the innumerable vibrating dimensions of the word as such. As technology pushes toward the ultimate elimination of "hardware," it asserts the primacy of the word itself. Philosophers, thinkers, and historians, as much as executives, will continue for some time to live in the shadow of the older "hardware."

The great law of bibliography, which now applies very obviously to newspapers and magazines, will soon apply to all printed and bound books:

THE MORE THERE WERE THE FEWER THERE ARE.
THE FEWER THERE WERE THE MORE THERE ARE.

The de luxe snob editions of eld are still plentiful and cheap. A single scrap of Elizabethan handbill is worth a fortune.

Another paradox of instant retrieval systems is that while on the one hand they create encyclopedic coverage and access, they also create a much greater need for precise definitions and classifications. If we consider the extent of new medical knowledge made available in the 2,500 specialist periodicals (in English alone), the problem is not one of possession but of access to what is tantalizingly present but unreachable.

Classification as Such Obstructs the Breakthrough into Process

In every field of study and research at present, the incidence of insight and new knowledge surpasses every means of systematic retrieval. The game reverts once more to the individual hunter. In the age of mass man and mass information retrieval, the solitary seeker rules again.

If a TV show were to be mounted in order to permit millions to participate in top research processes, there would be many invaluable insights among the audience. But *how* could *any* of these ever reach the program coordinators? A vast response of unique discoveries defies all existing means of processing even the most precious data. *The* cure for cancer could never get attention. However, it might dawn on many that "cancer" is not a useful category. We are beginning to recognize that all old categories obscure knowledge by lumping a multitude of independent processes under a mere heading.

THE RECOGNITION OF PROCESS AS PRIOR TO CLASSIFICATION IS THE
KEY TO RELEVANT DECISION.

This awareness may well be a major result of the new speed of access to existing data. New instant speed of data processing reverses the order of organizing any structure or procedure. Whereas mere headings were once specialist, mechanical catchalls, they now become the avenues of insight into complex organic processes. An obvious example is POLLUTION. It has always been a major feature of any environment. At high information speeds it presents a Gorgon-like and intolerable visage. It is no longer a category or nuisance, but a process that turns societies to stone.

Paradoxes and Problems

Paradox is the technique for seizing the conflicting aspects of any problem. Paradox coalesces or telescopes various facets of a complex process in a single instant. Our fathers sometimes encountered paradox in the jocular form of the "Irish Bull":

> When you see three cows *standing* in a pasture, the one that is *sitting* is the Irish Bull.

That is to say, the Irish Bull is a form of perception that wittily apprehends the contradictions of human existence. It is playful and supralogical.*

Consequences of Images as Images of Consequences

The process of complementarity is itself fraught with paradox. POVERTY has always been with us under the aspect of misery. When interfaced with affluence at high speeds of information movement, poverty is not a thing but a process that invades every level of action and awareness. So it is with such old accepted classifications as retardation, stupidity, ignorance, intolerance, war, disease, insanity, and crime. These and many such conventional classifications of social and psychic fact are no longer acceptable in the age of instant information.

Today complementarity is demanded in categories as in processes. Every side must be perceived simultaneously as in a cubist drawing:

> Client to marriage broker after sight of bride-to-be: "You didn't tell me she had squint eyes and her mouth sagged."
> Broker: "How should *I* know you hate Picasso?"

When Al Karpis came out of the pen after thirty-two years, he was asked by the press what he most looked forward to on his return to civilian life. His

---

* In her monograph, *Paradoxia Epidemica*, Rosalie Colie tells the story of the passion for paradox among the learned from ancient Greece to modern times.

reply was one word: "PRIVACY." That is a simple instance of complementarity. Solitude is not privacy. Privacy is generated by interface with a public, just as the "colored problem" is generated by interface with the white world. Without "whites" there would only be people. The white man's burden is the white man.

4

Extending

GIGANTISM: THE NEMESIS OF CLASSICAL ELEGANCE

Some executives still insist that only figures count. In this they are echoing the voice of the nineteenth-century physicist Lord Kelvin, who is often quoted as saying that "when you can measure what you are speaking about and express it in numbers, you know something about it; but when you cannot express it in numbers, your knowledge is of a meager and unsatisfactory kind."

The illusion created by figures and currency motivated the drive toward gigantism in all spheres of empire building:

> Guide to Texas visitors watching lion in front of a Chicago public building: "This is the longest unsupported lion's tail in the world."

Gigantism was, until recently, regarded as an effective solution for meeting competition and satisfying stockholders. Governments welcomed any increase of tax base regardless of the loss of human scale and community. The sudden upsurge of "intangibles" prompted by the devotion to tangibles did not merely take the form of gaseous smog but also appeared in the rise of organized crime and violence as the hidden support for democratic delegation of power and authority. Within business itself, the same delegation of power for the growth of massive *proxie plotz* led to the same loss of controls. Giant structures, hurried into new courses by technological speed-up, go for broke.

Magazines and movie empires could not adapt their vast organizations to the emergence of color technologies. The highly literate staffs of these enterprises could not be switched from narrative techniques to the verbal icon. The TV world itself is in the same bind of being staffed by literates who have no clue to the effects of color technology on their operation.

Gigantism is compelled to grow until collapse. Adaptability is absent. Survival demands an "unthinkable" reversal of scale and pattern.

At least, this megalithic monster of *moreness* tells us we are in the domain of Lord Kelvin, where everything can be said in numbers. It happens that Kelvin spent his life striving to reach ABSOLUTE ZERO: the giant omission. Little did Kelvin realize how the numbers racket would be developed in economics and in the studies of the psychologists. His dream of absolute zero has been realized many times in the social sciences but remains a mirage for the physicist.

THE CHALLENGE OF THE PAST

Obsolescence Is the Matrix of Innovation

Obsolescence provides the means of new hybrids and transformation. Until a service has permeated the world of producers and consumers alike, there are not the ideal conditions for maximal performance. With print, writing became obsolete, but the press spread literacy, which demanded new armies of authors and scribes. Every business and school was on the handwriting kick full time until the Remington entered the picture. Even then, handwriting continued to proliferate new uses. As Chesterton said: "Women refused to be dictated to, so they went out and became stenographers." That meant much more handwriting than ever.

THE OBSOLESCENT WILL ALWAYS BE THE PIGGYBACK ON
ANY NEW TECHNOLOGY

By merely looking at new game forms, one can see the latest obsolescent form. By the same token, the obsolescent will be used by the top brass to provide programming for their new toys. Were they aware of the developing situation they would use the old as *probe* rather than as *program*. The obsolescent "fun thing," which is useless as program, is indispensable for exploring the new boundaries of dynamic processes.

In the Ecological Present All the Old "Intangibles" Acquire Regimental Crusts

Today's executive is called upon not only to cope with standard accounting procedures but also to know when to use statistical methods, operations research, cost-benefits analysis, budget plans, computer programs, and general systems science. System designers are constantly developing new techniques for reducing more and more industrial production and human organization processes to BITS, the ultimate YES or NOT-YES choices of computers.

Computers can do better than ever what needn't be done at all.
Making sense is still a human monopoly.

Computers need only programmed instructions and codified inputs to handle sequential data and analysis to yield information more rapidly than people. But no computer "know-how" can transform breakdowns into breakthroughs without human insight. Knowing what to do is still a human monopoly. Only people can *make sense* by dislocating unfamiliar situations into meaning.

ULTIMATE TWO-BIT WITTEDNESS
WHEN MORE AND MORE IS DONE WITH LESS AND LESS

The new man of two words, a hippie: "Hi! Bi!"

In *The Social Impact of Cybernetics*, Robert Theobald predicts that "computer systems, not men, will first realize humanity's old dream of a universal language, and the subtleties and nuances of human thought will risk being mediated through the restricted and standardized symbols of computer communication." While artists like James Joyce can *make* a resonating universe with two words, computer programmers try to *match* universes of human knowledge and perception to the *two-bit wit* of their machines.

One-sense to Non-sense

The "exponential growth curves" of mathematics are well-known means of portraying not only "chain reactions" but any accelerated quantitative expansion whatever. Herman Kahn and Anthony S. Wiener provide a rich store of fantasy curves illustrating such trends up to *The Year 2000*. However, "Adam Smith's" hilarious observations of stock-market "chartists" in *The Money Game* confirm what Alexander Ross notes in the *Financial Post* (Toronto, October 25, 1969):

> Chartists aren't unanimous about anything. Not only do they quarrel about which indicators to trust, they even disagree about what the same indicators are telling them. . . . "Next year," says one chartist, "I'm going to look seriously at the relationship between astrology and the market. No one's done a serious study yet, but some of the correlations are absolutely amazing."

Well, why not?

Exponential Curves: The Accelerating of Accelerated Accelerations

There is, nevertheless, an irresistible temptation to extrapolate mathematical models either to breakdown or to nonsense, as Lewis Carroll knew, and Dennis Gabor, inventor of holography, recently warned: "Exponential curves grow to infinity only in mathematics. In the physical world they either turn round and saturate, or they break down catastrophically." Gabor would imply that there is no change possible except in quantity. It is like saying that traveling by jet is no different than traveling by donkey, provided you make your *connections*. Mere speed of travel makes no physical difference!

WHEN INNOVATION OUTSTRIPS OBSOLESCENCE,
INVENTION BECOMES THE MOTHER OF NECESSITY.

When this stage has come, Rolls-Royces literally carry the country-estate garbage to the metropolitan incinerators: the country must not be polluted; the city cannot be saved. When invention is an everyday job, then what has already been invented is garbage, from which only new invention can come. Let us recall the great lines of William Butler Yeats at the end of a career of artistic innovation:

> Now that my ladder's gone,
> I must lie down where all the ladders start,
> In the foul rag-and-bone shop of the heart.
>   "The Circus Animals' Desertion"

Every world must be reborn from its own ruins. Every discovery rises from the trauma of breakdown and ignorance.

Logic and Mathematics Never Question Their Own Axioms

Logicians are unaware that the world of "rationality" and "connectedness" is built on the visual sense alone and is meaningless to nonliterate cultures.

DO YOU FEEL ANXIOUS WHEN THE PACE SLOWS?

Technology Eats Itself Alive: Loops the Loop

John Platt, in *Science* (November 28, 1969), points out:

> In the last century we have increased our speeds of communication by a factor of 10^7; our speeds of travel by 10^2; our speeds of data handling by 10^6; our energy resources by 10^3; our power of weapons by 10^6; our ability to control disease by something like 10^6; and our rate of population growth by 10^3 times what it was a few thousand years ago.

John Platt is not really a worshiper of figures. One of his figures is wildly inappropriate, namely, his estimate of "population growth." The speed of travel increases the encounters of people many times more than the population increase by number. By mobility the number of people who now meet every day for the one and only time in their lives is far greater than the population of the world itself. These brief encounters create the illusion of growing density of population. The same flaw can creep into any form of statistic. One recalls the case of the statistician who drowned in a stream whose average depth was three feet.

What kinds of growth should we expect? Qualitatively, we can already observe the new general trend toward inverted evolution, or "imploded metamorphosis." Can we yet predict how much, and for how long, such trends will affect us?

In *Decision Making in National Science Policy,* C. D. Foster tells us what to expect from "cost-benefit analysis," which has now become fashionable for estimating the ratio of the services and disservices of any enterprise.

The sense of corporate criminality has become so pervasive in our all-at-once world of collective responsibility that it is quite common to find even experts and specialists writing books titled *Technological Injury: The Effect of Technological Advances on Environment, Life, and Society.* Yesterday the specialist would have stuck to his mathematics and not heeded the impact of computers on community values.

One Man's Mede Is Another Man's Persian

As an example, the effect of "cost benefit" to a big science foundation of accidentally backing a major scientific breakthrough could well be ruin for that institution. It would have to bear the costs of the social disservices arising from the new service. The Dutch elm disease was an unwelcome by-product of a sterile investigation. Many of the unhappy spin-offs of phosphate detergents tend to obscure the original service intended. (Eutrophication pampers the algae that swallow the men who feed them.)

Measurement Kills What You Love

As any fool can plainly see, Ah can see it.
                    Al Capp, *L'il Abner*

All "scientific" and "economic" measurements of human psychic and social processes are rooted in human preferences. In Renaissance Italy "Old Nick" (Machiavelli) observed how just men had become just prices, but he was unaware that this was an effect of psychic and social fragmentation intensified by the new Gutenberg "rim spin." Nineteenth-century mechanical technology pushed atomization still further to the flip of failure through success. But today's instant speeds are returning us, paradoxically, to human scale and involvement, to new successes through old failures. *Death and taxes are the only sure measures of life.* Case closed!

5

Probing

Statistics for X-Raying or Freudening?

Nothing is more uncertain than the duration of human life; nothing is more certain than the solvency of a life assurance company.
Sir Arthur Eddington, astrophysicist

The Economist (September 6, 1969) shows how statistical concepts have found application in all fields of science and technology, in public and private business alike "to introduce scientific method into the control of human affairs: reasoning in terms of certainty was replaced by reasoning, equally logical in terms of probability, and laws governing individuals by laws relating to aggregates."

Matchless Montagu the Excelsior Man:
The Average-That-Never-Was

All American business and sports gain yardage and report satisfactions by statistical play. But, as the skeletal ghost of new welfare services, are statistics taking the load off our backs, or pulling the rug from under our feet?

> Time hath, my lord, a wallet at his back,
> Wherein he puts alms for oblivion,
> A great-siz'd monster of ingratitudes.
> Shakespeare, Troilus and Cressida

The "fine print" ensures that the fruits remain high above the reach of human hands. As diet, statistics may be tasteless, but as an environment they are deadly proof. Today we are witnessing the end of the "average man" in both East and West.

$24 BILLION PER ANNUM NOW SPENT ON BOOZE IN THE U.S.A. PRO-HIBITION WAS AN ENORMOUS SUCCESS AS PROVEN BY STAGGERING FIGURES.

Wearied by his own part in the modern frenzy to compile information, William James's contention that statistical "science" is not only of late origin but also can be parochially Western is one we can sympathize with.

The Objection to the Rule

In his textbook *The Principles of Psychology*, James quoted a nineteenth-century Turkish official who answered a visiting Englishman's question in this fashion:

> My Illustrious Friend and Joy of My Liver:
> The thing you ask of me is both difficult and useless. Although I have passed all my days in this place, I have neither counted the houses nor have I inquired into the number of inhabitants; and as to what one person loads on his mules and the other stows away in the bottom of his ship, that is no business of mine. But, above all, as to the previous history of this city, God only knows the amount of dirt and confusion that the infidels may have eaten before the coming of the sword of Islam. It were unprofitable for us to inquire into it. O my soul! O my lamb! seek not after the things which concern thee not. Thou camest unto us and we welcomed thee: go in peace.

Some-antics of Statistics: The Average Is the Medium Is the Message

It is now proved beyond doubt that smoking is one of the leading causes of statistics.   Fletcher Knebel

Statistics prove that very few people die after ninety.
                                                     An actuary

No airliner has yet been blown up when two passengers are carrying bombs. So play safe. Carry your own bomb. It figures.   Anonymous

WHILE THE LAW OF AVERAGES PROVES THAT NOTHING AVERAGE CAN EVER HAPPEN, MURPHY'S LAW PROCLAIMS THAT IF ANYTHING CAN GO WRONG, IT WILL . . . AT THE WORST POSSIBLE TIME.

Number Mystique as Beat and Rhythm of Corporate Poetry When Money Talks and Figures Never Lie

> Eight statisticians out of ten
> Are blue-eyed, thirty-seven, men,
> Married, college graduates, called
> J. Wilbur, Protestant and bald,
>
> Own five-room houses, one-half a car
> And two and one-third kids—but are
> Unable to compute a way
> To live on civil service pay.
>   Mavor Moore, *And What Do You Do?*

Although meaningless in a tribal context, numbers and statistics assume mythic and magical qualities of infallibility in literate societies. The hidden *ground* of statistics is literacy itself, and the underlying assumption is that premises never change while quantities vary—*the myth of perpetual return:* "The thing that hath been, it is that which shall be; and that which is done is that which shall be done: and there is no new thing under the sun" (Ecclesiastes 1:8).

This is an eternal ebb and flow of *moreness* and *lessness;* of annual, decennial, centennial, and purgatorial cycles. But the Hertzian complementary of certainty through cyclicity is uncertainty through discontinuity: "When your number comes up"; the "terrors of the year 2000"; and "The Bomb."

The Zodiac-Fortune-Finder: A Bicycle Built for You

When the numbers racket really got rolling, it took off with cyclicity. The *figures* left the *ground* behind. This bicycle built for you is a fortune finder that can roam over any terrain in a wide domain.

THE RACKET OF NUMBERS

Stochastics: when figures run wild and impose the rule of accident.
Statistics: when figures close in and impel automatic sequences.

Especially when dealing with numbers, it is fatal to be unaware of the hidden *ground* of tradition. Numbers have been worshiped as powers from the time of Noah's Ark (forty days) to the latest "floating crap game." Mystical gambling rituals and faiths associated with "games of chance" provide much basic slang and folklore of the modern world: "Baby needs a new pair of shoes"; "Jokers wild"; "When my number comes up." As custodians of the hidden *ground* of number, the literary fraternity has been understandably weak in numbers and math, taking a dim view of numerology in general. Many literate people have probably never read the Pythagorean Prayer:

> Bless us, divine number, thou who generatest gods and men! O holy, holy *tetraktys,* thou that containest the root and the source of the eternally flowing creation! For the divine number begins with the profound, pure unity until it comes to the holy four; then it begets the mother of all, the all-bounding, the first-born, the never-swerving, the never-tiring holy ten, the keyholder of all.

All religions have recognized a social bond (resonance) between the world of numbers, names, and hidden divinity. Much of what we call the occult or ESP today is simply the recovery of awareness of nonvisual *ground* for the *figures* and configurations of our visual civilization.

The *visual ground* of literacy provides the rationale of connectedness and goals, without which "performance" and "progress" would be meaningless. But in today's new hidden surround of information flow, the old *visual ground* of hookups and hang-ups is transformed by electric speeds into a new *acoustic ground* of resonant interfaces. All boundaries become porous, the opaque becomes pervious, and goals move faster than measures of performance can. What is your telephone number for today?

SHEER WEIGHT OF NUMBERS

> It is a schizoid world in which numbers inexorably take over as our means of identification like lava threatening to fossilize all breathing life in its path.   Rollo May, *Love and Will*

When numbers take over, apathy sets in. Apathy is the strategy of numbing against numbers. "Who gave you that numb?" As James Joyce understood, to name or to number a thing is to classify and thus reduce it below the threshold of human curiosity. Can the hot line replace the hot number?

THE THIRD WORLD: WHERE PHYSICAL HARDSHIP AND PSYCHIC POVERTY MERGE

Affluence breeds poverty through expectation, but not hardship. A millionaire alone on a life raft may suffer hardship, but he is not poor. C. J. Eustace in *The Canadian Register* (June 13, 1970) used a statistical X ray to expose the apocalyptic presences in the Third World where "hardware" and "software" deprivation meet:

> Technology can remedy famine, and in some parts of the world this is being done. But chronic malnutrition is more destructive than outright hunger. In round figures three out of every four people in the world are suffering from hunger. Even in countries where people obtain sufficient quantitative nutrition, there is often concealed hunger caused by lack of vitamins and proteins. Such qualitative deficiencies have terrible effects—they reduce the physical and intellectual faculties, set up deficiency diseases in children which have lifelong effects. . . .
>
> Then there is the population increase in relation to resources. At the beginning of the Christian era there were 250,000,000 people; in the 16th century 600,000,000. In 1970 there are seven billion human beings. This rapid change is accompanied by a sinister phenomenon; the resources which this population has available for its needs are growing at a much slower rate. This—remember—is in a world where large quantities of food are destroyed because there is not a profitable market.

> Life's a comedy to those who think and a tragedy to those who feel.
>   Richard Brinsley Sheridan

The tender sensibilities of the man of feeling are easily exacerbated or exasperated into misery by mere statistics. By the same token, the beaming and ebullient "Bucky" Fuller seizes the helm of Spaceship Earth with a confident shout:

NOT WOE BUT GO!

Census or Sensus: Population Explosion or Congestion?

In his *Operating Manual for Spaceship Earth* Buckminster Fuller points out that there is "room for the whole of humanity to stand indoors in greater New York City, with more room for each human than at an average cocktail party." And in the final lines of *Number, the Language of Science,* Tobias Dantzig concludes that MAN IS THE MEASURE OF ALL THINGS, AND THERE IS NO OTHER MEASURE.

6

Gaming

Only Robinson Crusoe can achieve the greatest possible good for the greatest possible number, the number being one. In place of the notion represented by this aphorism, the theory of games establishes the concept of a strategy through which conflicting maximum desires can be reconciled in an optimum. It is the only economic theory, except that based on Robinson Crusoe, to explain the working of the profit motive.   John MacDonald, *Strategy in Poker, Business and War*

The Executive Poker Face Can "Put On" Private Rivals but Not TV Public: Like Dale Carnegie, His Good Nature Pours from Every "Seem"

The essence of poker, MacDonald continues, is not cards but money; its spirit is the bluff, and its supreme objective the inducement of a bet against an unbeatable hand. Poker concerns the management of money and people, whereas other card games concern the management of cards.

Poker may be a game, but it is a travesty on life, since it brings out all the repressions of a competitive society. The theory of games approaches economic life from an individual, microscopic point of view. It is in sharp contrast with the macroscopic, all-embracing economic systems of Adam Smith, Karl Marx, and Maynard Keynes. Games are less complicated than economics.

THE MACHINE IN THE GARDEN: TO HELL WITH EVIL*!*

In the Los Angeles *Free Press*, December 19, 1969, Gene Youngblood discusses Buckminster Fuller's "world games." Under the headline

PLAY THE WORLD GAME—BY-PASS POLITICS—SHAPE EARTH'S DESTINY —RESOURCES INVENTORY

Fuller himself explains:

The objective is to explore for ways to make it possible for anybody and everybody in the human family to enjoy the total earth without any human interfering with any other human and without any human gaining advantage at the expense of another. The programs that the computers will select as being most favorable for all humanity will go far beyond man's ignorant ways of assessing what he can afford. The computers will demonstrate that he can afford nothing short of the best, which is to make spaceship earth a successful environment for man. . . . Our greatest problem is the educational problem of getting man to realize in time what his problems are, and what the most effective priorities may be.

At electric speeds only simultaneous anticipation of both effects and causes by perception and understanding of all processes in action will enable us to navigate in ECO-land. The image of the world as a garden is the dominant biblical archetype. Man's role as gardener was to understand the properties of all the creatures in the garden. The work of Adam, the gardener, was the viewing and naming of creatures. In modern terms this means research into the hidden properties of things in addition to the enjoyment of their beauty.

> Good fences make good neighbors.
> Robert Frost

Voltaire's famous prescription for happiness is close to Fuller's dream for Spaceship Earth. Voltaire suggested that each of us simply tend his own garden, and a kind of pre-established harmony would ensure that the world garden flourish. The upshot of Voltaire's dream of private choice and private autonomy, insofar as the environment is concerned, is

PLANET POLLUTO

Fuller proposes the exact opposite of Voltaire's prescription. He is confident that in place of any pre-established harmony, man is now capable of eliminating all noise and pollution from the global environment. As much as Voltaire, he is innocent of any political dimensions or suggestions. Man, with his extreme limitations and obsessional appetites, does not figure in Fuller's earth plan. As Voltaire eliminated these factors by the aesthetic delight of pure reason, Fuller, unperturbed by the obliquities of the human past, pronounces the new regime of the computer as a substitute for human fallibilities and limitations. Convinced of the overwhelming power and accuracy of this new extension of man, he is confident that a benign future is entirely in our hands.

Nobody would deny that "Bucky" Fuller has enough personal benignity and good will to keep the computer on this course, were it within his control. In the Bucky Game there are neither fences, nor defenses, nor offenses. The simple fact is that the computer has been commandeered to perform all the old tasks of a bureaucratically confused mankind. Fuller is implying that once people have the relevant data concerning their physical environment they will orchestrate it for their needs and delight.

Emperor-cum-Clown of Dymaxionland

> You can deny seriousness, but not play.
> Johan Huizinga, *Homo Ludens*

The scientist is the environment builder who has hitherto shown little concern for the ecological world game. Too specialized to play, or to be his own clown, he tends to assume a resolute goal-tending attitude. Not for him the nonchalant ambling among the parameters; he long ago discovered the importance of being earnest. By contrast, Bucky is an unspecialized and unclassifiable emperor-cum-clown. Since he takes all territory for his world game and is consumed by an insatiable desire for knowledge and discovery, he is more than a match for the pedestrian specialist. As an old sailor he has often sailed to the holy city of Byzantium with its resonating domes.

Men at Play

In his classic *Homo Ludens*, the Dutch historian and philosopher Johan Huizinga reveals the essential qualities of play involved in creating all human institutions and well-being. It is here that the war game becomes a natural component in the ultimate cultural welfare of mankind. For Huizinga takes us on a tour of human institutions, social and political, to illustrate the unfailing quality of duality, interface, and dialogue that characterize all living and viable forms of existence. An example of how Huizinga is able to tackle the complex business of game is a passage in his chapter "Play and Contest as Civilizing Functions":

> It is very curious how the words "prize", "price" and "praise" all derive more or less directly from the Latin *pretium* but develop in different directions. *Pretium* arose originally in the sphere of exchange and valuation, and presupposed a counter-value. The mediaeval *pretium justum* or "just price" corresponded approximately to the idea of the modern "market value". Now while *price* remains bound to the sphere of economics, *prize* moves into that of play and competition, and *praise* acquires the exclusive signification of the Latin *laus*. Semantically, it is next to impossible to delimit the field proper to each of the three words. What is equally curious is to see how the word *wage*, originally identical with *gage* in the sense of a symbol of challenge, moves in the reverse direction of *pretium*—i.e., from the play-sphere to the economic sphere and becomes a synonym for "salary" or "earnings". We do not *play* for wages, we *work* for them. Finally, "gains" or "winnings" has nothing to do with any of these words etymologically, though semantically it pertains to both play and economics: the player receives his winnings, the merchant makes them.

Huizinga moves with equal ease and insight into the world of science:

> A game is time-bound, we said; it has no contact with any reality outside itself, and its performance is its own end. Further, it is sustained by the consciousness of being a pleasurable, even mirthful, relaxation from the strains of ordinary life. None of this is applicable to science. Science is not only perpetually seeking contact with reality by its usefulness, i.e., in the sense that it is *applied*, it is perpetually trying to establish a universally valid pattern of reality, i.e., as *pure* science. Its

rules, unlike those of play, are not unchallengeable for all time. They are constantly being belied by experience and undergoing modification, whereas the rules of a game cannot be altered without spoiling the game itself.

In contrast to the thought of Huizinga and Thomas Kuhn is the science-fiction fantasy of Lewis Carroll (the speculative mathematician Charles Dodgson.) In Carroll's world the *ground* rules are given a complete holiday as he swings into a twentieth-century orbit in good Queen Victoria's golden days. Between the philosophical quests of Huizinga and Kuhn's severe exposés of scientific limitations in our next chapter, the playful world of Carroll is pure donnish delight. (The reader of this book is likewise expected to enjoy freedom of travel on both sides of the looking glass.)

The Society for Basic Irreproducible Research

Writing in Toronto's *Globe and Mail* (July 29, 1970), Stan Fisher comments:

SCIENCE SATIRE

The Journal of Irreproducible Results is published tri-annually by the Society for Basic Irreproducible Research, (which has headquarters in Chicago) and is circulated among scientists in 36 countries, including Canada. . . .

A recent issue, for example, carried an item entitled "A New Ergometric Procedure and Its Application to the Domestic Horse," which, among other pertinent data, gives a detailed account of the difficulties involved in taking a rectal thermometer reading of a horse running across a hayfield.

Past issues has dealt with such significant subjects as "The Function and Significance of the Zipper (Zipper-dynamics)" and "The Vagaries and Sex Life of the Common Flatworm." . . . One of the scholarly satirists has reportedly been working on a paper entitled "The Reproducibility of Irreproducible Results," and it may have to be the very last article the journal can legitimately publish.

It was inevitable that as the integration of knowledge developed under ever-increasing speed of access scientific specialists should suddenly begin to savor the incongruity of their older specialist activities compared with the comprehensiveness of the new scientific dialogue. Countless men and disciplines that had long ceased to be on speaking terms now cultivate a daily interface and dialogue prompted by the new ecological drives. The invasion of the scientific area by the comic spirit had been heralded by the abundance of grotesque travesties of scientific activity in numerous movie and TV offerings, whether of the thriller espionage variety, or "Star Trek" and "Mission Impossible" type. The pretensions of scientists have been eroded steadily by these entertainment forms. They have participated in their own audience participation to the Point-of-No-Return.

THE SCIENCE GAME IN THE HOUSE OF MAGIC

Return of Pre-Socratic Nature

In *The Science Game: An Introduction to Research in the Behavioral Sciences*, Neil M. Agnew and Sandra W. Pyke consider the higher strategy of "grant grubbing" for self-perpetuating research programs aimed at 100 per cent pure "scientific truth." While denying the existence of any single agreed-upon scientific method, they propose various mixes of strategy and tactics to produce "science recipes." The "good scientist" is one who can cook up a tasty morsel of durable "software." Good scientists accept criticism from no one else but their peers in the acceptable scientific language of reputable scientific journals, published after the results may have ceased to be relevant. But who knows, and who will tell? Gerard Piel, in *Science in the Cause of Man*, affirms that "science still occupies the *House of Magic* . . . the most surely established house of knowledge in popular view." As both science planners and scientific planning increase their claims to national budgets, what may we expect from scientists themselves?

In *The Structure of Scientific Revolutions*, Thomas S. Kuhn discusses some hidden implications of the science paradigm:

> No part of the aim of normal science is to call forth new sorts of phenomenon. . . . One of the reasons why *normal science* seems to progress so rapidly is that its practitioners concentrate on problems that only their own lack of ingenuity should keep them from solving.

MODERN SCIENCE ORGANIZES KNOWLEDGE NOT IGNORANCE, LABELS RATHER THAN PROCESSES.

Chapter 5

The Quantum Leap from
Science to Art

1

Unraveling

Via Media

Whereas science links the present to the past via concepts, art leaps from the present to the future via percepts. Concepts isolate *figures*, while percepts relate *figures* and *grounds* as interplay.

Knowledge Breeds Ignorance
(*Just as Public Creates Privacy*)

In *The Sacred Wood*, T. S. Eliot points out that "the vast accumulations of knowledge—or at least of information—deposited by the nineteenth century have been responsible for an equally vast ignorance."

Astrology Died Hard
(*Like the Star System*)

J. Isaacs in *The Background of Modern Poetry* remarks:

> Astrology was the science which studied the specific influence of the stars on human destiny, and for this science a fixed universe was essential. Add but one star and "chaos is come again." Galileo added millions of new stars. Dante and Chaucer and Shakespeare are poets of the fixed universe. Donne and Milton are unstable as water, fluctuating between the Ptolemaic and the Copernican heavens. Astrology died hard. It still lives in the Sunday newspapers, and during the last war both Hitler and our counter-intelligence took it very seriously indeed. The new science had now passed beyond the scientists to the people.

Today, electronic retrieval of the occult horoscopic and the old movie stars alike is a built-in feature of the information environment. Thomas S. Kuhn points out in *The Structure of Scientific Revolutions* that "discovery commences with the awareness of anomaly, i.e., with the recognition that nature has somehow violated the paradigm-induced expectations that govern normal science."

In this context scientists unconsciously acquire a bias for choosing only those problems that they feel will not endanger the validity of their paradigm. Problems "not covered by the paradigm" are rejected as "metaphysical" or as the concern of other disciplines. Such is the plight of the specialists of "conventional wisdom" in any society. Their entire security and status emanate from a single form of acquired knowledge. Any innovation is for them not a novelty, but disaster. The amateur can afford to lose face but the professional must stand on his dignity.

> Dignity is a mysterious carriage of the body to conceal the defects of
> the mind.   Laurence Sterne

As the information environment reaches electronic speeds, the professional is left out of the world game. In a world of ecological awareness he knows not where to stand. The amateur is the hunter of "live game" and ever-new adventures of ideas. He plays the field with "his horn and his hounds in the morning," and encounters an *embarras de richesse*.

Gravity a Matter for Levity?

> *Gravitation,* n. The tendency of all bodies to approach one another
> with a strength proportioned to the quantity of matter they contain—
> the quantity of matter they contain being ascertained by the strength
> of their tendency to approach one another.
>
> Ambrose Bierce, *The Devil's Dictionary*

In his parody of professional scientists on the flying island of Laputa (Spanish: the prostitute) in *Gulliver's Travels,* Dean Swift implies that his comic hero, Newton, discovered "levity" not "gravity." People had often observed that apples fell off trees. Newton, by asking whether there could be an up pull as well as a down pull, reversed the age-old perception pattern. He then formulated certain behavioral characteristics of "gravitational fields" later refined by Einstein. For scientists gravity is only a mathematical relationship. Nobody has yet discovered the nature of "gravity," although the current hypothesis of "gravitons" has aided the cause of "levity" no end.

Meanwhile, teams of scientists, engaged in putting satellite embodiments of Newton's laws around both earth and moon, continue to ignore the psychic and social consequences of the invisible information environments they have inadvertently created. Scientists are strangely indifferent to the "total field" effects of their innovations.

VELIKOVSKY THE MEDIUM AS THE REJECTED MESSAGE

Return of the Hidden Ground

In *The Politics of Science and Dr. Velikovsky*, Alfred de Grazia, Ralph E. Juergens, and Livio C. Stecchini review the "acrimonious debate and bellicose maneuvers" of the scientific community over Emmanuel Velikovsky's humanist approach to cosmology, which scraps Greek "Nature." Most striking was the instant emotional counterblast in contrast to their puny counterevidence against this monster hypothesis. Scientists become as irrational and panicky as any other group when their basic tenets are questioned. Such is the strategy of corporate oblivion.

Velikovsky, by treating all the scientific *grounds* as merely incidental *figures*, has evoked an unexpected new *ground* that engulfs conventional science by means of a massive retrieval of ancient human tradition. The phenomenon of Velikovsky would be unthinkable except in the present age of instantaneous recovery of the most primal human experiences.

LIKE THE FUTURE, THE PAST IS NO LONGER WHAT IT USED TO BE

From the sixteenth century, the physical sciences fostered a mounting "hierarchy" of interlocking components and images, described in A. O. Lovejoy's *The Great Chain of Being*. "Scientific truth" became anything that could be solidly linked to "the great chain." This monolithic vision of "scientific truth" was dispelled by the biological encounter with the "missing link." The hierarchical image of "scientific truth" dissolved overnight, leaving "not a wrack behind."

Who will define "scientific truth"? Who will expound the hidden biases not only of scientists but of science itself?

THE A B C OF WESTERN SCIENCE

Scientists who condescend to treat language and literature as minor amenities for undisciplined minds have all the while ridden blithely on the coattails of literacy. Without literacy as *ground* for perception, there could be no *figures* for science or mathematics or logic. Even a merely classificatory science like botany was unable to move toward scientific status until after printing. The first step toward Western philosophy and science was writing based on the alphabet, as Eric Havelock explains in *Preface to Plato*:

> Before Homer's day, the Greek cultural "book" had been stored in the oral memory. . . . Between Homer and Plato, the method of storage began to alter, as the information became alphabetized, and corre-

spondingly the eye supplanted the ear as the chief organ employed for this purpose. The complete results of literacy did not supervene in Greece until the ushering in of the Hellenistic age, when conceptual thought achieved, as it were, fluency, and its vocabulary became more or less standardised. Plato, living in the midst of this revolution, announced it and became its prophet.

William M. Ivins, Jr., demonstrates in *Art and Geometry: A Study in Space Intuitions* that geometry itself did not achieve a pure state of science until printing freed it from nonvisual sensory influences.

Plato scorned the practical tribal encyclopedia of pragmatic wisdom stored in the Homeric, Hesiodic tradition, considering it as based merely on memory rather than insight into the specific "forms." Those who had not mastered geometry were not admitted into Plato's academy. In the *Phaedo* he uses geometry as proof of the independent metaphysical status of the soul. Socrates elicits the solution to a geometric problem from a "mere slave" to prove that knowledge is not simply recollection of some previous existence. T. E. Lawrence, in *Seven Pillars of Wisdom*, explains a similar conflict between East and West in exploring and contrasting "the interplay of the written tradition and the spoken tongue." In contrast to the compact and memorable oral tradition Lawrence points out that it is "not too much of an over-statement to say that the resources of literature constitute a blank cheque which the speaker in speaking can fill in to almost any amount."

In an oral society the *figure* of the written word stands out against the bardic or poetic *ground*. It stands out as a precise and abstractly visual *figure* against the resonant and acoustic *ground* of the collective oral tradition, just as the specialized industrial West stands out against the tribal Asiatic world. Today, in exactly the same way, the old visual written tradition appears as the merely humanist and intuitive world of aesthetic values and experience. It stands in contrast to the new scientific *figure*, contrasting with the nonvisual world of the new physics. It is this reversal that tosses literature and aesthetics into abeyance as an unquantifiable area of mere human preferences and satisfactions without scientific foundations. It is precisely the components of visual or "rational" space, which constituted Western science for two millenniums, that are now degraded into the status of mere entertainment. It is now obvious that the new nonvisual *figure* of the new physics will soon enough suffer the same fate as Euclid and Newton and Darwin.

The Snow Job

In short, as a snowdrift is formed where there is a lull in the wind, so, one would say, where there is a lull of truth, an institution springs up. But the truth blows right on over it, nevertheless, and at length blows it down.   Henry Thoreau, *Walden*

C. P. Snow is quite innocent of any knowledge about the dynamic origins of literacy, or of science in relation to literacy. Without the long written tradition of the West there would be no science. What Snow calls "two cultures" are the *figure-ground* interface of the components of the same culture. In Plato's time the new *figure* was written, and the old *ground* was oral. In our time the new *figure* of science is acoustic and the old *ground* is visual-written. With the absence of either the written or the oral tradition, the other becomes a cripple. A merely tribal society without writing and visual culture is as crippled as a merely literate society without the resonance of the oral tradition. Lord Snow's prescription for doctoring the myopic scientist is an occasional dose of stale humanist nostrums.

2

Unveiling

MAGIC AND REVERSE MAGIC

Science, a part of the interplay between man and Nature.
Werner Heisenberg, *The Physicist's Conception of Nature*

Scientists make their discoveries as "artists" or as "magi," using all their faculties—their human intuition—rather than their specialist knowledge. Any new laws they may discover always lie beyond *normal science*. In his preface to *Where Is Science Going?*, Albert Einstein insists: "There is no logical way to the discovery of these elemental laws. There is only the way of intuition, which is helped by a feeling for the order lying behind the appearance."

In *From Dream to Discovery*, Hans Selye also observes:

> Intuition is the spark for all forms of originality, inventiveness, and ingenuity. It is the flash needed to connect conscious thought with the imagination. . . . In the languages of the ancient Peruvian Indians there was only one word (*hamavec*) for both poet and inventor. . . . In discussing intuitive flashes with others, I find that most scientists have experienced them quite unexpectedly while falling asleep, awakening, or doing something quite unrelated to the problem at hand.

THE VISION AT THE INTERFACE BETWEEN
SLEEPING AND WAKING

The twilight zone is the moment of the birth of wisdom: "Minerva's owl takes its flight at twilight." The abrasion betwixt and between worlds creates the disturbance that is intuition or resonance. The intuition is born of the "interval" not the "connection" between events. This accounts for the strange aura of irrationality which surrounds discoveries. "Errors" (wanderings) are more productive of creative awareness than conventional knowledge.

Error is essential to the determination of truth.
Gerard Piel, *Science in the Cause of Man*

From Plato's *Republic* and Thomas More's *Utopia* to Samuel Butler's *Erewhon* and George Orwell's *1984*, the underlying assumption of all utopian planners has been that societies could be built "scientifically" free from human imperfections.

3

Reducing

Cybernetics Loops the Bloop

Cybernation is the computerized marriage of industrial automation and cybernetic control technology. It paves the way for producing on demand whatever anyone can define within known limitations of current "hardware" and "software" techniques. As John von Neumann put it in reply to a question about the power of computers to exceed human intelligence: "If you can tell me *exactly* what it is that a computer cannot do, I may be able to give you a computer that can do it" (quoted by Dennis Gabor in *Innovations*).

Cybernation is the breeding ground for a fresh crop of system specialists described by Robert Boguslaw in *The New Utopians*. They are the new prophets of

Ultima Laputa: Where Men Are Faceless Tentacles of Computers

The new utopians are concerned with non-people and with people substitutes. Their planning is done with computer hardware, system procedures, functional analysis, and heuristics. . . . The theoretical and practical solutions they seek call increasingly for decreases in the number and in the scope of responsibility of human beings within the operating structures of their new machine systems. . . .

A designer of systems who has the de facto prerogative to specify the range of phenomena that his system will distinguish clearly is in possession of enormous degrees of power. . . . It is by no means necessary that this power be formalized through allocation of specific authority.

By keeping their knowledge and plans secret, as any bureaucracy does, they can increase the importance of their professional know-how. Boguslaw notes that bureaucratic organizations tend to convert policy problems into administrative ones.

The absolute monarch is powerless opposite the superior knowledge of the bureaucratic expert.   Max Weber

Computer specialists go all out to reduce every human problem to YES or
NO questions demanding YES or NO answers. In the new translation of the
Book of Knowledge into a two-bit language, *only the gaps make sense.* John
Kettle in *Monetary Times* (Montreal, December, 1968) affirms: "Using
the computer to mediate between people is the prime technical goal, the
strongest wish, the most significant change promised in communications
technology." The new utopians are busily improving the invisible bureaucratic machinery for instant reduction of all human community and culture
to "bytes" of computer "bits." "Computer addicts" in the name of "management science" are making the latest attempt to establish a Swiftian
"Laputa," where man's wisdom is prostituted to the level of today's technology and man himself is forced to become its faceless tentacle.

Automation Automates Automatons: Human Vagaries Nullified

> Her vocal vagaries have killed the canaries
> And druv the gas back in the mains.
>
> English music hall song

The "five-year plans" of the new utopians are now high fashion; they are
the ultimate contribution of "hardware" thinking to our "software" world;
no defense establishment, no government, and no corporation can afford to
be seen dead without one!

4

Forecasting

Fashions in Forecasts

Forecasting is a difficult task, especially when it's about the future.

An Irishman

The Economist (September 27, 1969) reported from Madrid on three "Fashions in Forecasts" favored by short-term business forecast-mongers:

1. ECONOMETRIC MODELS are based on past relationships between such factors as income and employment, or capital investment and interest rates. The main difficulties are getting relationships correctly established, and obtaining correct data to put into the equations. The more sophisticated the model, the more input data are needed, and the more sensitive the results are to time lag. Such forecasting never catches up with the economic facts of life.

2. OPINION AND ATTITUDE TESTS report on what the spending tendencies of scientifically chosen samples of businessmen and consumers are likely to be, simply by asking them. The main snags are that people change their minds, and answers are often biased in favor of downturns or upturns, or even by fears of self-fulfilling prophecies.

3. LEADING INDICATIONS such as business expenditures on plant and equipment, share prices, labor costs per unit of output, and changes in hire-purchase debt habitually reach turning points well ahead of the general business cycle. The main trap is that, although such leading indicators give warning of a turn, they also give many false signals.

The Economist concludes that "opinion forecasts now indicate that the U.S. economy is likely to keep inflating while economic models predict the opposite."

AS FOR THE VIABILITY OF THESE MODELS, WHEN INVISIBLE THEY'RE INVINCIBLE

In our world of instant communication, the nonspecialist information consumer now dictates to the specialist information producer. Neither data nor models nor plans can be dealt with fast enough to keep pace with actual needs. But, as inventories of effects, questionnaires and polls can serve as PROBES to expose active causes. Like plans, questionnaires omit data that are always more relevant than what are included. The omissions are the future discoveries!

Tomorrows of Yesterday

Funferall in a notshall
James Joyce, *Finnegans Wake*

At the Fourteenth Annual Business Conference held at the University of Western Ontario on May 28, 1970, Eric Barry discussed the proliferation of organizations and literature devoted to the future of business. He stressed that a forecast assumes that the future is not predetermined: "The real trick is to predict the discontinuities, the places where there are going to be sharp breaks, either in the direction or rate of change."

THE MONSTER OMISSION

The priorities of the future were derived from the status quo.
Michael Harrington, *The Accidental Century*

Barry cited a prediction of the Marquis de Condorcet as the all-time blooper in social and political forecasting. In 1784, five years before the French Revolution, this nobleman, mathematician, philosopher, and revolutionary predicted:

> . . . the great probability that we have fewer great changes and fewer large revolutions to expect from the future than from the past. The progress of enlightenment in all the sciences . . . the prevailing spirit of moderation and peace, the sort of disrepute into which Machiavellism is beginning to fall, seem to assure us that henceforth wars and revolutions will be less frequent.

This was eight years before Condorcet himself called France to a war that was to ravage Europe for twenty-three years, and less than ten years before he was guillotined in the Reign of Terror. Barry noted that although a plan embodies a forecast, the reverse is not true. And he quoted Wilbert Moore as saying, "What you want is a plan of action based on all the environmental factors including the effect of the plan itself upon the world." John McHale also observes in *The Future of the Future*: "The number of professionals engaged in exploring the future is possibly matched only by the number employed in excavating the past." The danger is no longer that the future will be neglected but, rather, that it will be buried in the past by

The Specialist Treatment

Whereas the ancient oracle at Delphi gave all answers as new questions, the Delphi specialist of today gives only old answers to new questions. Among outstanding contenders for leadership of the "futurists" are Herman Kahn and Anthony J. Wiener, who dare to "think the unthinkable" in atomic strategy and who illustrate their thinking in *The Year 2000*.

Assuming All Possible Assumptions

In setting out to establish "standard projections and multifold trends" to the year A.D. 2000, Kahn and Wiener proceed to identify

> . . . important long-term trends which seem likely to continue . . . a complex long-term MULTI-FOLD TREND consisting of thirteen inter-related elements . . . quantitative changes in the combination of trends, and emergent properties, such as increasing self-consciousness . . . to construct significant baselines, statistical where possible, to project key variables in society . . . extrapolations of current or emerging tendencies . . . create a SURPRISE-FREE PROJECTION . . . a "standard world" and several "canonical variations," designed to raise certain issues.

They use

> . . . two approaches common in the study of political-military and other kinds of public policy problems . . . the SCENARIO and systematic context, or ALTERNATIVE FUTURE . . . scenarios are hypothetical sequences of events constructed for the purpose of focusing attention on causal processes and decision points. They answer two kinds of questions: (1) precisely how might some hypothetical situation come about, step by step?; and (2) what alternatives exist, for each actor, at each step, for preventing, diverting, or facilitating the process? (capitals added)

This is a paradigm trip to outer confusion:

> the wise gods seel our eyes;
> In our own filth drop our clear judgments; make us
> Adore our errors; laugh at 's while we strut
> To our confusion.
> > Shakespeare, *Antony and Cleopatra*

The "scenarios" and "alternative futures" of Kahn and Wiener are *surprise-free* projections precisely because their forecasts are concerned with *quantitative* variations of the old rather than with *qualitative* transformations to the new. Such thinking is typical of "futurists," who conceive of variation as normal and metamorphosis as either purely accidental or entirely unpredictable: "Any day has some chance of bringing up some new crisis or unexpected event, an historical turning point, diverting current tendencies so that expectations for the distant future must shift." But now that change is the *norm*, only the "unpredictable" needs predicting.

"Figures" Without "Grounds"

Projections in their book of "long-term trends," "gross national products," and "per capita incomes," considered in isolation, are far more frivolous than any horoscope ever kicked out by a computer. In fact, a horoscope is at least centered on human satisfactions and anxieties. The projections of Kahn and Wiener are abstractions that have nothing to do with human satisfactions past, present, or future. GNP and income projections of this kind merely rouse memories of the German inflation of the 1920's. They cannot be translated into human experience at all. *Penta-plans are pentagone. Only the artist can catch up with the model.*

Kahn and Wiener express all the warm human understanding and perception of most science fiction. Such merely quantitative projections have no human content whatever. Even as probes they are manifestations of human ignorance and insensibility. It says much for the desperate state of human values that quantifiers and planners of this ilk should be taken seriously. Until humanists have translated their projections into creative social dialogue, this kind of two-bit language can only eviscerate what remains of an embombers' world—awaiting its turn in the crematorium.

Only those who have learned to perceive the present can predict the future. They need only predict what has already happened by being the first to see through pattern recognition. FOR THE FUTURE OF THE FUTURE IS THE PRESENT.

5

Modeling

SUPER SYSTEM

Have you heard of the wonderful one-hoss shay,
That was built in such a logical way
It ran a hundred years to a day?
        Oliver Wendell Holmes, "The Deacon's Masterpiece"

All industrial systems involve both people and machines. Most of their present hang-ups are the result of piecemeal development and hierarchical organization. The telephone system, often cited as an ideal example of *system engineering*, was also its birthplace. Ludwig von Bertalanffy and Anatol Rapoport, well-versed not only in psychology and biology, but also in music and mathematics, were joint editors of the first *Yearbook of the Society for General Systems Theory* (1956). In their preface they stressed: "The utility of mathematical models of generalized systems stands or falls with their application to social and behavioural science." The authors were inspired by philosopher A. N. Whitehead's warning that twentieth-century science was still living mainly on the intellectual capital of the seventeenth century, now approaching exhaustion:

> The search for theories of generalized systems is an attempt to escape the extremely "analytic" viewpoint of classical physical science and to make the so-called "holistic" approach, rather vaguely eulogized by various philosophers since Goethe, more rigorous and explicit . . . to bring together areas of research with dissimilar contents but with similar structures or philosophical bases . . . to develop a common language and thus to stimulate each other more effectively.

Writing in the same *Yearbook* on "General Systems Theory," von Bertalanffy defines it as *the formulation and derivation of those principles which are valid for any system whatever*, and he discusses the urgency for developing such an approach: "The essential problems are the organizing relations that result from dynamic interaction and make the behaviour of parts different when studied in isolation or within the whole."

General Systems theory tends to ignore primitive problems, for example, how to choose companions for an arctic expedition. You might have to eat them! All theories are packages of concepts derived from repeated percepts. Regardless of the labels they bear, theories without direct human perception can never catch up to "where it's at" in the global theater.

THEORETICAL EXCELLENCE IS PAST PLU-PERFECT

Whose Concern Is the Concern of Forgotten People?

Tom Wicker, New York *Times* Service (March 9, 1971), cites Robert Penn Warren, who, while accepting the 1970 National Medal for Literature in Washington, noted this forgetfulness:

> Marianne Moore has said that her kind of poetry deals with real toads in imaginary gardens. The kind of poetry across the street here (in Congress) might often seem very similar to hers. It deals with real solutions to imaginary problems. Sometimes, however, it deals with imaginary solutions to real problems. When genius begins to be inflamed, it deals with imaginary solutions to imaginary problems of imaginary people.

WHEREAS REALITY IN THE NINETEENTH CENTURY MEANT "MATCHING" THE OLD, TWENTIETH-CENTURY REALITY IS "MAKING" THE NEW ON ITS OWN TERMS.

Monolithic Integration by Reducing All Living Gaps to Dead Connections

Know when to let go; hang loose.
                    A hippie

General Systems science, mathematical models, and computer languages alike are *media*. They impose their own "grammars" and hidden assumptions upon the user as *content*. But science, the child of literacy, has hitherto ignored the effects of literacy upon itself.

PARADOX OF PARADIGMS

Is there a life before death?
                    Anonymous

Thomas S. Kuhn, in *The Structure of Scientific Revolutions*, notes:

> Once a first paradigm through which to view nature has been found, there is no such thing as research in the absence of any paradigm. To reject one paradigm without simultaneously substituting another is to reject science itself.

Neither authors of subsequent yearbooks nor practitioners who proclaim the virtues of General Systems science have yet revealed any awareness of imposing a new tyranny of concepts upon the processes they are structuring. Pursuit of logical rigor kills the wholeness they love. What artists and philosophers have said of other conceptual schemes, Kurt Goedel reaffirms for mathematics:

. . . every set of premises must bear within it a contradiction or paradox. The contradiction can be resolved only by the addition of another premise to the set, but this stratagem ineluctably generates yet another contradiction.

Goedel's Theorem: On Formally Undecidable Propositions

It is precisely because of the breakdown of a form that it becomes understandable for the first time. An *antienvironment* reveals hidden environments. Disservices become manifest, not in themselves, but in relation to other services. It was recognized by Aquinas.

The Principle of Analogical Proportionality

Nothing has its meaning alone. Nothing is intelligible in isolation. Perception as such is a proportion among proportions apprehended in our sensory life. There is meaning in the sense ratios themselves.

From ONE-SENSE to CON-SENSE

Seeing is believing, but feeling is God's own truth.

Folk saying

"The First International Symposium on Computer Imitations of Brain Functions," reported by *IEEE Newsletter, Systems and Cybernetics Group* (September, 1967), indicates that for scientists "pattern recognition" is merely visual description and classification:

The first approach was the modeling of pattern recognition problems as a partition of measurement space . . . the second approach included mainly the need of a good dictionary for all the basic terms and the development of the grammatical machinery to connect these basic terms for pattern descriptions.

There is no inkling here that each sense actually makes its own space with its own distinctive perceptual structure. Only the visual sense is connected; all others resonate consensually. *Nature loves vacuums and plays the field while classifiers fill the spaces and spoil the sport.*

All paradigms are traps. Any philosophy that considers sensations and concepts as mere "reflections" or "copies" of material objects in the human mind fails to account for the continual transformation of sensory inputs into outputs of quite different kinds. Food for the mind is like food for the body; the inputs are never the same as the outputs! This pattern of nonlineality is evident in every human activity. AS "FIGURES," ALL SENSES CREATE THEIR OWN SPACES, WHICH ARE METAMORPHOSED BY INTERACTION WITH THEIR ENVIRONMENTAL "GROUNDS." "Causes" become "effects" *via concepts*, whereas effects merge with causes in process pattern recognition via percepts.

6

Re-cognizing

Languages and Cultures Transform Perception

Speak that I may see you.
Ancient plea

I've often seen it said.
Modern mode

Since Benjamin Whorf's pioneer work on the effects of language structures in biasing human perceptions, cultural anthropologists have begun to
develop a fresh approach to "general systems" by studying the psychic preferences and perceptual modes of preliterate peoples. By observing the
effects of interaction with their own literate cultural biases, these anthropologists are also learning how to anticipate these effects with their causes.
Natural interfaces are never neutral channels. THE MEDIUM IS ALWAYS A
BARRIER.

Through the Pane of the Present We See
the Ghost of the Past

In *Displacement of Concepts*, Donald A. Schon discusses how "the tendency either to obscurantize or to explain away novelty reflects the great
difficulty of explaining it. The difficulty comes in large part from our incli-
nation, with things and thoughts alike, to take an after-the-fact view." Or,
as Coleridge says: "To most men, experience is like the stern lights of a
ship, which illumine only the track it has passed."

We have already seen how most people are perceptually inadequate to
grapple with the immediate present. They prefer the familiar, even if this
compels them to retreat to an earlier period of their own culture. In our
own times this has taken the popular form of "camp" and the return to
country music. It is parallel to the nostalgic charade at Versailles, when
Marie Antoinette had the ladies in her court dress up as china shepherdesses.

Sputnik Reverberations

The unexpected prevalence of ecological and environmental studies has
become a popular pressure of panic proportions. It dates from Sputnik 1 in

1957. A universal consensus occurred in that year concerning the need for an enormous increase in the educational effort in America at least. It was unambiguous. The existence of Sputnik 1 indicated a lull in Western energies. Sputnik circled the planet triumphantly, proclaiming the Russian as *avant-garde* in technology. In the West, increased educational effort became explicitly synonymous with economic welfare. The new "software" military thrust became a parallel of the old "hardware" military establishment. The new information world revived the preceding world of specialized ghosts. Economic well-being seemed, then as now, to be inseparable from abundance of old "hardware" and consumer goods.

OLD WHEELS ARE NOW KEPT ROLLING BY
NEW ELECTRIC RESONANCE

In a single complex appears the convergence and the conflict of "hardware" and "software," specialism and integration, private goals and ecological obsession. It is very difficult to simulate any of the older forms of corporate behavior under the canopy of the new satellite environment. It is like living under an Oriental parasol as the West twirls East and the East dances West.

Today, the young are vividly aware of the unviable gap between current information sources, to which their environment exposes them daily, and the established modes of education.

> The sea has many voices.
> T. S. Eliot, *Four Quartets*

The poets and artists are masters in anticipating such gaps decades before they become dangerous. The poet and artist are in charge, as it were, of intensifying perception of the present and refurbishing the perception of the traditional forms of culture. Instead of merely discarding traditional forms, the poet and artist and inventor are engaged in supplying the ancient forms with youthful vigor. It is perhaps a type of cultural transplant of organs from one host body or culture to another. At a more commonplace level the "hardware" inventor transfers existing components or techniques from one area, or combination, to another.

The Displacement of Percepts

"Make it new," the Chinese say.

The art of remaking the world eternally afresh is achieved by the careful and deliberate dislocation of ordinary perception. Even the surrealist had this ambition—to attain a fresh vision of the world by unexpected juxtapositions of ordinary things. Most readers are familiar with Dali's "Fur-lined Teacup" and "Mona Lisa's Moustache." Charlie Chaplin performed this function by bringing the tramp into direct confrontation with the world of cops, robbers, and businessmen. Vulcan, the muse's anvil for inventing and hammering out the new, is an age-old legend of the relation between art and technology—"software" and "hardware." In the global theater, Chaplin plays the role of *clown as emperor.*

Encounter of East and West

The poet Ezra Pound saw that the telegraph press, with its mosaic coverage of world events under a single date line, had solved the problem of creating the new poetic vision for our time. In contrast, he pointed to the helpless fumbling of educated but conventional minds that scorned the popular media as major resources for innovation and insight.

Pound also saw that the telegraph mosaic of news items was an organization of experience that bridged the ancient Oriental and Western forms. In the *A B C of Reading,* Pound cites Ernest Fenollosa:

> In Europe, if you ask a man to define anything, his definition always moves away from the simple things that he knows perfectly well, it recedes into an unknown region of remoter and progressively remoter abstraction.
>
> Thus if you ask him what red is, he says it is a "colour."
>
> If you ask him what a colour is, he tells you it is a vibration or refraction of light, or a division of the spectrum.
>
> And if you ask him what vibration is, he tells you it is a mode of energy, or something of that sort, until you arrive at a modality of being, or non-being, or at any rate you get in beyond your depth, and beyond his depth. . . .
>
> But when the Chinaman wanted . . . to define red . . . how did he go about it?
>
> He . . . put together the abbreviated pictures of
>
> | ROSE | CHERRY |
> |------|--------|
> | IRON RUST | FLAMINGO |
>
> . . . the Chinese "word" or ideogram for red is based on something everyone *knows.*

Explanations that ignore the perceptual complementarity of EYE and EAR lead to conceptual conflict—the divorce of rhyme and reason.

Grammars for Languages That By-pass Print, the Inhuman Medium

Edward T. Hall's books, *The Silent Language* and *The Hidden Dimension,* are rich in examples that illustrate how people of differing cultures perceive both temporal and spatial relationships, often in strong contrast with our own ways. Edward S. Carpenter's essay, "The New Languages," published in *Explorations in Communication,* explains how the audile-tactile sensory biases of preliterate tribes and the visual sensory preferences of literate men reveal essentially different worlds.

Representation is never a replica.
  E. H. Gombrich, *Art and Illusion*

Every medium imposes its own structure and assumptions upon all data, while each favors either EYE or EAR, confrontation or transformation, MATCHING or MAKING.* All conceptual models or metaphors transfer or transform meaning from one sensory modality or field of being to another, just as the word "metaphor" itself presents semantic meaning under the guise of transportation. It can also be the reader who is "transported," as in Keats's sonnet "On Reading Chapman's Homer": "Much have I travelled in the realms of gold. . . ." You "put on" the poet's *medium* and become its *content* by adjusting yourself to use his poem in altering your perception of the world. Whereas this alteration is the *meaning* of the poem for you, its *message* is the totality of its effects, present and future, in the worlds of "software" and "hardware" alike.

Instant Alienation

In "TV Meets the Stone Age" (*TV Guide*, Toronto, January 16–22, 1971), Edward S. Carpenter describes the sudden transformation of the sensory lives of tribal New Guineans on seeing and hearing themselves for the first time:

> We take self-awareness for granted. It has been part of our culture for centuries . . . but with these natives, self-awareness came instantly and without warning. Suddenly the cohesive village had become a collection of separate, private individuals.

Like Matthew Arnold's scholar gypsy, they wandered "between two worlds, one dead, the other as yet unborn." Their world moves from EAR to EYE, just as our world is moving from EYE to EAR.

THE SPECTER OF OBJECTIVITY

Being overtaken by the future is the terror in the rear-view mirror! Objectivity is achieved only in short spurts by specialisms. Objectivity means leaving out all modes of awareness except the visual. James Joyce called it "the royal divorce" between thought and feeling. In *The Sacred Wood*, T. S. Eliot explains: "Aristotle had what is called the scientific mind—a mind which, as it is rarely found among scientists except in fragments, might better be called the intelligent mind . . . a superior sensibility." Aristotle lived at the interface of "barbarism" and "civilization," of preliterate and literate cultures. He was both information hunter and classifier, with the perception and awareness of "the borderline case."

* For more on this topic see *Understanding Media* by Marshall McLuhan.

The Miracle of Communication

I like the way he nods. He really communicates.
Corporation executive

Most specialists tacitly accept Hilaire Belloc's tongue-in-cheek formula for successful communication: "First I tell them what I'm going to tell them; then I tell them; and then I tell them what I told them." If they "turn off" their audiences by this semantic barrage aimed at matching responses to inputs, they don't give up; they just keep shouting! They have not yet perceived the message from the birds. The pathetic fallacy, that the *output* of a system can be trusted to be a reasonable facsimile of the *input*, has been in doubt as long as the ingratitude of children or the waste products of any body whatever.

RHYTHM   RHYME   REASON

Poetry can communicate before it is understood.
T. S. Eliot

We can have the meaning before the experience, but more often we have the experience without the meaning. We have had the experience of radio and TV, but their meaning may not be known for decades to come.

"Le Mot Juste"

The "right" word is not the one that names the thing but the word that gives the *effect* of the thing.

Experience is play, and meaning is replay and re-cognition. Far from being normal, successful communication is a rarity. It requires not only repetition of a common language, but also demands participation of both author and audience in the process of remaking from their old components a pattern that only the author may have perceived. *Communicating the new is a miracle.*

PUTTING ON THE MEDIA

The Viewer Is Monarch of All He Surveys

Hypocrite lecteur, mon semblable, mon frère.
Baudelaire

My shemblab, my freer.
James Joyce

It was very helpful of Charles Reich in *The Greening of America* to say that what McLuhan means by "the medium is the message" is that "the medium has no content." It is rarely that readers of anything explain what they think it means. However, most readers are eager to tell how what they read makes them *feel*. It is not very helpful to an author seeking to clarify a problem to be told that "you send me," on the one hand, or, on the other hand, that "it stinks." Sam Goldwyn ran into the same opaque wall with film commentators. They never had any insights into his problems, so he observed: "As for movie critics, don't even ignore them." To banish such criticism from one's mind might use up useful energies or even upset the indispensable processes of the subconscious in creating new vision. Professor Reich did not say how McLuhan's writings made him feel; he simply reported his idea of what was meant by "the medium has no content." Thus, with the electric light, it might seem natural to say it has no content. It simply creates an illuminated area. It makes a new kind of space—a lighted place.

In his truly illuminating book *And There Was Light*, Jacques Lusseyran reports the multisensory adventures of a person violently blinded when only eight years old:

> A very short time after I went blind I forgot the faces of my mother and father and the faces of most of the people I loved. From time to time I remembered a face, but it was always that of a person I did not care about.

The same thing happens to most of us on the telephone. We can scarcely visualize the faces of our own family while talking to them on the phone, but we find it easier to "see" those with whom we are not acquainted. Stockbrokers tell of their surprise on meeting men they have dealt with for years on the phone: "Never thought you looked like that."

Radio, in contrast to the telephone, permits the listener to fill in a good deal of visual imagery. The radio announcer or disc jockey stands out loud and clear, while the voice on the telephone resonates in isolation from the visual sense. Nobody ever wrote a lament about "all alone by the radio," but "All Alone by the Telephone," a classic of the twenties, is a resounding prophecy of high-rise living in the present time.

Seeing Through Voices

The telephone permits kissing, if not visualizing. The phone is an audile-tactile medium. Lusseyran notes: "It is strange that when laws men make are so ticklish in matters concerning the body, they never set limits to nakedness or contact by voice. Evidently they leave out of account that the voice can go farther than hands or eyes in licit or illicit touch." Lusseyran explains how, when one sense is sealed off, the others rally to new intensity: "Furthermore, a man who speaks does not realize that he is betraying himself. When people addressed me, a blind child, they were not on guard. . . . They never suspected I could read their voices like a book."

When one of our senses is closed down, the other senses create new patterns among themselves. This is especially so when the individual senses are given new magnitude and scope by technical innovations. Lusseyran's book is rich in illustrations of the changes that came over his sensory life through blindness. What he says of our senses applies also to the extensions of our senses in new art forms and in new systems of science and philosophy: "When I came upon the myth of objectivity in certain modern thinkers, it made me angry." To a blind man it is obvious that our ideals of quantitative stability are of visual origin. The visual sense alone provides the idea of uniformity, continuity, and connectedness:

> From my own experience I knew very well that it was enough to take from a man a memory here, an association there, to deprive him of hearing or sight, for the world to undergo immediate transformation, and for another world, entirely different but entirely coherent, to be born.

The radio generation of "jazz babies" and "hot mamas" in the 1920's encountered a new world, although one that was connected and traditional compared with the world occupied by the TV generation of the 1950's and 1960's. The TV generation imagines it has a totally new human mandate. It sees life returned to a primal state with all the rules of the game yet to be discovered. Such was the natural feeling of North American settlers when they seemed to be monarch of all they surveyed. This familiar phrase can teach us much about our current media of communication. The user of the electric media, whether radio, telephone, movie, or TV, has a powerful sense of being king and emperor, since he is the content of a total environment of electric services. These services extend to the moon and to Mars. Electric media transport us instantly wherever we choose. When we are *on* the *phone* we do not just disappear down a hole, Alice-in-Wonderland style. We are *there*, and they are *here*.

The English painter and novelist Wyndham Lewis devoted his trilogy *The Human Age* to exploring the condition of men as angels in the new *magnetic city* of the "wired" planet. By means of electric circuitry, men are now disembodied intelligences, capable of intellectual actions at vast distances. Lewis portrays this development beginning with the telegraph press in World War I. The moment of the telegraph was the moment of *mass* man. Mass man is created not by numbers but by speed. The mass audience is created by the simultaneous experience of the press or of radio. The book is not simultaneous for the reading public. The arrival of mass man was accompanied by the order

Give the Public What It Wants

There was an ingenious parrot breeder who managed to develop a bird that weighed three hundred pounds. He taught it to say, "Polly wants a cracker," and the bird straightway added, "AND I MEAN NOW!"

Keeping in mind that the user is necessarily the content of any man-made service environment or media, it is noteworthy that, with Sputnik, men put the planet inside its first man-made container. From that time people had an immediate sense of being the "content kings" of the Earth. As the content of the planet they suddenly noticed how poor a job Nature had done in keeping men in line. If "what the public wants" was the first child of the telegraph press, ECOLOGY was the first progeny of Sputnik. When processes moved up to electric speeds, it became obvious that "everything *causes everything*." For every cause there are many effects, just as every effect has many causes; this becomes apparent to those existing in an electric environment of information. Those existing as the content of a man-made environment never cease adjusting it to their own behavior, just as they adjust their behavior to the environment. "Programming" the environment had this form of slow adjustment earlier. However, for the residents of the "wired planet," or the magnetic city, the programming now begins to assume the character of rapid and extensive change, which we take for granted on radio, movies, and TV. Sputnik and the moon shots brought about, in effect, the institution of a new kind of global theater, in which all men become actors and there are few spectators. The population of the world is both the cast and content of this new theater. The repertory of the theater consists of a perpetual *happening*, which can include the retrieval or *replay* of any previous happenings that men choose to experience.

The replaying of past events in "realistic" ways began with the power of print to retrieve the ancient authors and historians. The Elizabethan stage projected scenes and characters of the past as a staple entertainment. Our power to reconstruct the past has grown steadily with media enlargement, till Hollywood made such replays into a major feature of this century.

Media Hosts

We can now see how any medium of communication can play host to many others. The principle that *the user* is the content clears the way to the observation that when TV uses or presents a movie, the prime content of the movie is the host medium, TV. A ball game or a bullfight *on* TV is, naturally, a TV experience. For those *at* the game or the fight, the content of the game or fight consists primarily of the corporate user. In the case of a spectacle with a large clientele, it is a question of just who the user is. Who "turns on" a ball game? Essentially, any game is a dramatization of some of the interests and motives of its audience. If the audience were absent, the "game" could only be a practice or rehearsal. It would have no content. The audience or the public is the user of all sports and thus their ultimate content. The public both makes and "turns on" the game.

If the public is the user and hence the content of spectator sports and entertainment, it is understandable why these forms must always "put on" or project the changing image of the public. The popular expression "where it's at" may say a good deal about the strivings of media people to bring language and images, song and dance into a perceptual focus. When we read a poem or listen to a song, we put on an extension of our language. Such extensions bring into relation to us the experiences of multitudes of lives. These experiences can be the means of enlarging or sharpening and enriching our private perceptions. However, when we "put on" an entire service environment, such as radio or TV, something more seems to happen than in the case of the individual means provided by a poem or song or book. There is a strange character in electric media, which we encounter even in the daily newspaper. The daily paper says in effect: "This is your world for today." It has been pointed out that by some miracle, just enough happens every day to exactly fill all the newspapers. It is the simultaneity of news coverage that makes possible this mosaic experience of the world for today. No connections are sought or found amidst the innumerable items. Everything is unified under date line rather than story line. If the paper carried yesterday's date or tomorrow's date, the items could be the same, but the effect would be totally different. If it were yesterday's date, we would drop the paper in disgust. If it were tomorrow's date, our eyes would pop out.

Hijackers of the Global Theater

There is something about the push-button dimension that changes our relation to our world. It raises the entire question of the place of advertising and sponsors in the world of the new media. When the printed book was new, there were no reading publics to speak of, and authors vied with one another to secure the most distinguished patrons possible, a dedication to who would win attention and promotion for the book. The patron played the role of the program sponsor now. The patron tended to fade from the book scene in the eighteenth century when newspapers enlarged the reading public almost to the point where it made up the entire literate community. Strangely, it is just at the moment when the *user* becomes the public at large that a change in attitude toward the medium takes place. Until the moment of inclusiveness it is natural for elites and specialist tastes and preferences to be accepted by the users of the medium. However, at the moment, when the entire public is involved in the medium, there occurs the cry of "what the public wants." It is as if some flip or reversal occurred that enabled the user to say with emphatic voice: "I am the content of this medium. I am the monarch of all that this medium reaches. Any outside considerations are mere interlopers." It is almost as if the medium had returned to the condition of a primal wilderness, where each individual feels like the king or an emperor and would tend to regard any intruder with suspicion and rivalry. Paradoxically, then, it is at the moment when public attention occupies every phase and feature of a new service environment of technology that there is heard, on the one hand, the dogma of what the public wants, and, on the other hand, the arguments against the dilution and pollution of commercialism.

When the movies were new, ads used to be injected on slides. As the movies became more and more an indispensable service environment, ads on the show or during show time became distasteful and unwelcome. This quantitative fact is important since, if the user *is* the content, then any other user of the medium will appear as an interloper. Let us test the principle that the user of a medium is the content. The response to the media advertiser in the push-button age of media service would tend to resemble the reaction of the inhabitants of a natural solitude or wilderness to the invading voices of real estate salesmen and strip miners. It is possible to hijack the whole culture, or world, by simply diverting this course or function.

Suppose that each time we turned on an electric light a voice told us that the ensuing illumination was by courtesy of our local car dealer? There is nothing illogical about such a possibility. However, it does contradict the principle that the user is the "content king" of the medium. Electric light creates an instant service environment of which the user is absolute monarch. That is why he is very sensitive to any rival royalty. By contrast, the space of the highway can be segmented and interrupted with commercial signs ad infinitum. Imagine, however, the dismay of an air traveler if the airways were punctuated by commercial or other announcements. It would be almost as disruptive as an announcement by a plane's captain: "We have a bomb aboard!" A bomb definitely challenges the space role of an airplane's passengers much in the way that a hijacker does. The aerial space allowed to the passenger plane is almost the equivalent of a natural wilderness.

Media Monarchs

It may indeed prove true that the service environments created by the electric media are so extensive and inclusive that their users become natural monarchs, if not tyrants, who will brook no interference from other media. In electric surrounds the user as content can only experience rivalry in the form of static or short circuit. For sponsors to attempt to "put on" an electric service environment such as radio or TV seems to present some of the brash effrontery of a royal usurper. When Shakespeare wrote his dramas of power politics among the medieval and Renaissance kings, the natural image for power, legitimate or illegitimate, was clothing. The media viewers and users regard those who would put on the electric media as private or stylish garments, as the usurpers of an integral and absolute territory.

We are already getting a very large breeze from this new quarter in the form of ecology. Ecological awareness is unmistakably the return to the Paleolithic outlook of the hunter; this attitude regards with scorn and hostility the mere planter and agrarian specialist who seeks to break up the unified domain of nature into small strips and patches. Electronic man, for good or ill, seems to be reclaiming the unity and integrity of the global environment as a natural inheritance of inviolate sanctity.

AT ELECTRIC-INFORMATION SPEEDS ART AND SCIENCE AND NATURE
CONVERGE THROUGH UNDERSTANDING MEDIA.

Chapter 6

Old Wars and New Overkill

1

PNR

The Ultimate Mass Medium: E = MC²
(Whatever Became of the First MC?)

Monster Merger of Inner and Outer

At exactly fifteen minutes past eight in the morning, on August 6, 1945, Japanese time, at the moment when the atomic bomb flashed above the city . . .   John Hersey, *Hiroshima*

The Peace That Passeth All Technology?

In the city set upon slime and loam
They cry in their parliament "Who goes home?" . . .
For there's blood on the field and blood on the foam
And blood on the body when Man goes home.
And a voice valedictory . . . Who is for Victory?
Who is for Liberty? Who goes home?
                    G. K. Chesterton, "Who Goes Home?"

NEW POINT OF NO RETURN

In the Toronto *Globe and Mail* (June 6, 1970) Zena Cherry reported from Hiroshima on her conversation with some Japanese university students:

"Well, you must have heard that since the A-bomb year of 1945, 1,000,000 persons have become corpses, in nine different wars. . . ."

"In the Tomb of the Unknown People are buried 30,000 skulls. . . ."

"The heat from the bomb blast lasted only one-ten-thousandth of a second but anyone exposed was burned to death. As it burst into the fireball the temperature was about 1,000,000 degrees centigrade. It corresponded to some 20,000 tons of TNT. . . ."

"Of half-a-million population 158,607 were left alive. There were only 14 buildings left in the whole city. . . ."

"Every morning for two months at exactly 8 A.M. American planes flew over Hiroshima . . . but soon we paid no attention . . . one stopped its engine and as it glided over the center of the city it dropped a single atomic bomb. Total instantaneous destruction."

Universal Service Environment

From the moment of Hiroshima and The Bomb we had positive proof that information as such had become the new sinews of war. By complementarity, the same pervasive use of information had created an environment of learning for war, business, and education alike. Paradoxically, the overkill via sheer knowledge returned men to sudden recognition of the precious significance of the human scale. The classic wisdom of NOTHING IN EXCESS was resurrected by this instant of hideous strength when everything was in excess. The human scale that had been submerged during a century of industrial gigantism was instantly and unforgettably retrieved.

Man-made Rim Spins Supplant Natural Cycles

Henceforth, the natural round of seasonal and biological cycles was supplanted by vehement new intensities of man-made "rim spins" demanding a new programming of the entire human enterprise. Perhaps some will say that this supplanting of the "natural round" (earth, air, fire, and water) had been assured earlier with the economic and experience cycles engendered by the speed of electric communication technologies.

THE "NEW" SCIENCE IS PERCEPT NOT CONCEPT

The Abnihilisation of the Etym.
James Joyce, *Finnegans Wake*

Here Joyce is referring not only to the splitting but the splintering of all etymologies or the scrubbing of all human perceptions. The *Etymologiae* of Isidore of Seville in the sixth century A.D. was a compendium of the arts and sciences. Etymology was understood to include the secret principles of all forms of being, physical and spiritual. In the seventeenth century Vico's *Scienza Nuova* reasserted those ancient principles of verbal resonance as comprising the keys to all scientific and humanist mysteries. James Joyce, who incorporated not only Vico, but all the ancient traditions of language as science, alludes to the principal feature of this kind of "new science" in *Finnegans Wake*: "As for the viability of vicinals, when invisible they're invincible." The allusion to Vico is environmental (*vicus*: Latin for neighborhood), indicating the irresistible operation of causes in the new environments issuing from new technologies. Since these environments are always invisible, merely because they are environments, their transforming powers are never heeded in time to be moderated or controlled.

Having ourselves created new environments of invisible powers, embedded in such things as The Bomb, we are unprepared to encounter the psychic consequences of these powers, but we find ourselves baffled and dismayed at the occult obsession of young and old, ignorant and learned, which accompanies the new electrotechnical environment. Like all other new environments, these situations are made up of whole clusters and communities of causes, whether "formal," "efficient," or "material." Innovations re-establish contact with long-forgotten "causes" (*e.g.*, Zen, Yoga, and acupuncture) kept in abeyance by past environments.

In *The Sacred Mushroom and the Cross*, philologist John M. Allegro lyrically proclaims the recovery of the subterranean cult of the mushroom god—*amanita muscaria*. It is, of course, no coincidence that the subterranean should mime and portend the superterrestrial action of the mushroom cloud. The biological blastoderm and the atomic blast merge in a grotesque existential pun. Philology and etymology have become once more the basis for the metaphysical in Martin Heidegger. In Allegro's study we have once again the wedding of philology and theology: the return of the mushroom god that mocks both God and man by the maximization of the minimal. Allegro fulfills the prophetic and ominous vision of Poe's *Raven*:

> Once upon a midnight dreary, while I pondered, weak and weary,
> Over many a quaint and curious volume of forgotten lore—

DEFENSE AS EXPOSÉ

Peter Drucker's *The Concept of Corporations* shows how the speed-up of any large business organization, in effect, instigates civil war among various levels and groups in our society. Every technological innovation is itself war. The new technology eliminates the old world and the old image of identity, while at the same time it inspires a new world and a fight for a new image of identity. Today, the electric speeds of technology promote wars to be conducted on the front pages of our newspapers, and on the TV screens in our living rooms. The "space race" between Russians and Americans is a repeat of the territorial interplay that occurs more intimately in the media. But for countries lacking the new industrial technology, war is their "crash course" in technical education.* It is easy to view wars in terms of technological development:

WORLD WAR I—A RAILWAY WAR OF CENTRALIZA-
TION AND ENCIRCLEMENT.
WORLD WAR II—A RADIO WAR OF DECENTRALIZA-
TION CONCLUDED BY "THE BOMB."
WORLD WAR III—A TV GUERRILLA WAR WITH NO
DIVISION BETWEEN CIVIL AND MILI-
TARY FRONTS.

The new overkill is simply an extension of our nervous system into a total ecological service environment. Such a service environment can liquidate or terminate its beneficiaries as naturally as it sustains them.

Backlash of the Iron Age

John Huizinga in *Homo Ludens* describes how the mood has changed:

Modern warfare has, on the face of it, lost all contact with play. . . . In contemporary politics, based as they are on the utmost preparedness if not actual preparation for war, there would seem to be hardly any trace of the old play-attitude. The code of honour is flouted, the rules of the game are set aside, international law is broken, and all the ancient associations of war with ritual and religion are gone. Nevertheless the methods by which war-policies are conducted and war-

* See *War and Peace in the Global Village* by Marshall McLuhan and Quentin Fiore.

preparations carried out still show abundant traces of the agonistic attitude as found in primitive society. Politics are and always have been something of a game of chance; we have only to think of the challenge, the provocations, the threats and denunciations to realize that war and the policies leading up to it are always, in the nature of things, a gamble. . . . Despite appearances to the contrary, therefore, war has not freed itself from the magic circle of play.

WHEN JOHNNY COMES MARCHING HOME,
HE'LL HAVE A TICKER-TAPE PARADE.

WAR IN PEACE OR PEACE IN WAR?

The Artful Dodger

In many tribal societies war is institutionalized as a way of life. War with deadly intent is practiced as both pastime and as a means of maintaining the hunting skills of the society. Few people are killed in these deadly encounters because of their high training in evasive action. Proportionately far more people are killed by our motor traffic than in these tribal war games. The corresponding skills of survival in our society are found less on the highway than in "tax dodging."

ESP-ION-AGE

U.S. LAUNCHES SATELLITE TO SPY ON RUSSIA, CHINA
Headline, Toronto *Star*, June 19, 1970

I have eyes upon him,
And his affairs come to me on the wind.
Shakespeare, *Antony and Cleopatra*

War Is Dead? If It Isn't, We Are!

At the overkill peak of no return, war went dead. The moment of overkill created an environment like the Nessus shirt of Hercules that shredded the human hero. At this point there occurred the inevitable retrieval of the unexpected from the remotest primal period of pretechnology—the peace that passeth all technology. Like the poverty of the Third World, World War III is a secret dimension inherent in our own technology.

The commander imposes himself from above whereas the leader exposes himself to the dangers below. So far as "hardware" is concerned, most executives would now readily concede the point of the adage "We are always magnificently prepared to fight the preceding war." Since many people in business have actually been involved in military establishments past and present, they feel a natural empathy for the forms of organization that dominate the military life of their times. In *The Sexual Cycle of Human Warfare*, Norman Walter observes:

> In wartime every individual "matters" to the State. *Barriers between* classes become less forbidding, and the common danger revives sympathy and fellow-feeling throughout the warring group. . . . The result of all this is that many people look back with a sense almost of nostalgia on the war period, as the brightest and most vital in their lives.

The afterglow persists in both "hardware" and "software." Old generals keep refighting old wars and insisting, "Ve vont lose de next von." As long as some persistence and continuity of military technology can be assumed, a general-staff plan for the next campaign is likely to have some degree of relevance, whether in business or military matters. But this continuity of technology is precisely what has disappeared today. *Now change alone has any semblance of reality.*

3

TOP

The Public

F. W. Howton, in his useful historical survey of the multifarious patterns of executive activity, *Functionaries*, cites the Napoleonic example. In life and in fiction, Napoleon had many imitators. A whole new genre of heroes emerged, from Stendhal's Julien Sorel of *The Red and the Black* to Raskolnikov in Dostoevsky's *Crime and Punishment*, to the hard-bitten "tough guys" of thriller fiction and movie lore. There is an unbroken line of such figures. Since Nature imitates art, the equivalent types begin to appear in the business world a bit later. Mighty corporation chiefs of Bismarckian quality and Teddy Roosevelt enthusiasm became standard properties of every well-managed enterprise. These types were prepared to impose themselves on every situation. Commenting on the new "citizen soldier" of the Napoleonic era, Howton notes:

> Command is imposed; leadership is won. Command implies a top-down structure of authority; leadership implies a bottom-up structure. All bureaucratic structures make use of both principles, but the emphatic shift in Napoleon's time from command to leadership was exhilarating because it expressed the new spirit of the nation-state.

Pentagon Poverty of Polity?

It is an excellent example of trying to live in two incompatible worlds as if there were only one world. William Beecher reports in the New York *Times* Service, October 15, 1969:

GENERAL DEFENDS WAR
Sees Vietnam as Live Test Site

> "I see battlefields on which we can destroy anything we locate through instant communications and almost instantaneous application of highly lethal firepower."

This is the plight of the goal-oriented man and his victims at all times. Today's organization charts with their "line" and "staff" functions are still patterned after the needs of nineteenth-century military organizations. But as Napoleon understood:

La politique est la fatalité.

The fifth element is mud.

The *Times* of London, December 27, 1969, quotes George S. Ball, former United States Under Secretary of State: "The U.S. hasn't prepared for the possibility it might not gain objectives."

War is now a useless concept, an effete category that confuses all our thinking about the new situation. At instant speeds the abiding war is the war of icons and images, achieved by alliances and misalliances in a sequence of unholy deadlocks.

FAREWELL TO ARMOR

The main military "armor," both in war and in peace, is now recognized as consisting of information via espionage. The fact that espionage heroes have become the stock in trade of entertainment is an index of their having been by-passed by the latest technology. *The plain fact is that the only way to keep up with enemies or rivals is to be ahead of them—by sheer design.* As A. C. Clarke put it in *Profiles of the Future:* "The only runner in the much-vaunted space race is—man."

Not only are the old forms of war dead but the most recent forms of espionage obsolete. THE NEW WAR IS TO RECOVER PERCEPTION OF OUR HIDDEN ENVIRONMENTS—MOST OF THEM MADE BY OURSELVES. The old hunter foraged in alien territory; the new one sharpens his perceptions at home.

4

GHQ

The New Hunter Lives in Wartime and Surrounds Everyman

The automated presidential surrogate is the superlative nobody. One of the little-known effects of current military need for rapid communication with all parts of the world has been a blizzard of innovation that has ignored private and national boundaries alike. In Latin America, for example, the arrival of transoceanic cables, microwave, and satellite communication have been the consequence of military needs. To assure effective intercom between the Latin American governments and Washington in resisting political subversion, United States defense has fomented telecom networks. The same drive to arrest subversive developments within the existing regimes in both the Middle East and the Far East occurs in the same fashion. Preliterate Africa is perhaps the only area beyond the present reach and control of American military HQ. This media blizzard, like many other technological events, is unrelated to the local cultural needs.

C.I.C. and President: Chief Autocrat and Democratic Chief

Today, the Commander in Chief, President Nixon, is looking rather fragile and inadequate simply because his advisers are so brittle and specialist. *One right way—the American way.* And legal specialist Nixon himself shuns the "laying on of tongues." He wants it in writing. *One right word for every meaning.*

> Killing men is the king's game.
> Nursery adage

Julius Caesar (circa 50 B.C.), as much as any C.I.C. today, maintained power-at-a-distance through bureaucratic controls. But he was above all an encyclopedic humanist, as was Charlemagne (A.D. 742–814). Libraries had already become a major military resource in Roman times and in medieval Byzantium also. Barbarossa (circa A.D. 1500), whose domains included both Sicily and Prussia, France and Italy, was equally dependent on the literates and lawyers and libraries. Today, telecoms and computer memories have bypassed libraries as military and business resource alike. Yet libraries are growing bigger and more diverse than ever before—obsolescent, but far from dead.

When President Eisenhower went to South America in 1960, he carried with him the entire electronic umbrella. It is not only inconvenient for the United States President to do this wherever he goes in the world, but increasingly tricky and dangerous. It is now impermissible for the American President to be more than twenty minutes out of touch with over-all world events. The President now has to live in these "world overalls" somewhat in the way Churchill occupied his "siren suit." So crucial is this time factor that it can no longer be left to a wake-a-day working President. A much more reliable substitute has been devised for this fallible and limited human. According to Herbert F. York, who explains in "ABM, MIRV, and the Arms Race" (*Science*, July 17, 1970):

THE "LAUNCH-ON-WARNING" DOCTRINE

The time in which the decision to launch must be made varies from just a few minutes to perhaps 20 minutes. . . . This time is so short that the decision to launch our missiles must be made either by a computer, by a "pre-programmed" President, or by some "pre-programmed" delegate of the President. . . . In effect, not even the President, let alone the Congress, would really be a party to the ultimate decision to end civilization.

If launching *our* missiles on electronic warning does not seem so bad, then consider the situation the other way round. . . . Foreign Minister Gromyko last summer said (Report to the Supreme Soviet of the U.S.S.R., 10 July, 1969) . . . the command and control for arms are becoming increasingly autonomous, if one can put it that way, from the people who create them. Human capacity to hear and see are incapable of reaching to modern speeds. . . . The decisions made by man depend in the last analysis on the conclusions provided by computers.

Only a few months later the Associated Press (February 22, 1971) reported:

WRONG TAPE TRIGGERS NUCLEAR ALERT

*White House calls for full report on sounding
of false national emergency alarm*

The National Emergency Warning Center frantically tried to cancel the message several times, but was unsuccessful until it found the proper code word—"impish"—to indicate that the cancellation was authentic.

Achilles and the Tortoise

Neither the President nor the businessman finds it convenient to lumber about the world with the new means of playing safe. The need, therefore, is to equip the tortoise or slow-moving territories with the latest speedy tele-

coms. Homogeneity of world culture is mandatory to assure the defense of
the big powers. The result is a cultural "blitz" on "backward" territories.
The tortoise must be supplied with the most speedy forms of locomotion,
even though they smash its shell and pattern alike. The Latin Americans
may endure these "culture shocks" by reminding themselves that Achilles
can never catch up to the tortoise.

It is America that has now undergone "culture shock" from its own electronic services. The justification for these cultural blizzards imposed abroad
is no longer felt by young Americans at home. They too have been blitzed
and now prefer the most "backward primitivism" to the most "advanced
standards of living." It is their counterstrategy against

Instant Homogenization to Cultural Sawdust

Turning over the American military establishment to the Vietnamese as
a university has the same purpose. The United States, hung up on its old
centralist "hardware" pattern, which has lost it a nineteenth-century style of
war in Vietnam, is now trying to impose the same homogenized programming on the world—magnetic city itself. Totally misunderstanding both its
own antiquated pattern and the new involvement of everybody in magnetic
city, it persists in attempting to connect everybody "by wire" to the HQ of
its C.I.C. This centralism is as futile electronically as it had been militarily
in Vietnam.

WAR BY AUTOMATION

Ultimate Specialist Programs for Solving
Warfare-Welfare Problems

A UPI release from Washington, July 6, 1970, cites an accusation by
Senator William Proxmire against the Pentagon for spending nearly $2 bil-
lion "to develop a totally new method of waging ground warfare" using
complex electronic equipment such as sensors, lasers, and computers. The
resulting *automated battlefield* would be a natural substitute for *automated
welfare* or G.A.S.

The obsession with such nineteenth-century patterns at once explains the
American obsession with territorial intrusion, where no advantages of
ground or resource appear to be in play. It also clarifies the equally irrational obsession with keeping "Communism" out of the territories it has
wired to HQ. The Pentagon is bewildered by both the goals and the direction and the effects of its own policy, as the defense forces communize and
homogenize the world.

THE GREAT SOCIETY

If the Child Is Father to the Man,
the Environment Is Alma Mater

In his classic *The Great Society*, written in 1914 on the very eve of war, Graham Wallas devoted his opening chapter to doubts about the mechanical inventions that had made the Great Society possible. He expressed misgivings that had become general in 1914, when people compared the consciousness typical of the Great Society with those states of consciousness typical of more primitive organizations. These misgivings led Wallas to scrutinize the Great Society and its assumptions.

At the very entrance to the twentieth century, inclusive consciousness had once more become necessary for social navigation and survival alike. Exclusiveness and specialism had swiftly brought the West to the 1914 threshold of misery.

World War I, in effect, created a more efficient market for "hardware" products and for fragmented "hardware thinking" than any available in peacetime. Today, having got into a "software" or electric information war, we have reached another kind of saturation point, this time involving "software" technologies. In 1914, men had decided that war was the only remaining market for the effective exchange of "hardware" products. Today, we are asking ourselves whether war has any residual advantages as a means of motivating and organizing our new technologies of "software" information and programming. Even in World War II, "hardware" had become incidental as a commodity in comparison with propaganda and image making and prestige maneuvers.

Parallel shifts in the business establishment are perfectly familiar to the ordinary scanner of the press. With Jacques Ellul's *Propaganda*, wars are back again in the world of resistance to total occupation. Today, resistance has become our preoccupation—a way of life. Now we seek to resist total occupation of our territories by our own technologies. The smoke of battle, a universal smog, hangs over us.

Invasion from Within as Undergrounds By-pass All Fronts

We are hanging out our washing on the Siegfried Line.
British popular song of World War II

Modern industrial "hardware" met its classic defeat in the Spanish Penin-
sular War, from which we have the word *guerrilla* (Spanish: little war).
Napoleon and his generals were helpless to establish a *front* against the innumerable pockets of Spanish *guerrillas*. What mud had done to Napoleon,
what "hardware" and terrain did to the big battalions in the early nineteenth century, "software" and the new information environment are doing
at present. It is not possible to establish a military *front* in the new communication jungle. The prototype of the guerrilla warrior is the North
American Indian. When the European invaded Indian territory, both regarded it as their own. Only the guerrilla can use the total environment as
resource against the invader. China had always swallowed invaders whole
and made them Chinese. Passive guerrilla warfare—a variation of the old
pattern—is using the environment as a major weapon to envelop the enemy.
For all the targets and techniques of conventional warfare there are coun-
tertechniques and territorial environments for guerrilla warfare. But overkill
—killing to the last man—makes war absolutely meaningless and irrelevant.

The New Communication Jungle

Since World War II Western military operations have been conducted
according to the most conventional industrial thinking of yesteryear. One
of the more fantastic episodes, illustrating the centralist drive of the old
military machine, concerned the *Pueblo*. This ship, which bore the most
advanced electronic equipment, depended upon a control contact with
GHQ in Washington, where the ordinary paperwork of the bureaucracy
had fallen behind. The most advanced and centralized technological control operation in military history was consigned, as it were, to a wastebasket.
Consider the *Pueblo* episode as a microcosm of the entire Western
world. Its bureaucracies have no means of sensitive response to the changing environments of information. The only possible upshot of this impasse
is the dissolution of the entire "hardware" operation and its underlying
structures and assumptions. Only so far as it is alerted by the cash nexus
does the sensitivity of the market place exceed that of the military sector.

The Shot-gun Wedding of Specter and Antispecter

The very phrases "cold war" and "where it's at" (1940's and 1960's) mark new eras of human organization and development. Both are much more complex than their predecessors' "shooting war" and *"avant-garde."* Each era rallied the media to present its mode in the most vivid light. The nineteenth-century mind mistakes the "war of images" for a "cold war." "Cold war" marks the end of nineteenth-century "hardware" in the Western military scene. By the same token, it has become enormously expedient to dump old-fashioned "hardware" on all the undeveloped areas of the world. Such dumping grounds are new "markets" for old industrial garbage or surplus. These hapless lands help us to bridge our old Stone Age to the new—from poison arrows to "death rays."

War readiness is bread and butter for the Paleolithic hunter. So it is becoming now for the industrial warfare-welfare state. Paradoxically, warfare has become the *ground* for the new *figure* of the welfare state. To take it one step further, both warfare and welfare states are *figures* against the new *ground* of ecological man on Spaceship Earth, even as Spaceship Earth is now new *figure* against the old galactic *ground* of the cosmos.

Gross National Product Equates Killing and Curing

The warfare-welfare state highlights the service/disservice character of a world of accelerating innovation. In GNP terms it is now difficult to see the distinction between costs and benefits of warfare and welfare. This distinction is further confused by a growing awareness of the technological benefits conferred by "advanced" societies on their "backward" military foes. The speed-up of "benefits" received by backward countries during current hot wars has been reckoned to take some of the sting, and all the stigma, out of death itself. Instead of *dulce et decorum est pro patria mori,* "backward" peoples are inclined to note how economically advantageous it is to have a little scrap going with some big advanced foe (*The Mouse That Roared*). World War I, *Kaiser Bill's Grand Opera,* was an early instance of "War as Horror Comedy" (*Time,* June 15, 1970):

> Naturally, anyone who wants to get out of combat isn't really crazy. So, supernaturally, anyone who says he's too crazy to keep flying is too sane to stop.

"Hardware" war, now a completely passé form of power struggle, has once again become a "sport of kings" in accordance with the familiar dynamic of *"past times are pastimes."* Current events have surpassed the most sophisticated and cynical speculation on the nature of war games. Wherever there is grievance, there is comedy. The *horror comedy* consists in the action of the war game advancing every field of human service: technology, education, and entertainment alike.

CLICHÉ — TOUCHÉ — RETROUVÉ

With the innovations and new services accruing from military operations and the exertion of the sinews of war, there goes the complementary recovery of roots and traditions, the return of forgotten technologies and wisdom. A familiar journalistic example is the new relevance of old elephant and tiger traps in Indo-China.

Tommies and Indians in Belfast

An Associated Press dispatch, August 1, 1970, reports:

> RIOTERS USE BOWS AND ARROWS AGAINST TROOPS IN BELFAST
>
> British troops ducking arrows fired tear gas and heavy streams of water . . . at rioters. . . . An army spokesman expressed concern at the introduction of arrowfire. . . . "It's a lethal weapon, and it's particularly difficult to deal with. At the moment, we don't know where the arrows are being fired from and it's causing us some concern."

Thus the return to guerrilla fighting is not limited to the Far East. It has been from the first the method of the student activists. But in Belfast it has suddenly acquired a Stone Age form with nostalgic overtones of childhood games of "cowboys and Indians." Typically, the "advanced" military unit with its specialist techniques is easily unbalanced by the antique. The very ancient and the very modern have much relevance in common.

6

ART

Anthony Lewis, writing in the New York *Times* Service, September 25, 1970, notes:

> Technological development in the past 50 years has made killing a more remote, impersonal process. . . . Bombs are dropped from planes so high up that human victims can scarcely be imagined. Shells are summoned by radio and aimed by computer. Helicopter gunships spray whole areas so that every living thing is eliminated.

> *Look 'em straight in the eye and kill 'em dead:*
> *Electronic aim-by-eye for automatic fire-by-pushbutton*

The same technology that permits us to perpetrate atrocities-at-a-distance also creates instant feedback of empathy. The functionary in any part of the Establishment, military, business, or educational, feels untainted. The New York *Times* Service (January 12, 1971) reports from Fort Benning, Georgia:

> The man who said he helped Lieut. William Calley slay more than 100 unarmed South Vietnamese civilians, including children, at My Lai, testified yesterday that he and the army officer were only "doing their job!"

He is doing his job—like the hangman, like the hammerman in the slaughterhouse. You have, on the one hand, the name of the game and the actors, and, on the other, the audience whose patterns of life are represented in the game. Miniaturization and etherealization of weaponry make possible not only action-at-a-distance, but callous irresponsibility and trancelike unreality.

Man Becomes the Slave of His Servants

Commenting on the memoirs of Albert Speer, *Inside the Third Reich*, *The Observer*, London, April 9, 1970, remarks:

> He . . . symbolizes a type which is becoming increasingly important in all belligerent countries: the pure technician, the classless bright young man without background, with no other original aim than to make his way in the world and no other means than his technical or

managerial ability. It is the lack of psychological and spiritual ballast, and the ease with which he handles the terrifying technical and organizational machinery of our age, which makes this slight type go extremely far nowadays.

On September 2, 1970, writing for the London *Observer* Service, Arnold Toynbee notes:

> Today, from all quarters of the globe, we are receiving well-authenticated reports of cold-blooded torture. . . . We realize now that Hitlerism was not just an isolated aberration. It was an ominous sign of the times. . . . We have learned how to fly and to split the atom, and how have we used these technological achievements? The answer is given by the names of five cities: Guernica, Coventry, Dresden, Hiroshima, Nagasaki. . . . Even more disquieting is the increasing brutality of domestic strife.

TORTURES, LIKE GAMES, ARE THE ART FORMS OF WORK IN ANY CULTURE

So-called violence in modern entertainment can be seen as "monster" or *merger of figure-ground*. When work is intensified and projected as a separate art form, it appears as "torture." Torture in the Western world is highly specialized, whereas in the Eastern world it is tribal and involving. That is, Chinese tortures are a mime of their work and society insofar as they are totally involving—slow, leisurely, carefully intervaled. North American Indian tortures, on the other hand, were mimes of their harsh hunting lives and were spectacular in their demands of endurance and dramatic courage, from "puberty rites" to braves "running the gauntlet." They took great pride in their power to endure torture and admired the bravery of those who underwent it. Indian scalping derived from bounties offered by the fur-trading monopolists. Initially, the scalps served to confirm the "body count" of free-enterprising *coureurs de bois* eliminated as threats to the market. Indians turned this into art form. What had been cash for the bounty hunter became ritual instead.

WORK AS TORTURE

Note the exact parallel with our own workaday pride in being able to "take it." There is a merger of *figure-ground* in our creation of a horrible environment of noise and smog by means of the work process itself. The work has become torture and merely existing in the environment has become work. Hence the seeming insensibility to tortures is made possible by an anesthesia borrowed from the work of the world. The more specialized and savage the forms of work, the more ruthless the torture. In this context the nineteenth century retrieved work as a sacrament (*laborare est orare*— working is praying) in the midst of the new industrial horror. In the twentieth century, we have recovered leisure as a by-product of the work process, and leisure has been degraded to idleness—the interval that torments, since most of it is enforced.

From Torture as Art to Art as Torture

We torment others by "hardware," using the old organization chart, and we participate in this torment through "software" by holding the new media mirror up to old Nature, as it were. This process transforms the torture of work into the refined torture of art—the primal curse laid on man: he will earn his bread by the sweat of his brow. Today the sweat is empathy, and the self-knowledge that is the most awful form of torment is awareness of one's own sordid motives manifested in their consequences.

ENVIRONMENT AS TORTURE

"Après moi le déluge"

Paralleling torture as art form is the twentieth-century use of the man-made environment as torture. Note that littering the streets since TV is an attempt to regard the man-made environment as Nature. The old Nature is now regarded as completely polluted art form. The bottles and papers are left like residuous leaves from a former Nature, whereas the rivers and streams are now being cleaned up or restored to the pristine condition of pre-Nature. We look forward to the time when we can drink river water, while we pile up streets with litter. *We are polluting Art as fast as we are tidying up Nature.*

Torture as Entertainment

In the nineteenth century a huge literature of torture appeared in the form of psychological casebooks and psychological histories—the world of the Marquis de Sade and Leopold von Sacher-Masoch. The outer goals of nineteenth-century industrial society created the inner trip of psychiatry as a new kind of purgation and a new specialism.

Today, science fiction uses science instead of society as *ground* (while business uses market as *ground*). It is somewhat like the paintings of di Chirico and Utrillo, who painted metropolitan areas minus people. Science fiction is much like the police state where the police act as *ground* in place of society. Hence the close resemblance of the two art forms of thriller fiction and science fiction. The hidden *ground* of the workaday world is absent from both. Note the relation of this to torture as *games people play.*

ENTERTAINMENT AS TORTURE: THE TOP TEN

Pollution of Services

Skyjacking as a war of airways is made possible by air waves. The EYE-oriented Westerner views aircraft as a means for rapid transport of "hardware." The EAR-oriented Easterner understands airliners as a still more powerful means of transporting viewers via media as "software." Piracy in the skies and activism in the streets are new forms of the guerrilla "war of the icons"; they are made possible by media resources far bigger than the events themselves. Without media coverage they would have no powers of action-at-a-distance.

The Custom Job Replaces Assembly Line

The mystery of retrieval of ancient forms amidst innovation has been universally manifested in the recovery of the Middle Ages in many of its forms by the young TV generation. More potent still, there is the drive back to the "cottage economy" under the impulse of computer technology.

FROM STEEL TANK TO THINK TANK

Creativity Specialists Soggy with Ideas

Shape without form, shade without colour,
Paralysed force, gesture without motion.
T. S. Eliot, "The Hollow Men"

As a descriptive term, "think tank" is extremely ambiguous, but also revealing. It conveys the suggestion of an oil tanker laden with energy resources. It strongly suggests a place for tank-farming ideas, *i.e.*, ideas with no roots or soil, like chemically force-fed tubers. It also conveys the image of a swimming pool peopled by intellectuals at play, where philosophers can be "kings for a day." The drab fact about "think tanks" is that they are contrived for the mass production and packaging of scenarios and programs for the harassed Establishment. These secluded hunters under "security" conditions show all the spontaneity and enterprise of a "trap shooter" knocking down "clay pigeons." They have reduced the old hunt of the operations research team to "managerial" proportions. The game is "in the bag" before the hunt begins. By contrast, Operations Research was born in the urgency of World War II conditions, when the *ground* rules were the dynamic hazards of war itself. Since results alone counted, it was found necessary to invite the nonexperts. Experts are not only poor at dialogue but are opposed to discoveries. Breakthroughs discredit experts who are necessarily custodians of the known. They who know also know "it can't be done; we've tried everything." Specialists treat the disease according to its name, rather than its nature.

The Real Game Is Outside

The fate of "military science" and "management science" and education alike, when their specialisms are pushed into top gear, is the emergence of encyclopedic awareness. It is as unexpected a change as the flip back to private tutorial and dialogue that accompanies the computerizing of the curriculum credit modules. Having weighted them evenly for speedy bureaucratic handling, it is found that courses can only be interrelated by private personal discourse. The older lecture procedures are useless with the new modules. In the same way, the distinction between a modern general and a "think-tank" generalist has disappeared. The military executive may now be recalled from the "field" for dunking in a "think tank" in order to acquaint himself with the total field of human awareness. The military *field* has become a tiny "plot" far removed from the wider world of operations. This plot is no longer "where it's at." It's no longer training for "war on the playing fields of Eton," but in the electromagnetic field of communication.

7

GNP

Communication is power.
>Senator J. W. Fullbright

He made the news.
>Folk saying

GNP no longer indicates the full scope of economic activities in an information age, just as "war" no longer defines the areas of military effects or the real range of military activities. You can no longer "nip in" and "nip out" again. Quite apart from deliberate raids and espionage, there are the hidden environmental effects of the visible impacts. For example, one of the effects of war today is the institution of news coverage and distribution on a scale even greater than the war itself. Today, we must include in war coverage the TV audience as direct participants in military actions. The TV audience is naturally far greater than the number of military personnel involved on both sides. It is therefore not surprising that the young have decided to become actors in the political scene of our time, since they are already combatants in the military, both at home and abroad. Like the economists who can no longer draw a line between services and disservices in the GNP, the young can find nowhere to draw a line between war and industry, or education and politics.

THE BIG BUSINESS OF AMERICAN MILITARISM:

Who Profits? Who Pays? Who Commands? Who Dies?

In an article under this heading (*Look*, August 12, 1969), Eric Sevareid quoted Senator J. William Fullbright as saying, "A nation's budget . . . tells what a society cares about and what it does not care about."

D. S. Greenberg reports in *Science* (November 28, 1969) on the "New SIPRI Yearbook of Armaments, Disarmament Documents, the Direction, Pace of the Arms Race":

>Worldwide military expenditures rose nearly 30 per cent between 1965 and 1968, with the result that they today exceed spending on education by more than 40 per cent, and are more than three times worldwide expenditures for health purposes. . . . Military research and

killing powers far outstrip the growth of expenditures. . . . Each
new weapon spurs the development of counterweapons.

The *Yearbook* further observes that "since 1960, the emphasis of U.S. military assistance policy has shifted from the defence of states from possible
external attack, to the defence of governments from possible internal insur-
rection." What the *Yearbook* does *not* say is that the emphasis of the
Pentagon's defense of the United States itself is now also shifting from the
"external" to the "internal" enemy.

Budgets in Hiding

In this context, Sevareid remarks:

> This nation has spent around a thousand billion dollars on arms and
> men-in-arms since the end of World War II. . . . No conspiratorial
> cabal planned it this way. There is no monolithic "power elite" in this
> country. . . .
>   There are two major reasons for the suffocating growth of the
> military-industrial-academic-labor union-congressional complex. One is
> that world realities have changed faster than our perception of the
> change and much faster than our institutions and practical processes
> could change. The other is that bureaucracy inevitably takes on a life
> of its own. . . . Government is becoming ungovernable . . . we are
> closer to becoming a "bureaucracy state" than anything else. . . . No
> one in Washington even *knows* how many Federal programs involving
> aid to states and cities now exist.

"Management by objectives" is no longer relevant for enterprises of such
scale and scope in the age of speed-up. For the objectives themselves
change faster than any traditional management can.

THE WARFARE-WELFARE STATE

From Market Wars to War Markets

The sheer scope and scale of modern warfare blanketed the traditional
economy as effectively as the technological service environments have
blanketed Nature. This, in turn, created the illusion in many quarters that
the warfare and the welfare state were complementary or correlative. The
state could do anything. Without attempting any definition of "government," without probing into its character, and without questioning its new
modes of existence, Peter Drucker comments:

> In the seventy years or so from the 1890's to the 1960's, mankind,
> especially in the developed countries, was hypnotized by government.
> We were in love with it and saw no limits to its abilities, or its good
> intentions. Rarely has there been a more torrid political love affair
> than that between government and the generations that reached man-

hood between 1918 and 1960. Anything anyone felt needed doing
during this period was to be turned over to government—and this,
everyone seemed to believe, made sure that the job was already done.

The Age of Discontinuity

In wartime the civil procedures are in abeyance. Any kind of restriction
on social and economic life can be imposed at any time. The entire social
"machine" goes into top gear. War as such is speed-up or "inflation." The
"depression" that is the backlash of this inflation is the casualty list and the
destruction of amenities—physical, psychic, and social. In the warfare state
built and experienced during the first part of the twentieth century, the ebb
and flow of depression and inflation have become a way of life.

The main advantage of studying the processes of a war economy is that
all the peacetime features stand out starkly, as strongly marked *figure*
against the new *ground* of war. Features that in peacetime are obscure become major processes involving far larger energies and personnel. In short,
mere exaggerations of the war economy reveal the structure of the peacetime economy. In peacetime one can also study features of the war economy that during actual warfare are little noticed. The heat of battle is a
notorious anesthetic.

Markets Black and White: Cheek by Jowl

American armies in Vietnam encounter untapped markets for army supplies, much as Caesar did in Gaul. This inspires Mephistophelean entrepreneurs to provide consumer services for those about to die. In peacetime
black markets are minimal, whereas in war they become much enlarged.
You cannot have a written tradition of *white markets* (fixed prices) without an oral tradition of *black markets* (haggle).

Joseph Heller's *Catch-22*, both the novel and the film, presents an extended study of World War II flight missions as part of an elaborate
"black market" presided over by a "syndicate" and oriented toward postwar
"welfare" for the servicemen. The "entrepreneur" behind the syndicate is
the blond WASP-type, cheerful, ebullient, and irresistible charmer—a man
for all seasons. This operation is a parody of a peacetime market overlaid on
a wartime technology. Those involved in the war seem as mad in their goals
as those engaged in the syndicate. War and peace appear as complementary
forms of the same cultural performance.

The reflected light thrown by this syndicate operation aimed at private
welfare matches the light thrown by our peacetime economy on the war
operation. When pushed into top gear, each of these enterprises nullifies
the other. Incidental to these complementary "hardware" processes are the
hideous psychic and physical torment of the entire personnel.

There is a natural complementarity between the enemy outside and the
enemy within the economy. A war effort directed toward the "containment
of Communism" reminds us of the "stress theory" of Hans Selye, which

says that irritation and inflammation and disease are in fact efforts at containing a malignant thing that threatens to spread. The "enemy" in modern warfare is necessarily part of a single body politic, namely, the global community. War against any part of that community inevitably reverberates with inner and outer assonance.

The Enemy Is in the Eye of the Beholder

In a word, the outer enemy reflects a fear that in fact originates at home. In seeking to stabilize the existing setup by an external war, there is the recognition of the danger of a social breakthrough at home. *Every move taken to stabilize the existing situation has in fact the opposite effect.* We become what we fight in the very act of fighting. There is a kind of perverse mimesis, which causes the thing we fear to come upon us.

8

SVC

In the warfare-welfare view of the state, warfare is simply the disservice side of welfare service environment. The hidden assumption in this paradox is that innovation of any kind causes intolerable imbalance among the components of the system. Of course, this assumes that the system is self-contained. In fact, the *interfaces* among the components of any system perpetually create new and unexpected forms that do not match any existing system whatever. It is only for the harassed and hurried journalist that the fixed categories of capitalism, Communism, barbarism, and civilization are the convenient means of throwing together his daily "copy." The mere demands of speed and repetition require that every writer have a handy supply of familiar labels. Perception of what is actually going on would eliminate such writers from "professional" journalism altogether. The artist, or the man of perception, is inevitably the enemy of the conventionally wise.

The Warfare of the Assimilator Is in Low Key

The tremendous impact of war and innovation in a centralized industrial society may be contrasted with relatively small changes that occur in a decentralized society such as Vietnam, where two decades of warfare have scarcely rippled the surface of the lives of its people. Any form of continued and accelerated innovation is, in effect, a declaration of war on one's own civilian population. War is any process of innovation or change at high speed. An act of war directed against another civilian population involves that population in revolutionary adjustments, such as we now take for granted on the home front in an age of rapid scientific advance. For example, the cities of North America have been devastated, not by bombing, but by renewal, in the past decade. The citizens have undergone as much barrage and displacement as any population in a state of siege by a visible enemy. The enemy within is far harder to oppose than the old-fashioned variety. One can no longer discern one's friends. The arms race at home is at least as destructive of social peace as the exploding of its product in "enemy" territory. In the Global Theater of the Absurd we can no longer identify our enemies either.

OLD "GROUND" FOR ECONOMISTS

Market Place Usurps Place of Nation

Both Drucker and Galbraith yield to the plausible pressure that leads to identifying the processes of war and the total economy. They do this without considering that the major aspect of war in the age of information is espionage. These economists are still centered in their thoughts and observations on the processes of nineteenth-century industrial "hardware" and the related markets. In fact, the main action and aggression and innovation have long since shifted to the areas of information hunting and image making. Writing from New York in Toronto's *Globe and Mail*, August 8, 1970, Barry Lando notes one aspect of defense secrecy:

CASE OF THE SECRETS THAT ARE NO SECRET

A Pentagon bid to keep a secret label on information in a Congressional report seemed like a spy's delight. Now there are requests for the document from all over.

The weapon of secrecy is not what it used to be.

9

MAD

MEGA-DEATHS BY MICRO-MEANS

The Pentagon is fond of acrid acronyms such as its strategy of "Mutual Assured Destruction" (MAD). One means of implementing this strategy is referred to as "Chemical Bacteriological Warfare" (CBW). These are closely related to the management technique of "cost effectiveness," which in Pentagon context demands more bangs for the buck. The result of applying cost-effectiveness thinking to this or any other social situation leads to something that has been called "value engineering." Stripped to the buck, the human psyche desperately embraces the value engineer.

A recent instance of specialist blindness to the effects of military innovation was the episode of the unwanted nerve gas. This new chemistry of mega-deaths by micro-means parallels many other features of the wedding of industrialism and military technology. The hydrogen bomb itself, a "miniaturization" of the uranium bomb, carries many of the consequences of miniaturization as such. It offers the immediate threat of concealed portability. The popular image of this is the concealed bomb on passenger vehicles.

THE RETURN OF THE ALCHEMIST

From Finger in the Dike to Pill in the Pond

When the little waif with a capsule can end the world, the atom bomb is a military dropout.

> This is the way the world ends
> This is the way the world ends
> Not with a bang but a whimper.
> T. S. Eliot, "The Hollow Men"

"The Hollow Men" and *The Waste Land* by T. S. Eliot manifest inclusive consciousness, anthropological and archaeological, of the human condition, *i.e.*, how inflation of human knowledge can breed deflation of human values.

The compression of extreme power in minute form, which also characterizes the new means of chemical and bacteriological warfare, would enable a juvenile activist to pop a pellet into the metropolitan water supply and end a city as readily as could an atom bomb.

10

c‑⁂‑ɔ

DRE

At electric speeds every type of human enterprise is pushed to its limits. At this point the return becomes a transformation or metamorphosis.* We have already seen how war becomes education. No matter whether it be exposure of "backward" people to advanced weaponry and organization or whether it be the competitive endeavors of "advanced" peoples to over-reach one another in weaponry, war in both instances hastens the spread of knowledge.

In the world of advertising, the sales campaigns of large general staffs, backed by the resources of the entire entertainment and information indus-tries, swiftly developed forms of advertising that initiated new features in the communication arts. The "cost-benefit" demand for measuring results insured the use of top talents and top energies drawn from every field of the cultures of the world. The target of the advertisers had somewhat the same effect as the military targets of CBW. The operation was hidden as much as possible, but the agents engaged in this "Operation Frogman" had no wish to be branded as the purveyors of a rich new culture. Big business is as horrified by being enmeshed in the toils of "culture" as the military fear the civilian backlash from their specialist aim at the enemy "outside." Both the military and the admen have become "double re-agents" in activating proc-esses antipodal to the ones they envisaged.

The admen (backed by logistics and psychologists) sought to approach the lowest levels of motives and intelligence in the public at large; they hit upon the primal sources of primitive magic and myth. Advertising has had to accept the accolades of "culture vultures" as a fringe benefit of its utterly degraded motives and ambitions.

Double Re-entry

The intended disservices flipped into the public service division with "Sesame Street." This heavily subsidized educational experiment for pre-kindergarteners drew on the talents of Madison Avenue and garnered aca-demic and educator acclaim. This, of course, was the mere tip of the ice-berg. The budget for advertising greatly exceeds, item for item and minute

---

* *Culture Is Our Business* by Marshall McLuhan is devoted to illustrating and explain-ing this transforming process as it embarrassed the world of advertising.

to minute, the budget for feature entertainment. The discovery of the most primitive and iconic symbolism as a basis for ad effectiveness relates ads to the major art movements of our century. The difference is that the advertisers have vast budgets, and the artists have none. There is a correspondence in this relation to that of the R and D establishment and the mere private inventor. Another relevant difference is that the artist seeks an audience for his work with the intent of *awakening* perception and sustaining and nourishing vital impulse. The advertiser, on the contrary, seeks to submerge perception and motive in a collective sound-light show of turbulent sensation. It is merely his avid pursuit of the most effective means of moving people that has turned him also into a "double re-agent" of culture and education. As information levels rise, the noble and ignoble become simultaneous. You don't choose your friends in a rat race or at a fair!

The same double re-agent status that befalls all highly developed activities in our time is as manifest in the art of what was formerly called "propaganda." In Rome the College of Propaganda is the department devoted to Christian missionary activity. In the sense of "teaching," the term has significantly attached itself to many of the activities of our time. Many people have joined the enterprise of spreading the word that "they have the answers." All they ask is: "What are the questions?"

WAR OF THE ICONS

Grinding the Looking Glasses

In *Propaganda: The Foundation of Men's Attitudes,* Jacques Ellul flips the usual approach by stressing propaganda as the total *ground* of any culture as it confronts any individual *figure.* The interface between these, between, say, the French language and the child's acquiring his perceptual and affective life with the aid of French, is the relationship of propaganda to teaching. In its popular sense as a degrading relationship, propaganda would seem to date from the full impact of the mass media (mass media being necessarily electric or all-at-once). It cannot be stressed too often that a book, no matter how popular, is not a mass medium, since it never finds all its public simultaneously.

Jacques Ellul's inclusive approach to propaganda is taken for granted in cultural anthropology. The name of Benjamin Lee Whorf is associated with this approach in linguistics. Instead of approaching language as a vehicle for transporting data, he regards each language as a unique and infinitely complex mode of encoding or apprehending the world. Language becomes a total encounter with being. To push this approach into the world of nonverbal media enables us to see propaganda, not so much as a message, but as an environment or a total way of life.

This is how, for example, we Westerners appear as propagandists to the Chinese. To them we seem to be trying to foist off a ridiculous and irrational style of existence on our betters—the Chinese. Dennis Bloodworth explains this in *Chinese Looking Glass:*

> The [Western] barbarian then appears, on the whole, as a lamentable creature. Seemingly devoid of any philosophy that might enable him to live in harmony with the world as it is, he is at best a clever monkey, burning himself out in a feverish struggle to change everything all the time. The culture of the men who laughed at the bound "lily feet" of the ladies of Imperial China has produced a series of ludicrously unnatural and unhealthy distortions of the human frame and its packaging, from the Victorian wasp waist to the stiletto heel. And many of their habits hardly bear mentioning in mixed company. They kiss in public, pass you things *with one hand only* (extremely impolite among Chinese, who always use two), open presents you give them *in front of you*, and rudely say "thank you" all the time in order—quite obviously—to shrug off their obligations. They eat, as a Viceroy of Canton remarked more than one hundred years ago, with kitchen implements.

When a Westerner looks at China, he is likely to discover, with Bloodworth, that the conflicting varieties of social experience that we now find so confusing have long been the staple in the fabric of Chinese culture.

While the world has tended to think that the critical struggle of our time is between the superpowers, well supplied with old "hardware" and "software," it may finally prove that an even more crucial struggle has been going on within the superpowers themselves.

11

EAR

The Great Divorce of Thought and Feeling

As electric technology drives the West inward and Eastward from eye to ear dominance, young Westerners acquire a passion for the Taoist anarchy that has torn China for 2,500 years. The "square world" of Confucius, characterized by the strong bias or preference for visual order and repetition, has been given institutional opposition by Taoism, the anarchic world of discontinuity, and the resonant interval.

The ideologies of the visual man locate the enemy *outside* his boundaries. The Chinese have long known the enemies were *inside*. That is why the Chinese are prepared to wait for the outside enemy to destroy himself by his own inner conflicts. The Chinese have learned how to live with the complementarity of EYE and EAR, of "square" and "beatnik." We prefer to denounce them or to "put a tail on them"—in Darwinian style. Both Russia and America in the pursuit of industrial efficiency have achieved unintended "hippie" bliss.

Of course, the attendant loss of identity in America is complemented by the quest for private identity in Russia. The "self-expression" with which the Westerners are satiated is a passionate hunger of the Russian. In China "face" is still the accepted collateral. Will the Chinese ever go all the way to EAR or EYE?

The Inscrutable West—a Basket Case?

What had been the inscrutable East of the nineteenth century is now an open book whose language has been translated into the West by the latest computer technology. The Eastern *ground*, transferred to the Western scene, has made the West even more inscrutable than the East. We have lost the war in the East by crude application of nineteenth-century centralist assumptions to a decentralized oral culture.

While fighting the visible war abroad, we have lost the much larger struggle with invisible bureaucracies on the domestic front. Our management strategy is now as irrelevant at home as it still is in the East. In this process we have totally enveloped our own territories with electric technologies destructive of our traditional mechanical "hardware."

The ancient Roman, having divided Gaul into three parts, was occupied in turn by Alaric and his Huns. We, having conquered the East in the same way, find ourselves on the home front totally preoccupied with Orientalism, quietism, and inner trips. We have become the thing we fought. We now live in occupied territory, not knowing who to fight or where to resist. The West is unable to perceive the lineaments of the disaster it has etched upon itself. The occupation of Paris by the Germans was nothing compared with the occupation of our territory by our all-transforming "software" weaponry. The enemy is not merely inside our territory but inside ourselves.

INSIDE LEVIATHAN

Occupation as Environment

In *And There Was Light,* Jacques Lusseyran recounts the organization of the Resistance paper *Défense de la France* during the German Occupation: "Ours was not a political paper. Not one of us at the *Défense de la France* had any commitment to a doctrine. . . . We had no partisan cause, no material interest to defend." Lusseyran also observes that the focal images for the organization of their energy were variously De Gaulle, Churchill, and Roosevelt. These men, in that radio era, were tribal chieftains. Each, in his own way, embodied a unique combination of qualities needed for survival of a system of values. In the TV age this quest for leader images as "unwobbling pivots" that would permit the survival of complex value systems took on an even more obsessive character.

Under the German Occupation, which created a totally new environment, all the old goals disappeared. The Occupation became the preoccupation of a unified resistance.

12

EYE

CLASS WAR AS RIGIDITY OF POSTURES

Class war originates when the market usurps the social *ground* by extension of its specialist functions to organize and homogenize all social forms. The *figures* of worker and owner alike are frozen into immobile stances. By 1865, this development was sufficiently startling to inspire Dickens's *Hard Times*, on the one hand, and *Our Mutual Friend*, on the other. In *Hard Times*, the miseries of the new factory workers and miners leading a subhuman existence were described. In *Our Mutual Friend*, Dickens created the "Veneerings" and the "Podsnaps" as expressions of "conspicuous consumption" and "confidence gamesters." In the words of Professor Hillis Miller, "*Our Mutual Friend* is about money, money, money, and what money can make of life."

Karl Marx had derived his "revolutionary" categories of "class struggle" from his study of nineteenth-century industry. He had himself come out of a world structure of preindustrial skills and castes. This traditional *ground* of his experience gave great salience in his mind to the new *figures* and forms of mechanization of emergent industrial man. Later, Thorstein Veblen, with a similar European background, found it easy to ridicule the *parvenu* postures of the American consumer-producer world. Having established his categories in the current new developments of industrial England, Marx proceeded to validate and project them by free use of past and present history. Following the nineteenth-century obsession with the new "hardware" service environment of road and rail, he saw the entire historical process as a struggle between the "productive forces" of "hardware" technology and the "production relations" or social hierarchy created through the ownership of that "hardware"—the song of the "steal" men. His proposal to resolve this conflict was for the production workers to take over the production "hardware," instead of exploiting the new "software" environment and the new knowledge industries created by the mobility of the nineteenth-century "hardware." The "Rose of Castile" (the Joycean pun in *Ulysses*) interrelated the worlds of art and industry and the world of the press and the book to the world of the railway. Joyce asked: "My producers, are they not my consumers?" IN THE ELECTRIC-INFORMATION AGE, EMPLOYER AND EMPLOYEE MERGE AS AUDIENCE.

Trade Unions as Apostles of Moreness

The eleventh edition of the *Encyclopaedia Britannica* (1910–11) begins its section on trade unions with these words:

> They were considered to be contrary to public policy and were treated as conspiracies in restraint of trade. Those who were concerned in them were liable to be criminally prosecuted . . . and to be punished on conviction by fine and imprisonment.

In contrast, the 1947 version opens:

> Efforts have been made to trace the lineal descent of the trade union movement of the 19th and 20th centuries from the guilds of the middle ages. But trade unionism as we know it was the creation of modern industrial conditions.

What had begun as a criminal activity became a social ideal, a typical example of reversal by stress. During the battle for social mobility via the labor market, the workmen became what they fought. Trade unions became large centralized bureaucracies, eager to impose their homogeneous forms on all sectors of society. They shared the idea of "moreness" with their masters: Oliver TWIST, a typical "Black Hand" against the "Hidden Hand." Like the secret societies of masters and workers, criminality and the Mafia are attempts at liberation from market rigidities. George Bernard Shaw declared that "every profession is a conspiracy against the laity."

Pushed to extreme, class conflict resumes tribal warfare. Another reversal effect of trade-union growth was a return to conditions of tribal rivalry (jurisdictional disputes) and warfare, with a simultaneous revival of universal family structures in the "magnetic city."

CASTE, CLASS, AND RACE

One gets a new perspective on Western development of "class" structures from the experience of India. What we now refer to as their "caste system" began as a guild structure of crafts and skills, with doors open for change and mobility. With successive Moslem invasions, the guilds froze into the present rigid caste form. G. B. Shaw's celebrated *Pygmalion* is a classic of new integration and liberation achieved with the British class system by speech transformation. The British public schools, in effect, created a new "upper-class" system by homogenizing the "lower-class" diversity of speech patterns. This power of class formation and liberation by auditory intonation draws attention to the basic *ground* of all tribal societies as auditory and acoustic. "Race," on the other hand, is a visual *figure* or pigment against this tribal and resonant *ground*.

The Chthonic Boom Is the Sound of Rock

The age that has stripped itself of all community by the pursuit of private goals finds itself back on the *ground*. The TV generation happily concurs with the outlook of our aboriginals. We have not seen the last of the Mohicans when the Mohawks dominate the high steel of Manhattan.

Back to the Indians

One can get a sense of bearings in this kind of buzzing hubbub by looking at a totally removed cultural eventuation. Tribal societies, when threatened by invasion or envelopment by enemies, resort to organization patterns quite the reverse of their habitual ones. Just as Lusseyran describes a reversal of customary pattern of interests and energy direction in the French Resistance, Wilfred Pelletier, an Odawa Indian of Canada, tells of "childhood in an Indian village" (*This Magazine Is About Schools*, Toronto, Spring, 1969): "We didn't separate our learning from our way of life; we didn't separate our work from it either." Change came "only in times of war and disaster." At such times the habitual, easygoing structure of a completely decentralized society suddenly shifted to a vertical structure: "The war chief would designate various jobs to various people and use that vertical structure." The ordinary leadership of this Indian society did not consist of "leaders" and "work," as we look at them today:

> It was a different kind of leadership in that the person who was leader had special abilities, say, in fishing or hunting. He took the leadership that day, and then discarded the leadership when he was finished with the job. He had power only for the time he wanted to do something. That power came in all forms of all the things he did in the community, so that he used power only for the things he wanted to do, and then he immediately shed it so that someone else could pick it up and it could change hands several times in the community in a day or a week or whatever.

Just as resistance during the Occupation destroyed all the peacetime patterns and goals, so, under intense stress, the patterns of the most archaic preliterate tribal societies could briefly take on the character of our industrial specialism and delegation of jobs. This is to say, we have, by intense use of new specialist technologies like writing and printing, instituted a perpetual state of wartime energy organization.

OVERKILL HAS LOST FACE

From Territorial Boundaries to Cultural Interfaces

I've never seen an Asian nation so preoccupied with saving face as the
United States.

                    Senator Frank Church, quoted in Toronto *Globe and Mail*,
                                                        February 24, 1971

In warfare, as in all other phases of our time, there are areas that illustrate the recovering or resuming by a kind of *replay* some of the most private modes of military contest. Among the most deadly of these ancient
types of contest were the "slanging matches" or *flytings* (as our Anglo-
Saxon ancestors called them). To people who regarded words as possessing
magical powers of efficacy, there was nothing funny about those contests.
The equivalent in our time would be in the "loss of face" of some massive
prestigious corporation. In our age of information and "software," the most
deadly weapons are images used to deface images. Corporate images, built
up by the putting on and wearing of vast media audiences as mask and
costume (as in the once-famous "Bell Telephone Hour" of radio decades),
enable a new type of "corporate force" or image to emerge. Huge corporate
or collective images made up of whole markets, publics, and nations can be
slammed at one another or bashed together in a single headline. It is warfare elevated to the level of the ethereal encounter of angelic substances.
What we have called "ideological warfare" in this century has much of the
character of primitive name-calling or *flyting*. Scholars will one day make
inventories of such political slang as "beefsteak Nazi," a Berlin epithet of
the 1930's for a fake Nazi (*brown* outside, *red* inside). *The new "fronts"
are not "hardware" boundaries but "software" interfaces of total cultures in
action:* THE DING-DONG OF PING-PONG POLITICS.

LEADERS BY EAR AND EYE

As explained in *War and Peace in the Global Village*, both Alexander of
Macedon and Napoleon of Corsica had the advantage of coming from
tribal and relatively backward territories. This enabled them to by-pass the
military establishment of their day. In the same way, a backward country
today can start with the latest rather than with nineteenth-century technology. (The United States started with Gutenberg and by-passed the guilds.)
Alexander and Napoleon both took advantage of the new technologies of
their times. Napoleon is more familiar because nearer in time. His secret
was speed-up of both transport and communication, "hardware" and "software." Witness his right rule for road traffic and his optical telegraph from
Rome to Paris. Alexander and Napoleon had no obligation to *match* the
errors of their predecessors. They *made* the histories of their times.

END OF MILITARY MANAGEMENT

On July 28, 1970, the Associated Press reported from San Clemente, California: "Vietnam cost cut in half, Laird says . . . from $29 billion to $12.5 billion a year." The strategy of using old military "hardware" and assembly-line thinking in "backward" territories goes bankrupt. It has become "management by objectives in reverse," as the mission goes backward. The conventional response is merely for *more efficiency*—a bigger dose of specialist medicine as a cure for the disease of specialism. Instead of seeking solutions *inside* the process patterns of the problems themselves, conventional management persists in looking outside for answers.

PENTAGON PURGATION

The Associated Press reported from Washington, D.C., on July 29, 1970:

> A presidential commission recommended yesterday a radical reorganization of the Defense Department—including the removal of the Joint Chiefs of Staff from involvement in military operation—and a number of other steps designed to achieve more efficiency and save money in weapons procurement.

Such leaders, whether military or civilian, are merely *matching* the errors of the past rather than *making* the history of the present. Consultants and executives alike are made into nineteenth-century men by their nineteenth-century production-line thinking. *By trying to control the twentieth century with such means, they are elaborately qualified to make use of the nearest egress.*

MILITARY LEADERSHIP TODAY IS
SITTING IN THE EJECTION SEAT

Chapter 7

Tribal Chiefs and Conglomerate

Emperors

From Whiplash to Profit Lash: Purebreds Sink
as Mongrels Rise

One of the nicest things about being big is the luxury of thinking little.   Marshall McLuhan, *Culture Is Our Business*

cancellation of a world

"Wafted by a whiff of grapeshot," *l'ancien régime* merged dramatically with Napoleon's line and staff: "*Carrières ouvertes aux talents.*" The *ancien régime* collapsed as *figure* when its centralized agrarian *ground* yielded to industrial "hardware" as the new *ground*. In the whole story of "hardware bureaucracy" from Napoleon onward, the *figure* merges with his GOAL. Napoleon's continental system anticipated the *ground* of the European Common Market idea, just as his *figure* anticipated the industrial tycoon.

While Napoleon concentrated on centralizing power through his land armies, the British were engaged in decentralizing power through their navy and overseas empire. Naval power gave their nascent "hardware" industries access to materials and resources everywhere. Britain became the "workshop of the world." The accelerated manipulation of the misunderstood leads to a familiar situation in the present.

SPYING ON EACH OTHER KEEPS U.S. INTELLIGENCE AGENTS BUSY
WASHINGTON (AP)—Congress was told yesterday that the military's domestic surveillance often is a case of spy vs. spy, like the time 53 agents watched one another among 66 civilian demonstrators.
Toronto *Globe and Mail*, February 26, 1971

We live in a world where data processing (mostly hidden) has become the major occupation; it has ended the distinction between "blue"- and "white"-collar workers. The rise of data processing to supremacy has also ended the distinction between work and entertainment. Our work force has become a show-business cast of role players. Jobs are disappearing, along with human identity. Unemployment becomes a curve on a chart like the DJ index. Naturally, at this extreme there occurs a violent flip. Just as jobs become irrelevant, job hunting becomes an obsession. An extreme example of jobless role playing "show-biz" style is the complementarity of the FBI and the Mafiosa. During the radio age of jazz and booze, the first wave of hijackers arrived. The fast-driving, all-American bank robbers—John Dillinger, "Pretty Boy" Floyd, "Machine Gun" Kelly, "Baby Face" Nelson—provided J. Edgar Hoover with the headlines needed to obtain government support for his G-men.

1

Tribal Chiefs on Changing Premises

In *Ramparts* (August, 1970), Andy Tuskier comments on William Turner's *J. Edgar Hoover and the FBI: The Man and the Myth:*

> The FBI MYTH, as Turner's book makes clear, was not an accidental creation. . . . Hoover realized the political power that could accrue from building an independent base of popular support. During the 30's, Hoover immortalized his "G-men" by writing stories for the conservative *American* magazine . . .
>
> One can imagine J. Edgar Hoover reasoning that the fight against crime and communism depends first and foremost on the prominence of the FBI and on his hold over it, and that consequently whatever is necessary to his power is justified.

What Tuskier ignores is that "G-men" and "James Bond" and "The Man from U.N.C.L.E.," like the "cowboys and Indians" before them, are "past times as pastimes." As such, they proclaim that the "action" has now moved elsewhere to the T-men, the tax men who catch the big game. To be a "leader" today, when change itself has become environmental, requires perception and mastery of new rules for high-speed navigation. It is a replay in new context of the old Newfoundland skipper's awareness. When asked if he knew where *all* the rocks were, he replied: "I don't rightly know where they all is, but I knows where they ain't."

The phantom of the new *Operation Information* is the service environment itself. That means there can be no more stars like those in the Hollywood Looking-Glass World. Today, both the *figures* of the new knowledge industries and the *ground* of the new information environment are "software" that merge and destroy old boundaries. Tammany becomes a legal Mafia. The new *figures* are swamped.

WHY IS A KINGDOM NOT A BUSINESS?

Because it's a service. In business, money is the measure. In kingdoms, man is the measure. Every *service* is paid for by huge *disservices* to the community. Count your blessings, but don't try to evaluate them!

Do-gooders in Spite of Themselves

The old vertical organization put up its dukes and came out fighting. The new horizontal organization spreads around the earth and becomes emperor of ether with neither private nor corporate identity. The old visually oriented *figures* are submerged in the new acoustic *ground*. They are replaying an ancient drama in reverse.

The Unceasing Conflict of Oral and Written Traditions

In the fifth century B.C., the Roman dictator Cincinnatus was alienated from the politics of his time by the threat of a written code of laws whereby all men would be equal. This drove him back to the plough. The innovation of a written legal code threatened the whole oral tradition of his culture. His disillusionment is overmatched today by the universal alienation of management from a written code that has sustained the Establishment for centuries.

HUNG UP BY THE TANGIBLE INTANGIBLES

Gerald T. Dunne, writing in *Harvard Business Review* (May–June, 1970), asks:

CAN THE FINANCIAL COMMUNITY BRING ITS ARTIFACTS INTO THE ELECTRONIC AGE BEFORE THE PAPER BLIZZARD BURIES US ALL?

The author of this article maintains stock certificates and checks have taken on qualities apart from their meaning as symbols of corporate ownership or monetary value. These cultural trappings are inhibiting the advent of electronic methods of securities and fund transfers.

The computer retrieves the compiler. The computer with its high-speed operation has, in effect, resurrected the resonant patterns of oral culture in management as in popular forms of music and entertainment. But all the manager can *see* is:

> Paper, paper, everywhere
> Nor any scrap of sense

This is not an information explosion but a failure to understand the effects of speed-up. Buried under the superfluity of expendable paper, the managerial elite, whether civil or military, can find little time for attending to events and environments created by the speed of computer technology. The need is no longer for *Management by Exception,* but, rather, for *Bureaucracy by Exception.*

Today, the markets of our electric world are returning to preindustrial haggling, horse trading, and wheeling-and-dealing. The "big deal" ends as the environment itself becomes the biggest staple. It can be neither bought, sold, nor stolen. Only the "scraps" remain to do business with.

Going West as Coming East

In the new computer age the young have responded by the revolt against intense specialism in all its forms, pulling down the house-that-"Jack"-built, with its minutely fragmented bits of alphabet and movable types. In the electric age it might easily occur that populations of the West would shun the acquisition of the most basic skills of civilized technological continuity. The "West" may soon have to import people from the "East," who have discovered the necessary motives for acquiring Western modes of specialist behavior. For the Oriental, the older Western ways have all the appeal and excitement of a new game.

O Brave New World That Hath Such Technics in It!

In the electric world we have discovered that all along we have paid for specialism by a loss of manhood. Man became "thing." The ancient Roman was proud to be regarded as a "brick" in the impregnable wall of civilization. The British public schools aimed at the same classic uniformity of product and polish for their elite as the ancient Roman brick factory for its imperial administrators.

More than the British, the Romans were committed to a centralized, hierarchical kind of land empire. Their military bureaucracy left open careers for competitive talents. Military bureaucracies never undervalue "hardware" assets. The period during which Cicero and his contemporaries turned to the cultivation of books and eloquence as power and control was considered decadent. It was in the later Roman empire that the book and the library supported the battlefield. The turning of Rome toward paper "software" was the period when its "knowledge industries" achieved peak performance. The growing dependence upon papyrus as a basis for power proved a great weakness when the Egyptian supplies of papyrus failed through blight and river pollution. By whatever stages or crises, papyrus faded from the Roman imperial scene in the early Middle Ages and was replaced by parchment. The small supplies of parchment sufficed for the monopolies of knowledge of the age. It was with the coming of paper once more, from the Chinese world in the eleventh century, that life began to flow again through the old Roman system of roads and commerce and education. The twelfth-century Renaissance saw a new flowering of Roman culture in the West.

PAPER BRIDE AND PAPAL FUN

Whereas the Roman imperial structure was a communication system of roads, couriers, and papyrus, modern chemistry and engineering can now span chasms with bridges made of skin-stressed paper. Rome spanned nations, tribes, and centuries with the written word of command and the accumulated wisdom of generations all committed to paper. Between the couriers and the library, Rome created connections that endured for ages.

Related almost by contradiction and opposition has been the contemporary and co-terminus structure of the Roman Church. The centralist

Roman "hardware" structure of connected bureaucratic communication collapsed, only to be revived by the decentralist "software" of monasticism. The "guerrilla" task forces of monastic labor and learning sustained and restored Roman literacy and bureaucracy during the Roman decline. With Gutenberg and the full recovery of pagan knowledge and political organization, there is a startling parallel with the effects of electric technology on the even larger political structures of the Oriental past.

The Roman pontiff is, in an organizational sense, the greatest tribal chieftain in the world. He is the earthly head of a single family. Tribal structures are necessarily family-oriented. The authority of Peter (Greek *petros*, rock) and his successors is necessarily oral and decentralist at the same time. This paradox is contained in the pun on which the church was founded: "You are Peter, and upon this rock I will found my church."

The boundless resonant space of the oral church has always been at odds with the visual and bureaucratic spaces, beginning with the written word itself: "It is written, but I say unto thee." The character of the papacy has been buffeted not only by the written-oral clash but by the endless changes of bureaucratic structure within the many parts of the church. These changes have been prompted by everything from the disappearance of papyrus to Gutenberg in the Renaissance.

Shifting "Grounds" Transform "Figures"

The complicated question of whether *authority* rested in the pope or in the laity or in the church in plenary council fluctuated wildly with the conditions of travel and information movement from the beginnings of the church to the present. This fact becomes apparent today when there is no more geography in the world as far as verbal intercommunication is concerned. The telegraph, telephone, radio, and teletype have caused the disappearance of physical space and national and cultural boundaries, and have restored the most primal conditions of primitive Christianity. At the same time, this instantaneous character brings down an avalanche of historical, bureaucratic confusion upon the new oral church. The electric technology that abolishes central bureaucracy and organization also retrieves the entire past of the church—oral, written, bureaucratic, and historical. We begin to live a kind of Dantesque vision that merges all pasts and presents.

Today there is much talk about the "de-Romanization of the Catholic Church." To some people this might sound like detribalization. In fact, it is the exact opposite. The Roman organizational structure in the time of the Caesars had departed as far as was then technologically possible from tribal patterns. The Roman Church, as opposed to the Greek Church, continued this civilized hierarchical form of management. It is necessary to use the word "civilization" in a technical sense today, when electric speeds have gone far to retribalize the whole of mankind. As the human race becomes conscious of a unified family interrelationship via electric speeds, all older forms of civilized or specialized structures stand out harshly and incongruously. Civilization is a management pattern of delegated jobs and specialized tasks. It still manifests itself to an eminent degree in military and industrial structures, insuring their current obsolescence.

THE POPE POPS IN

The Chair of Peter Jets Around the World

In the first decade of radio, politics began to acquire some of the old tribal forms once more. Hitler and Mussolini began to "put on" their publics as political attire and to communicate their personal being to the entire body politic. In more WASPish territory, Churchill and F.D.R. strove to do the same. Political commentators are naturally ignorant of the causes of the emergence of these strange images, since understanding of *processes* is not "their bag." The Roman hierarchy after Gutenberg had acquired a great deal of the organization chart patterns of specialism and rigidity. Improved written communication made possible the development of a huge Roman bureaucracy, transforming the Roman pontiff into a chief executive. Further improvement in travel and communication brought the pontiff into more immediate personal relation to his subjects. Even the President of the United States need not govern from Washington, D.C.

ELECTRIFYING NEWS NOW AVAILABLE

Nonresident memberships in a state of mind.
Current ad

What, therefore, is called the de-Romanization of the Roman Church is quite simply its electrification. The managerial changes resulting from such deepening personal ties between the pontiff and his subjects are identical with those that have occurred in every other sphere of politics, government, business, and education. The nineteenth-century bureaucrats who assembled at the Second Vatican Council in 1962 were naturally as unaware of the causes of their problems and reforms as the representatives of the church at the Council of Trent (1545–63). There was not a single individual present at the Council of Trent who understood the effects of print on the spiritual schism and psychic distress of the religious and political life of that time. At the Second Vatican Council, the participants paid no attention to the causes of their problems in their new policies and prescriptions. Whether politics and business have always been conducted with the same total obliviousness to *causes* of change may be left an open question.

It seems necessary to postulate a profound motivation for such universal somnambulism. People in general seem to have a built-in intuition of the safe limits of their human awareness at any given time. Until this century the limits have been set well below the threshold of rational control of the total environment. At electric speeds it is quite futile to set the limits of awareness at that level.

ESP Is Old Hat When Effects Precede Causes

The patterns of formerly hidden processes now begin to obtrude on every hand. Prescience, prophetic vision, and artistic awareness are no longer needed to establish an understanding of the most secret causes of personal and social processes. Mere electric speed-up makes X-ray awareness natural. Any administrator today is aware of his environment as a universal teaching machine. Even as late as the 1940's, it was possible for historians of the Third Reich to make documentary films of the rise and fall of Nazi Germany without even alluding to radio.

> I am afraid that conglomerates will be the stranded giants of the next
> decade.   Peter Drucker, *Management Today*, May, 1969

New forms of tribal structures and leadership are developing today in unexpected areas. The terms "consortium" and "conglomerate" refer to business structures and organizations that deal with individual businesses themselves as members of a single family or tribe. Whereas the old take-overs used to add a business to an existing one for the sake of its "hardware" resources, the new conglomerates merge complex structures with existing enterprises for the sake of their knowledge and information. The "etherealization" of "hardware," as with the chemical bond (Arnold Toynbee considers this trend away from "hardware" and toward "software" as the over-all pattern of modern history), appears to be the obsessive trend in commerce, *i.e.*, the increasing ability to do more and more with less and less. The human bond in the medieval period had been familial and tribal in the degree to which communications were slow and communities were tightly bound together in their relative isolation. The Gutenberg speed-up gave great impetus to the commercial spirit of trade and exchange by making uniform products and prices easy to attain. The tight personal loyalties that had gone with the oral medieval community opened up.

Today, in terms of structure and organization, the situation has been reversed. It is the little man who tastes the big thrills. The big man merely collects the kudos and the credit rating. The shift from medieval corporate loyalties to private calculation and Caesarism was the traumatic experience for the people of that time. Today misery and suffering are felt for exactly opposite reasons. Now, involvement is so mandatory and loyalties so corporate that extremely individualistic or civilized societies are in the position of having to scrap their entire experience and establishments in order to survive.

If anyone supposes that this situation favors Communism, he need only look at the plight of China or Russia, where ancient corporate structures are grinding themselves into fragments of individualistic specialties in order to achieve economic success. Communist China and Russia are ancient feudal regimes that are now scrapping themselves in order to achieve the nineteenth-century goals of the Western world. The Japanese were saved from such goals by their craft skills and their tribal habit of consensus.

Just why "backward" countries should feel the overwhelming need to go through the nineteenth-century "hardware" phase in the electric age is somewhat baffling for the analyst. The Japanese, for example, seem to have leap-frogged over the nineteenth century. The Hindu scholar Jitendra Kumar suggests that one reason why the Japanese were able to by-pass the nineteenth century was because of their shortage of "hardware" materials. The same leapfrogging may to some extent also apply to Germany. In principle, "backward" countries can start with our latest electric technologies. It is easier to introduce radio as an educational means in Africa than to build innumerable buildings.

MEANS CREATE ENDS FOR THE SOMNAMBULIST
ENDS CREATE MEANS FOR THE ENTREPRENEUR
MEANS BECOME ENDS FOR THE BUREAUCRAT

Nyerere, in Tanzania, could govern by helicopter when he had neither radio nor rail to establish parliamentary institutions. By the same token, in "advanced" countries, airplanes, not to mention telephones and later devices, have brought representative governments into great difficulties. In Latin America there is a clearly discernible pattern of the latest light-ware preceding the old heavy-ware in the contemporary world; airplanes have preceded railways as well as automobile highways throughout the continent. Castro governs Cuba directly by television, acting as teacher as much as politician. But if a North American government were to permit TV government by education to supplant government by delegation and representation, all the bureaucratic arrangements of our government would collapse. New means create new goals and erase old ones. During speed-up means and goals merge in process.

As these patterns and processes thus become perceptible, the question arises: If something can be done, should it be done? How much innovation is compatible with social viability or with a critique of human satisfactions?

In a fat corporation the oily executive rises to the top.

In *Management and Machiavelli*, Antony Jay, addressing himself to the problems and characteristics of modern management, compares corporations (with their chief executives) to historical states: feudal Tudor, eighteenth-century Spain, and Renaissance Italy, *e.g.*, he considers barons analogous to the "line" organizations, and courtiers to the "staff." Corporations engage not only in making war but also in making peace treaties. Both have their orthodox conformists and their dissenters. Jay sees the presidents and chief executives of business organizations as resembling Bismarck, or George I, or Czar Nicholas II.

One of the best instances of starting from the market and not the factory is the Prussian war against Austria. Bismarck did not say, "There's my army, now what can I do with it to make Prussia as great a power as Austria?" He started the other way round, decided that uniting the North German states under Prussia would achieve the object, and that victory over Austria would be a necessary preliminary.

In other words, Bismarck started with the effects and invented the causes.

Inventing the Market Before the Product

Bismarck instinctively heeded the great discovery of the nineteenth century: the discovery of the "technique of discovery," which is to trace a process backward from its ultimate effect to the point at which to begin to produce that effect, *i.e.*, to invent the market before the product. This was the discovery of Poe in detective fiction, and Baudelaire in poetry. The twentieth-century discovery was, in the words of Bertrand Russell, that of the "technique of the suspended judgment." This is the awareness of process without involvement. It implies the possibility of by-passing the disservice effects previously attendant upon all innovation. The myth of the Machine in the Garden is the conviction of inviolable purity, that new technology cannot harm utopia. The current "mission orientation" of the defense establishment is a pure case of nineteenth-century mechanism. Jay's approach is to "attempt to analyze current and relevant management problems in the light of experience, observation, and history." His stress is on "leadership," *i.e.*, low-intensity "generalship," but always *from above*: "The real pleasure of power is the pleasure of freedom . . . to control his environment."

Jay compares the English baron of the twelfth century with the English manufacturer in the early nineteenth century. Both enjoyed unfettered power with profound insecurity. He draws parallels between Tudor monarchs and the Vanderbilts, Rockefellers, and Carnegies in the realms of railway, oil, and steel. Jay considers the key conflict as one between owner-bosses and professional managers—between capricious authority and corporate efficiency:

> The powers of government pass away from the dynasty to the professional meritocrats, to the politicians and top civil servants: the powers in industry pass away from the family to the professional managers. In politics it is called "the century of the common man," in industry "the managerial revolution."

King Lear delegated his powers to simplify his life. The result was that his executives wanted the rest of his power in order to complete their own effective power. Expansion by delegation is the specialist formula for death.

The Moreness Principle of Trevor-Roper

> Any society, so long as it is, or feels itself to be, a working society
> tends to invest in itself.
>
> Hugh Trevor-Roper, *The Rise of Christian Europe*

Hierarchical organizations thus tend to repeat the procedures and qualities that brought them success in the past. They share the assumptions
based on experience suited to the slow changes of the past. Such organizations collapse in the context of today's electric speed-up. As Antony Jay
points out, change intensifies the rivalry between "barons" and "courtiers."
The parallel with Gresham's law is that the bad drives out the good in
management as well as in currency. It puts those who reach the top on
naked display for all to see. The Peter Principle could have been extended
to the dilemma of the "naked ape" who climbs a pole. The higher he goes,
the worse the image—the more you see of his backside!

The Bigger the Business the Shorter the Odds?

> That puts it not unto the touch
> To win or lose it all.
>
> James Graham, "My Dear and Only Love"

There are parallels to the historical role in Jay's pageant, in military history, and in commercial and industrial warfare. No successful commander
ever risks everything on one throw. Milton's Satanic dropout illustrates this
theme: "Better to rule in Hell than serve in Heaven." Like a state, every
corporation needs a noble ideal. It also fights deviants. This faith is based
on the assumptions upon which their success was founded—their experience. It cannot be proved. *Old colonialism* exploited the raw materials, *i.e.*,
"hardware." *New colonialism* exploits productive capacity and skilled management and labor, *i.e.*, "software." Economic nationalism of governments
is thus defeated by economic inter-nationalism of corporations. What is
good for General Motors may ultimately be great for everybody but the
United States.

No Standing Room at the Top

With paper and print came the machinery, the yardsticks, and the fixed
slots of the organization chart. This fragmentation and homogenization
opened careers to talents. Machiavelli's *aut Caesar aut nihil* (Caesar or
nothing) became for his disciples *aut Babbitt aut nihil*. Such competition
ensures a dead, flat level of indomitable mediocrity. Those who are hung up
on the chart have to put up with and learn the art of being ruled—endurance of stupidity and boredom.

It was the competitive crowing of the nineteenth century that flipped enterprise into bureaucracy—risk into safety. With the art of being ruled came first the "press gangs" and then the press barons. "Civilization" in the sixteenth century opened the closed system of the feudal age. In feudal times the only career that presented any possibility for talents was the church. The church alone had an open hierarchy and organization chart. Rapid rise presupposed much learning. The church had that much in common with the Chinese competitive examination system. The churchman could not only rise within the hierarchy but his services were in demand with the monarchies. Like Becket, "the Cheapside brat," or Cardinal Wolsey, the butcher's son, or Cardinal Richelieu, a churchman could assume the power of monarchy itself. The churchman, as a man of erudition and eloquence, was indispensable to the man of experience, the mere militant baron. In Russia this pattern lasted until Rasputin in the twentieth century. Within the tight early feudal framework of interlacing loyalties, the layman of talent was too deeply immured in the local affairs of the dynastic structure to be a mobile consultant for all parts of any organization. A churchman, free of family ties, could move more freely than knight or baron.

As the laity broke the clerical monopoly of knowledge via the printed book, the competition between the churchmen and the laity for secular control became intense. The new secular power developed mechanical industry by extending Gutenberg technology. In England the army and navy remained the sphere of the aristocracy and resisted the invasion of middle-class learning. Until after the Crimean War they offered careers to gentry, not to talents.

2

East to West to East

Just when the West unloaded the feudal bureaucracy of the clergy, the new entrepreneurs of an expanding commerce began to contact the Orient. The spices and silks and treasures of the Indies had the paradoxical effect of establishing a massive new monopoly of knowledge in the West. Many people are aware that the famous Indian Civil Service (I.C.S.) competitive examinations had roots in Chinese mandarin methods of rigor and discipline in training their bureaucracy:

> The class of *scholar-officials* (or mandarins), numerically infinitesimal but omnipotent by reason of their strength, influence, position, and prestige, held all the power and owned the largest amount of land. This class possessed every privilege, above all the privilege of reproducing itself, because of its monopoly of education. But the incomparable prestige enjoyed by the intelligentsia had nothing to do with such a risky and possibly ephemeral thing as the ownership of land; nor was it conferred by heredity, which after all can be interrupted; nor was it due solely to its exclusive enjoyment of the benefits of education. . . . Their social role was at one and the same time that of architect, engineer, teacher, administator, and ruler. Yet these "managers" before their time were firmly against any form of specialization. There was only one profession they recognized: that of governing.
>
> Etienne Balazs, *Chinese Civilization and Bureaucracy*

Just why this Chinese form should have reached Britain through India is little known. The fact is that the Indians had picked up the Chinese competitive civil service examination system long before the British made contact with India. Another area of relative ignorance about India is its relative indifference to Buddhism. Most people think of India in terms of Kipling or of Herman Hesse. "The Road to Mandalay," title of a poem by Kipling, has familiarized the English-speaking world with

> Bloomin' idol made of mud
> What they called the great god Bud. . . .

The Buddhist thing is specialist and visual in bias. Buddhism entered India with the Moslems and the Mohammedans in the thirteenth century, and with Mohammed Akbar of the sixteenth century (see *The Root and the Flower* by L. H. Myers). The ruler types who invaded India at various times were those who specialized either in *this*worldliness or *other*worldliness. The Mohammedans and the Buddhists were both individualistic and "visually" biased in comparison with adherents of the natural religions of India, which were really nature processes of an exceedingly complicated kind.

Caste as Role and Class as Job

The structure of Indian society, insofar as it exploited "caste," was tribal rather than economic, *i.e.*, caste meant role, not "class" or job. In India to this day, any man can change his caste by changing his role, by moving from plumber to doctor, from carpenter to priest, or from lawyer to professor. This flexibility of the caste system was both consolidated and hardened by the invasion of alien cultures. The Moslem, for example, rendered Indian society rigid with hostility. The Moslem tended to separate the roles of men and women, and the Purdah costume was devised to enable women to hide their faces from the hated invaders. Perhaps the caste system was partly the result of trying to maintain the old system against the foreigner, the intruder. It seems contradictory that the British should have sought to preserve the caste system in India. After all, Thomas Babington Macaulay in the middle of the nineteenth century brought the organization chart to India. The British aristocracy still had enough of the old feudal system in its inner life to find much that was congenial in India, as in any backward society. The British retained enough of the old feudal system of personal loyalties in their make-up to find class and caste quite acceptable.

In passing, it can be said that the continuing British stake in nonspecialist feudalism inclined them toward plantation patterns of social and economic organization everywhere in the world. The Northern Yankee is the extreme form of the "civilized" specialist in thought and action. He carried the new Puritan middle-class literacy and efficiency into every phase of life and business. The Southern planter was typically from more genteel British stock, and the rootedness of the large plantations fostered his paternalistic streak. Whether in the West Indies or the East Indies, large holdings encouraged the settler in patterns of the old feudal times. Even on the Western frontier a big fraternal clan occasionally popped up to "pollute" with its kinship system the specialist pattern of the individual settler.

It is therefore one of the paradoxes of history that the Indian caste system, strengthened by Moslem invaders, should have emerged in an advanced industrial country in the nineteenth century under a new paternalism. The "mandarins of Bloomsbury," including the "posh" author E. M. Forster (*A Passage to India*), owed much to the caste system of India. Its caste system is both the creation of Moslem rigor and Chinese "inscrutability." (The word "posh" is a slang monument to British rule in India. It is an abbreviation of the phrase "portside out, starboard home," meaning a first-class passage to and from India, *i.e.*, the cool side of the ship.)

Ruth Benedict's classic *The Chrysanthemum and the Sword* describes the stark contrast between Eastern and Western attitudes to war. This contrast expresses the extremes of "visual" and "aural-oral" bias as they happen to occur in Japan in relation to the United States:

> The very premises which Japan used to justify her war were the opposite of America's. She defined the international situation differently. America laid the war to the aggressions of the Axis. Japan, Italy, and Germany had unrighteously offended against international peace by their acts of conquest. Whether the Axis had seized power in Manchukuo or in Ethiopia or in Poland, it proved that they had embarked on an evil course of oppressing weak peoples. They had sinned against an international code of "live and let live" or at least of "open doors" for free enterprise. Japan saw the cause of the war in another light. There was anarchy in the world as long as every nation had absolute sovereignty; it was necessary for her to fight to establish a hierarchy—under Japan, of course, since she alone represented a nation truly hierarchal from top to bottom and hence understood the necessity of taking "one's proper place."

Eye-to-Eye Pushed to Extreme Becomes Eyeball-to-Eyeball

Naturally, the Japanese conception of hierarchy is feudal and based on roles, not jobs; it is total involvement, total loyalty, and total commitment. This tribal attitude was, of course, identical with Hitler's logic, which automatically eliminated the Jews from any role in Germany or Europe. Tribal societies coexist with difficulty. Whereas the Japanese were accepting the logic of their ancient institutions, Hitler was an upstart using radio and confronting the modern electric world. He had revived the ancient feudalism of involvement and loyalty as a social means of accommodating the latest electric technology.

The Japanese were in a much stronger political position than Hitler, who was by comparison an ideological *parvenu*. It is important to understand that both Hitler and the Japanese had the totality of the latest electric technology built into their cause and their psyche. When ideological enemies of such regimes appeal to mere concepts that condemn such political structures, they tend to overlook the fact that these structures are the product of our own latest technologies.

The Wedding of Eastern Feudalism and Western Organization Chart

Management News (October, 1970), reporting on "Japanese Managers Stress Work Group," notes:

> "In Japan, the business organization is not a mere mechanism geared to work; it is a *Gemeinschaft*, a human group. . . . Individual em-

ployees are an integral and organic part of the organization," according to Jiro Tokuyama, director, International Operations, Nomura Research Institute of Technology and Economics. . . . Business is done through a group approach, characterized by limited authority but unlimited responsibility, that fosters a sense of "obligation to contribute to the company." Although individual efficiency may be low, the total performance of the company resulting from collective behavior is high. This is one reason for the impressive growth of many Japanese companies, he indicated.

DECISION MAKING: ANSWERS OR QUESTIONS?

Doing What Comes Naturally

Peter Drucker, writing on "What We Can Learn from Japanese Management," comments:

> With us in the West, all emphasis is on the *answer* to the question. . . . To the Japanese, however, the important element in decision making is *defining the question* . . . to decide whether there is need for a decision and what the decision is about. And it is in this step that the Japanese aim at attaining "consensus." The answer to the question (what the West considers *the* decision) follows its definition.
>
> *Harvard Business Review*, March–April, 1971

Obtaining consensus in Japan is too cumbersome for small questions, which are left to take care of themselves. On the other hand, Drucker observes, nothing causes more trouble in Western organizations than management concern with answers for too many petty decisions. The Japanese have discovered the relevance and efficacy of their traditional habits of consensus. In the electric age private points of view are self-destructive. They lead to multitudes of trivial answers to fragmented questions. The Western individual with his private perspective can scarcely be expected to grasp the coherence of large issues and patterns that emerge with high-speed data processing. He can find the answers for the individual only. The Japanese, unable to imagine a private point of view on anything, are not tempted to waste their time. They go for consensus that *happens* to be the need of our time.

We now begin to understand why the Emperor of Japan is not a private person at all and is in no sense the "head" of the country. To be the "head" of an organization is a strictly "visual" or private individual assumption of power by diligent goal seekers. To be the actual emperor of a vast population is not to have any private ambition whatever. Even the phrase *noblesse oblige* is sufficiently a relic of feudal corporate life to help us understand that the nobleman, whether of hereditary family or political hierarchy, has no private desires or wishes whatever in behaving disinterestedly, courteously, and impersonally.

Emperors and Clowns

The emperor and clown are complementary. The clown is the emperor's private self seeking contact with the people and situations that he embodies corporately in his *role*. The clown is free to spoof the emperor, to test his moods for the benefit and entertainment of the court. The clown is a type of audience researcher or consultant, just as our audience researchers and consultants have become the clowns of our culture. Today we see the emergence of a new type of executive who can switch roles from clown to emperor to probe the environment through his own awareness.

THE ECONOMICS OF PRESTIGE, HOOTCH, AND POTLATCH

War of the Tribal Credit Cards

Ruth Benedict's classic account of potlatch among the Northwestern Indians in *Patterns of Culture* is almost an anticipation of today's "war of icons and symbols" in the electric information environment. Miss Benedict is quite conscious of this when she says:

> Wealth had become not merely economic goods, even goods put away in boxes for potlatches and never used except in exchange, but even more characteristically prerogatives with no economic functions. Songs, myths, names of chiefs' house-posts, of their dogs, of their canoes, were wealth. Valued privileges, like the right to tie a dancer to a post, or to bring in tallow for the dancers to rub on their faces, or shredded cedar bark for them to wipe it off again, were wealth and were passed down in family lines. . . .
>
> The manipulation of wealth on the Northwest Coast is clearly enough in many ways a parody on our own economic arrangements. These tribes did not use wealth to get for themselves an equivalent value in economic goods, but as counters of fixed value in a game they played to win.

Production Not for Exchange but for Prestige as Use

Wealth becomes an end in itself when it provides its own context and relates to nothing else but itself. Wealth then becomes symbolic in the strict sense of being a set of effects for which the causes are either hidden or irrelevant. When a thing creates a world of its own, only play remains. The Northwest Indians understood the principle of play as gambling: either to win or lose all could achieve status by symbolic form. The Indians had reached the same awareness that the Elizabethans had on the frontier between the medieval and the modern worlds. The Indians, like Ibsen in the nineteenth century, were trapped and outraged on a frontier between their traditions and the encounter with the white man's world built on totally antagonistic premises to theirs. All these people had the opportunity of perceiving the effects before the causes came on the scene.

ICONIC POWER

We are now in a position to unscrew the inscrutable East, since the West has become far more inscrutable. The West is "uptight" precisely because its old "hardware" is in immediate danger of dissolution. What is inscrutable to the tribal East is the specialist methods used by the fragmented West. Today, as the West goes East and the East goes West by an exchange of technologies with their attendant physical, psychic, and social effects, it becomes quite easy to empathize with the Oriental at any level. As our political machines strive desperately to invent corporate images for political candidates, to say nothing of other commercial products, we begin to understand the need to "put on" the public as a mask of power. We know that the private face produced by means of literacy or photography is powerless to create the involvement and participation of a total audience. That is why the Negro or the Indian is so much more effective in color TV patterns than the hapless WASP. "Black is beautiful" recognizes iconic power. The West can only present a private countenance that alienates the corporate audience, since it offers no means of empathy.

IS THE NEW FRONTIER ALREADY HERE?

Planet Earth as Unhappy Hunting Ground

The United States had the unique fate of commencing to build its establishments—political, economic, social, and educational—without any previous commitments to the European feudal or handicraft worlds. Just as Africa or areas without a nineteenth century tend to commence their development in the twentieth century with the latest electric technologies, so the United States began with the latest technologies, by-passing the preceding craft technologies. Indeed, the American triumph was to translate the old European crafts into new mechanical form. The United States was further able to convert the unskilled and ignorant individual into a participant in the most advanced processes of a machine economy by following the process of extreme specialization and fragmentation of effort. It may be questioned whether today the same process can be duplicated under electric conditions. We may well inquire whether similarly semitrained personnel can quickly become involved in a computerized program enterprise. Can the computer perform the miracle of the pons asinorum? Can we be merely reducing the world into two heaps of categorized and uncategorized data, achieving the electronic miracle of eliciting sophisticated knowledge from ignorant people? Can specialism ultimately achieve comprehensivism?

In the new age of knowledge industries the optimist is necessarily one who considers it possible to perform this feat of the pons asinorum. The computer consultant may well be tempted to consider that the feat of the pons asinorum can be performed by the computer.

The miracle of the American achievement in the nineteenth century was the conversion of European skills into mechanized and unskilled processes; today the twentieth century is asked to translate the mechanized processes in turn into the integral electronic circuitry of instant and ecological programming. The price paid by the extreme specialism of the nineteenth-century converters of crafts into assembly lines was the converters' break with tradition and with human community in the interests of affluence and a huge flow of consumer goods for the common man. The price exacted of the twentieth century for reversing this process is a return to involvement in the most primitive modes of human consciousness.

Hunting the Africa Within: Return of
the "Astoneaged" Muse

A foretaste of this return to Paleolithic caveman awareness came in the 1920's with radio. While America was going to extreme "division of labor," it was also, via the American Negro, creating primitive jazz that integrated the world on African terms—miming the new environment as catharsis. American technology became the PA system for this new primitivism—a replay of "production for prestige as use."

FROM ENTREPRENEURIAL RISK TO CORPORATE SAFETY

Money as Metaphor Translates Everything as A-greed

> The prince who conforms his conduct to the *spirit of the times* will be fortunate; and in the same way will be unfortunate, if in his actions he disregards the spirit of the times. . . .
> I conclude, then, inasmuch as Fortune is changeable, that men who persist obstinately in their own ways will be successful only so long as those ways coincide with those of Fortune, and whenever these differ, they fail. But, on the whole, I judge impetuosity to be better than caution.   Niccolò Machiavelli, *The Prince*

Machiavelli's putting on history as the "spirit of the times" became the idea of a great psychic environment, called *Zeitgeist* by naïve eighteenth- and nineteenth-century thinkers. Civilized man calmly switches it off, as he would any other tiresome "factor" in his environment. Tribal man, however, is eager to latch on to the *Zeitgeist*, hoping to enhance his power, *e.g.*, Hitler in the twentieth century. We now know *Zeitgeist* to be the hidden service environment created by our own technologies. We are both their "content" and their servants.

INFORMATION: THE EMPEROR'S NEW CLOTHES

Clichés Retrieve Archetypes: "Ground" Creates "Figures"

This is another reminder that we have reached that state of awareness necessary for man's total programming of the human enterprise. Every new service environment automatically junks its predecessor while unexpectedly retrieving a much earlier set of environmental components. The rational eighteenth century was strong for the Gothic revival. The mechanistic nineteenth century plunged into primitive anthropology. The "cool" TV has revived the "hot mamas" and tunes of the twenties. Daniel Boone girls wear crew cuts, while men wear hair to the shoulders. THE MANAGER AS ENTREPRENEUR WORKS WITH RUBBISH, WHERE ALL DREAMS BEGIN.

The Diehard Tries to Conserve Nonexistent Stability

Donald Kircher, president of the Singer Sewing Machine Corporation, described a familiar dilemma:

> Its very success led to the assumption that all the answers were found, and that all one had to do was do what one's predecessors had done before. Everything became ingrained. There were no outside influences acting on the Company. It became withdrawn into itself.
>
> *Management Today*, June, 1966

The old pathways to success broadened out as new highways for failure.

Superenterprise

The classic statement on this subject is the opening passage of *Monopoly* by Joseph C. Goulden:

> This is not a story about a business or about free enterprise, for A.T. & T. is neither; rather, it is a unique monopoly whose profits are guaranteed, whose investment is risk-free, and whose conduct is largely outside the control of government, the customers it serves, even the 3,000,000 individuals and institutions that share its ownership.
>
> A.T. & T. is a corporate state, a Super Government if you will, whose presence in the United States is felt more keenly on a daily basis than even that of the federal government.

The superenterprise, like the superaudience, works for itself.

3

Heroes as Villains

HERO BECOMES ANTI-HERO

Perhaps the film classic on this subject is *True Grit*. It is the epitome and the last windup. John Wayne plays a parody of himself. He turns the traditional Western hero into an anti-hero. All the resourcefulness and daring of the frontiersman are poured out on the cowboy's coffin, as it were—a whole crock of red-eye, but it has first been processed through his kidneys. The savvy of the great frontiersman has been purchased for twenty-five bucks by a young New England girl who seeks to avenge her father's murder. She buys the individual skill and daring of the frontiersman, making sure to have him sign legal documents at every turn. She is the New England matriarch, skilled in all corporate defenses of legalism. In short, *True Grit* is a capsule summary of both the Western hero as entrepreneur and the eastern lawyer as the creator of corporate safety.

IT IS CHARACTERISTIC OF ALL SOCIAL PROCESSES THAT THEY BECOME MANIFEST AND CONSPICUOUS AT THE MOMENT OF THEIR DEMISE. Patterns only emerge at moments of intense stress, and such stress is the result of overload. Such is the world of medical symptomology, for example. The medical man is trained to recognize only acute symptoms, just as he is trained to treat such symptoms rather than their causes. (The Chinese doctors are paid not to cure but to keep their patients well.) In his book *The Stress of Life*, Hans Selye demonstrates that all illness is the effort of the body to restrain the spread of invading organisms. This applies, naturally, to "sick" jokes as much as to sick people or societies. "He has a fine head of skin."

The Protestant Ethic in Reverse

The WASP cannot see culture as fun, nor can he see "pop kulch" as serious: "Life is short; our faces must be long." His plight reminds us of Tarzan's last desperate cry: "Who greased my vine?" What the WASP ignores is that the "serious man" is one who can perceive and relate to the psychic and social processes that are active in his own time and place. Perception inspires levity, not gravity.

True Grit, by manifesting stark symptoms of the extreme form of individual enterprise and the extreme forms of corporate legal safety, calls attention to massive changes in these areas. The conglomerate as a form of hijacking in current business developments expresses the end of the corporation as a safety mechanism, as much as *True Grit* underscores the end of heroic individualism.

The anti-hero became a theme in art and literature as early as Thackeray's *Vanity Fair*, the "novel without a hero." Characteristically, the "hero" of the book is Becky Sharp, the "mother" of Scarlet O'Hara. The heroism of New England's Pilgrim Fathers has gone through the vanishing point. Thomas Hanna, in *A Primer of Somatic Thinking*, describes the Protestant ethic as the complementing of the monastic *laborare est orare*. It is the Calvinist tenet that "God's elect must justify their pre-ordained salvation by a serious devotion to the business of labor—to relax and behave as if he *knew* his salvation was certain would appear to be sinful presumption that one knew as much about the future as did Sovereign God."

Benjamin Franklin's *Autobiography* explains the "system" for attaining perfection. The autobiography is in the tradition of Montaigne's essays. Montaigne was the first to discover the meaning of the printed book: "I owe a complete portrait of myself to the public." At the other end of the spectrum is J. P. Morgan, proclaiming, "I owe the public nothing." The portrait becomes the sitter.

Specialism has often appeared as a mechanical means of diminishing the effects of "original sin." Idea people are oral people. They have time on their hands. The oral man tries to overcome original sin in human organization by a system of total involvement and loyalty. The visual man attempts to diminish the traces of original sin by extreme fragmentation of man and work, *i.e.*, nobody has much opportunity to be very wicked. You cut Satan up into little bits and throw the pieces in his face.

Modern hierarchy and division of labor are born of the conviction that even vicious people can be made useful by carving their energies into small pieces. The Western world, with Gutenberg, discovered a way of by-passing "original" sin by getting rid of the integral person in the work process. The integral person, to be useful, must be loyal and devoted. When the integral redskin met the specialist redcoat, the latter was defeated by his own skill. Printer Franklin's system for attaining perfection appears a few generations later in a document printed in 1852.

OFFICE RULES IN 1852

- Godliness, Cleanliness and Punctuality are necessities of a good business.

- *This firm has reduced the hours of work, and the Clerical Staff will now only have to be present between the hours of 7 a.m. and 6 p.m. on week-days.*

- Daily prayers will be held each morning in the Main Office.

The Clerical Staff will be present.

- *Clothing must be of a sober nature. The Clerical Staff will not disport themselves in raiment of bright colours, nor will they wear hose unless in good repair.*

- *Overshoes and top-coats may not be worn in the office, but* neck scarves and headwear may be worn in inclement weather.

• A stove is provided for the benefit of the Clerical Staff, coal and wood must be kept in the locker. It is recommended that each member of the Clerical Staff bring 4 pounds of coal each day, during cold weather.

• No member of the Clerical Staff may leave the room without permission from Mr. Rogers. The calls of nature are permitted, and Clerical Staff may use the garden below the second gate. This area must be kept in good order.

• No talking is allowed during business hours.

• The craving of tobacco, wines or spirits is a human weakness and, as such, is forbidden to all members of the Clerical Staff.

• Now that the hours of business have been drastically reduced the partaking of food is allowed between 11:30 a.m. and noon, but work will not, on any account, cease.

• Members of the Clerical Staff will provide their own pens. A new sharpener is available, on application to Mr. Rogers.

• Mr. Rogers will nominate a senior Clerk to be responsible for the cleanliness of the Main Office and the Private Office, and all Boys and Juniors will report to him 40 minutes before Prayers and will remain after closing hours for similar work. Brushes, Brooms, Scrubbers and Soap are provided by the owners.

• The New Increased Weekly Wages are as hereunder detailed:

Junior Boys (to 11
    years) 15c
Boys (to 14 years) 25c
Junior Clerks 1.05
Senior Clerks (after 15
    years with the
    owners) 2.50
The owners recognize the generosity of the new Labour Laws but expect a great rise in output of work to compensate for these near Utopian conditions.

THE SELF-MADE MAN
and
THE AMERICAN STORY

Marshall Fishwick, in *The Hero*, has a list of "self-made men," beginning with the first use of the phrase by Henry Clay:

A poor Virginia orphan named Henry Clay first used the term "self-made man" in an 1832 Congressional debate. Five years later, Horatio Alger, Jr., was born. He would carry the message onward and upward, telling time and again "the American story" that became the indelible stereotype at home and abroad, to last through generations and style-changes, good years and bad. . . .

There is no better example of the fateful contraries that lurk in any intensely stressed form than the case of Henry Ford. Just as much as John

Wayne in *True Grit,* he became the parody of the self-made man simply by pushing it to the extreme. Fishwick points this out:

> Many turned the Alger words into flesh, but none with more lasting impact than Henry Ford. He stands at the spot where the farm and the factory meet. People who have never heard of Washington, Boone, or Bunyan know the name Ford well. It bounces over the world's highway daily. Under his guidance, the automobile became for us what the cross had been for the Emperor Constantine: *inhoc signo vinces.*

The Ford car, by speeding up the old horse and buggy and by putting everybody on the open road to pursue distant goals and dreams, destroyed both the open road and the goal and dream. It all came to rest in Greenfield Village, as much a cemetery of forgotten values as any garden city.

Men of Extinction: Bulldoze and Be Damned

The old order changeth and lasts like the first.

James Joyce

In *Management and Machiavelli,* Antony Jay playfully surveys management patterns of the past as though they were still dominant. The British and the Europeans are now actually engaged in taking over some of the rather tired and blind American management practices. Jay's failure to grasp the irrelevance of many of the current American practices in management is matched by his minimizing the advantage of many of the past British practices: just now, when the gentlemanly tribal code (word as good as bond) is acquiring new salience in the espion-age of James Bond .007, when no bond except the resonant oral bond will hold.

Management Science

At the very opening of his book Jay reveals his illusions regarding the "science of management":

> The simple days of just the boss and the labor force are over: between the two has come the "hierarchy," the "management structure," the "chain of command." For the last hundred years, and with increasing rapidity in the last fifty, we have seen the small companies merging with larger groups: today, most business organizations are far too large and complicated to be run by a single policy former and decision taker. They have to be managed.

Jay is still trying to catch up to the nineteenth century.

All Boundaries Now Gone with the Ether

Jay's study belongs to the old "hardware" world of thought of the nineteenth century in which people stood firmly and symmetrically on their predecessors' shoulders. In the "software" world of today, progress and development no longer take this hierarchical form. Instead, progress often consists of dancing on another's toes. Major General Gordon T. Gould, Jr., U.S.A.F., HQ, in discussing "Computers and Communications—Touchstones of Tomorrow" at the seventeenth Joint Engineering Management Conference in Montreal, October, 1969, noted:

> Software is an *art*, not a science as some would suggest. There are few scientific rules yet identified as applicable to the art of software design and production. Thus, software is not susceptible to the same management processes that apply to hardware. . . . Producers of software stand on the toes, not on the shoulders, of those who have gone before. Each attempt is, in effect, a beginning all over again.
>
> *The Engineering Manager—Survival in the Seventies*

The general is as hung up in his thinking as Antony Jay. The general still assumes the old Machiavellian manipulation of the isolated individual as norm. In his own time, Machiavelli had made an important breakthrough, whereas the general, instead of treading on Machiavelli's toes, is satisfied to stand on his old ground.

4

Services as Disservices

The New York *Times* Service (February 23, 1971) reports:

> WASHINGTON—The friendship of an army general cost Vietnam's lead-
> ing Post Exchange profiteer "at least $1,000 a month," Senate investi-
> gators were told yesterday, but the testimony indicated it was a bar-
> gain . . . [for he] protected storage space . . . discouraged legal
> interference . . . promoted agents' raids against a competitor.

In *Catch-22*, the *figure* of the black market and the *ground* of war merge
into a monster presided over by the syndicate. *When war and market
merge, all money transactions begin to drip blood.* What has happened to
war and market in today's new "software" age is that both involve total
commitment in contrast to the specialist "hardware" world of the nineteenth century. The contrast can be observed in the *figure-ground* relations
of the slave market compared with the labor market. Labor is one thing;
man as a commodity is another. Today, modes of business and warfare alike
tend to blur these distinctions. The mercenary or professional of yesterday
was a specialist, who became the industrial worker of the nineteenth century. The military engineer (*e.g.*, Leonardo da Vinci) preceded the *civil*
engineer. And, whereas in the past the military engineer graduated into *civil*
engineering in peacetime, today it is the "civil" engineer who dominates
military technology. A similar confusion reigns between the industrial and
military establishments. Young activists have been reconciling themselves
to the use of the educational establishment for commercial and military
purposes. Napalm serves as a kind of "connection" or "hang-up" for all
these areas. By the time the hyphenating of "industrial-military" complex
has become cliché, it is obvious that the realities have moved elsewhere.
The information world cannot sustain any of the divisions and boundaries
between such functions.

The price war has become impractical. It was based upon the possibility
of one region enjoying a lower price level than an adjacent rival. The period
during which it is possible to exploit such discrepancies has been reduced to
zero by communication speed-up—the end of the "muddle crass."

Payment for Pains

In the early stages of the nineteenth-century labor market, skills were translated into cash. Parallel action today consists in translating into cash all the psychic dissatisfactions of tedious labor routines and specialized jobs of all kinds by endlessly renegotiated labor contracts. The mechanisms of the market resume the patterns of the most primitive haggle and barter as blood money is extracted for every dissatisfaction. Meanwhile, the economists continue to distract us with calculations about the drop in "productivity" resulting from these negotiations. They miss the obvious point that the negotiations are an end in themselves and a way of life through corporate violence.

Haggling as a Way of Life

Is this a private fight, or may anyone join in?
                                                    An Irishman

There is an obvious parallel with the university president who spends his term haggling with students who want the right to haggle with professors and with boards of governors. The students use the Establishment's rule book to clobber the Establishment. There is a corresponding interruption of university function and learning processes in the big new knowledge industries of the campus. The desire to haggle in direct personal encounter is the revenge for frustrated learning aspirations. Student, faculty, and administration alike have been frustrated by packaged, specialized learning as much as the industrial work force has been degraded by specialized repetitive tasks. There is no monopoly on this process in any part of our community. The medical establishment has parcelled out the human anatomy to groups of noncommunicating specialists, knowing *More and More about Less and Less.*

The old story about the astonishment of the debutante who enquired about the handsome officer in a navy uniform may apply.

"Who is he? What does he do?"

"He's a naval doctor."

She gasps. "They go in for the smallest things nowadays!"

Except for miniaturization of the anatomical specialisms, nothing has changed since this popular joke of the 1920's. The old GP was patient-oriented, visiting his patients in the midst of their family. In the age of the mobile home, the doctor need no longer worry about house calls. The new specialist processes his patient in a large hospital plant, where the nurses are expected to be as impersonally specialized as the doctor, chained to his oar.

WELFARE AS WARFARE: THE FURY OF THE GOOD SAMARITAN

Welfare acquired this centralist specialist character on the then new assembly line early in the nineteenth century. Dickens's *Our Mutual Friend* shows how money turns people into objects, rising or falling on the universal scale of a society dominated by money—a vain mirroring of nothing by nothing. In Chapter 41, Dickens describes the human misery under the Poor Law bureaucracy and the constant "horror of falling into the hands of Charity. It is a remarkable Christian improvement, to have made a pursuing Fury of the Good Samaritan."

Oliver Twist's poignant request for "more, please" disrupted the mechanical gears of a mechanical system by injecting a single human note. The human *figure* in Dickens suddenly stood out against the inhuman *ground* of the mechanical welfare system. It is worth paying attention to Dickens's names for these characters. Mr. *Gradgrind* in *Hard Times* is the inhuman and fact-oriented pedagogue of the industrial world. His name stands as a kind of symbol for the process of gradual, grinding dehumanization. Oliver bears a name famous in the ancient romantic phrase, "A Roland for your Oliver," which evokes all the chivalry of an earlier age. But this chivalry is now *twist*ed and distorted beyond recognition in the conditions of a workhouse. Nevertheless, Oliver rises to the noble role, indicated by his name, of a champion of Christendom. Oliver unexpectedly translates the degraded welfare system of the nineteenth-century poorhouse into the high plane of medieval military romance of a battle of champions. The universal popularity of *Oliver Twist* vindicates our suggestion that there is a mysterious resonance in the gap between warfare and welfare. By the mouth of the child Oliver more *moreness* is translated into a widely acknowledged spiritual value.

In both warfare and welfare, intensely specialized and bureaucratized communities can be seen to seek new illusory wholeness through sacrifice, which in fact leads only to further fragmentation through intensity and speed-up. The editorial in *Life*, July 31, 1970, brings it home:

> Welfare now is "a colossal failure," as President Nixon says, "a wheezing, overloaded machine" . . . headed toward complete breakdown because it hadn't the capacity to help the poor humanely.
>
> The "permanent welfare population" of the cities . . . in New York City there now numbers one million, or one person in eight . . . the total number of Americans on welfare roles today [is] more than 10 million . . . an incentive to remain on relief.

The man who stays on welfare longest is the welfare bureaucrat. He is now achieving the least with the most. IN WELFARE, IT IS THE UNEMPLOYED WHO ARE THE EMPLOYERS, JUST AS IN ENTERTAINMENT, IT IS THE AUDIENCE WHO EMPLOYS THE PRODUCER.

"After Such Knowledge What Forgiveness?"

The Indians were indispensable to the fur traders who opened up North America. Theirs were the hands that gathered the pelts from trap lines, just as the imported "hands," Negroes, were employed to pick cotton in the fields. Both these groups, deeply endemic to the soil and character of that continent, quickly became expendable as the economy developed. They were herded into reservations and ghettos and subjected to a process of "welfare" bureaucratization. It is only as the young TV generation of the white population has adopted tribal ways that the black man and the red man and the Eskimo have resumed their place in the total culture. The price we pay for this process is the total alienation of the young people of our day. The young have declared war on the ESTABLISHMENT and are inclined to regard their elders as candidates for some monster welfare reservation of has-beens. The skills and talents of Negro and Indian alike were not appreciated in the age of mechanical industry. Today, it is quite different. The Negro gifts for mime and masks and ritual entertainment are now part of the largest industry in the world—show business. The hippie, by the same token, has become a hunter again. Aritistically and occupationally, he finds new affinities with the aborigines. The industrialist, no longer interested in hiring "hands," goes hunting for talents and as likely as not encounters "heads."

WHEN EACH REMEDY IS BETTER THAN THE NEXT

Boris Kidel, writing on "A Growing Longing for a Better Life" for the London *Observer* Service from Paris, August 1, 1970, describes the French obsession with the outmoded patterns of Napoleonic centralism and Frenchmen's emulation of the more intense American version of the same. Just as Tocqueville's *Democracy in America* describes the ease with which the Americans surpassed all forms of European egalitarianism, so in their industrial phase Americans were uninhibited by a preceding feudal agrarian structure, such as constrains France even today. It seems incredible that after two world wars of intense industrial pattern France still considers itself an agrarian economy.

Sirvan-Schreiber, author of the popular *Le Défi Americain* (*The American Challenge*), implies the time is ripe for France to take over the obsolescent American know-how that is proving so embarrassing and cumbersome in the electronic age. Just when electric speed-up is giving new relevance and meaning to all decentralized and "backward" ways, just when the "hippies" themselves have discovered a sympathy for all surviving forms of European feudalism—just at this time the French have resolved to do a more drastic centralizing job on themselves. Having developed the old hierarchical pyramid of the organization chart in their military and educational establishments, the French are now hoping to adopt outdated American know-how that goes with their updated industrial plant. Michel Crozier, a French sociologist, has written in *La Société Bloquée* (*The Stalled Society*): "We've gone to the extremes of centralization, to the very point where we are blocked in a system that defies reforms."

This situation includes the basic components of hang-ups that are worldwide. On the one hand, there is the temptation to accelerate old "jalopies" to jet speed, and, on the other hand, there is the complete overlooking of the fact that jet speeds have long been outmoded by telephone, Telex, radio, radar, and TV. At every level of human organization there are teams of specialists prescribing more intense specialism and speed for fragmented "hardware thinking."

Consultants Abroad

The advantages that Tocqueville detected in revolutionary America are now on the side of a retarded France. But the French leaders do not have a single insight into how to relate to the twentieth century. This is clear from their willingness to ape America, which has manifestly failed to relate to this century. It is easier to recognize one's difficulties mirrored in those who are remote from us.

On August 1, 1970, Richard Wigg, writing from London for the *Times*, surveyed the Cuban impasse, diagnosing the need for a more highly trained bureaucracy, and describing Cuba's futile attempt "to fuse administrative and party functions" in a frantic striving for "efficiency." Mr. Wigg would prescribe for the Cuban sugar patch the "French disease" of superliterate bureaucracy. Of course, Mr. Kidel, in his *Observer* article, and Mr. Wigg would both prescribe the "American disease" of "efficiency" as a cure for both countries. Just why intensified efficiency should destroy "effectiveness" at this phase of social organization eludes the journalists and the management consultants alike. NOW, EUROPE IS THE PLACE WHERE AMERICAN IDEAS GO WHEN THEY DIE, AND WHERE DOES THE "HARDWARE" GO? *"Efficiency" is no longer effective in an electric society that requires informal participation and involvement as a basis for any operation whatever*. It is this hidden environment that makes nonsense of all the most brilliant sociological discussions. The Japanese, with their more detached cultural vantage point, call it NEO-FORDIAN.

As an example of "resonance," on the same date line (August 1, 1970), Peter A. Cumming wrote in the *Globe and Mail* about the Eskimo fear of the Ottawa bureaucracy in Canada. It is interesting that a small community of Stone Age people should confront an enlightened and highly developed bureaucracy with the charge of total indifference to environmental ecology. Industrial developers, in the name of "efficiency," are eager to provide jobs in oil and mining for Eskimos, while destroying their environment and their prehistoric way of life. Cumming noted: "The Sachs Harbor people fear their livelihood will be destroyed and that after a few years as labourers for the white man they will sink into the morass of welfare and alcoholism which has befallen many people of the Eskimo communities." In the satellite age, when ecology has become a sentimental theme song, it remains for a handful of aborigines to denounce their "enlightened specialist protectors" for ignoring all ecological principle.

In all these areas in America, Cuba, France, and the Eskimo North alike, what appears as the hallmark of the "stalled society" is the impossibility of adapting to any change whatever. The editors of *Time*, March 23, 1970, describe:

AMERICA THE INEFFICIENT

*A land governed by Murphy's Law: If anything can
go wrong, it will—and at the worst possible time.*

The editors make a Kafkaesque inventory of disservices created by the new service environment. A cartoon by Joseph Ferris illustrates their theme with a husband trying to explain to his wife:

> You won't believe this but I couldn't call you because all the phones were out of order. The elevator got stuck. The train was late leaving and then broke down twice. My car wouldn't start at the station. Those phones wouldn't work either. I cried. I went to a bar. I got drunk. I staggered home. Here I am.

One can note here the drunk as dropout, trying "to get in touch"—bridging a complex situation by superinduced flexibility. *The paradox is that as services for everyone become environmental, private services for anyone vanish. We return to do-it-yourself.*

THE SEVEN-YEAR NICHE HAS GONE

The Scientific Systems of the Technical Age Have Become Art Forms

As we approach "instant" speeds of information, we have no choice but to anticipate the pattern of change itself. All contemporary decision making confirms the habits of the past in reacting with a futile attempt to adjust. Reaction is the age-old attempt to adjust to the old, which is seen as "present" and "future." At instant speeds all reaction and adjustment are inevitably too late to be relevant. *To keep up we must be far ahead.* It would have been proper to say "ahead with the poets and the artists," if they had not become so eager to adjust to the consumer mores. Now *they* are what we have to adjust to. Whereas the arts used to be navigational, the role of the arts can no longer be the same in the satellite age, when the Earth has become art form itself.

GOVERNMENT AS BIGGEST CONGLOMERATE MERGES HEALTH-EDUCATION-WELFARE-WARFARE

(*Measures Performance by GNP That Equates Services with Disservices*)

Government had begun in a modest way as the figure of the helmsman. The ship represented the entire human community. Today, the rudder has become much larger than the ship. The number of helmsmen are coextensive with the community. At the same time that government has spread its activities to cover the planet, the planet has contracted. Electric communications literally "send" the sender to the remotest corners and back, and bring the remotest people to us. The stretching of the bounds of government has coincided with the contraction of the social membrane. The differences between "inside" and "outside" have been eliminated at the same time.

Bureaucracy the Bugaboo Becomes the Business

Le trahison des clercs.
Baudelaire

In the age of the information environment all government and social functions are scrambled. Bureaucracy, the "bugaboo" innovation of the nineteenth century, was anathema as long as it was a mere *figure* in a vast social *ground* of private enterprise and decentralized community. With the spread of massive community services like the railway, traditional communities broke up. Central organizations of both social and commercial enterprise resulted. It was in this industrial *ground* that Max Weber, the German sociologist, undertook his classic analysis of bureaucracy as *figure*. In the words of the *International Encyclopedia of the Social Sciences*:

> According to Weber, a bureaucracy establishes a relation between legally instated authorities and their subordinate officials, which is characterized by defined rights and duties, prescribed in written regulations; authority relations between positions, which are ordered systematically; appointment and promotion based on contractual agreements and regulated accordingly; technical training or experience as a formal condition of employment; fixed monetary salaries; a strict separation of office and incumbent in the sense that the official does not own the "means of administration" and cannot appropriate the position; and administrative work as a full-time occupation.

What Max Weber, with his "visual" bias of Western scholarship, could not perceive was the dynamic change occurring in the pattern of bureaucracy itself, as the social *ground* shifted into the *aural-oral* mode. The classic parody of Weber's ideal is by Ellis Parker Butler in *Pigs Is Pigs* (1905).

How could the post office decide the sender's claim that a pair of guinea pigs were "pets" and that he could therefore send them through the mail for twenty-five cents postage? Explosive growth of guinea-pig population took over the entire Establishment before the Supreme Court handed down its decision: whatever else they might be, "Pigs ıs Pigs."

Presidential Ploys and Vibes

Time, June 8, 1970, contrasted presidential management styles in the White House:

> John Kennedy . . . deliberately organized his staff to circumvent the massive federal bureaucracy [by dialogue]. Nixon prefers an orderly organization that frees him to concentrate, mostly alone, on one big question at a time [by memo].

George Reedy, President Johnson's press secretary, observed plaintively: "From the President's standpoint, the greatest staff problem is that of maintaining contact with the world's reality that lies outside the White House walls."

EXECUTIVE AS EXILE

> Cry cry what shall I cry?
> The first thing to do is to form the committees:
> The consultative councils, the standing committees, select committees
>   and sub-committees.   T. S. Eliot, "Difficulties of a Statesman"

In Toronto's *Globe and Mail* (January 6, 1971), John Sewell describes his initiation into the Toronto political establishment:

ALDERMANIC DISMAY

> I certainly learned things. I learned that the Executive Committee controls Council and that almost nothing slips through its fingers. . . . I found that it has been almost impossible to do anything in Council itself. Council is a place where people exchange speeches, poke at each other with questions and then vote. Nothing close to debate takes place there. It's a talking freak show, "full of sound and fury, signifying nothing."

What Alderman Sewell had discovered was the age-old fact that all committees are in-groups necessarily devoted to gossip rather than to dialogue or to doing business. That is why the strategy for even small accomplishments through committee requires outrageous motions. The job of the committee is then to moderate and gloss the outrage. Monstrous proposals, when moderated by the committee's "wisdom," are readily passed. The proposals may still be monstrous, even when tidied up. Such has been the history of city "development." Sewell continues:

> One of my most dismaying discoveries has been to learn how much people want politicians to be traditional. Presumably people do like to be ruled more than they like to rule, and thus they are all too quick to let the alderman make the decision, rather than tell him what they want him to do.

Sewell found the mere position alienated him from his constituents with whom he had worked closely before. He also found that "power isolates." He was isolated from the struggles involved in small discussions. This bred resentment. Equally frustrating was the relation of the media to all his activities: "They never seemed to report the crucial things." When he walked dramatically out of a council meeting, the media ignored his reasons for leaving, but played up the walkout and the name calling. His concern is that if the media cannot cope with the processes and the issues, what are the people to do?

The aristocrat may be the one who never cramps *his* style, but the organization chart soon dictates what the style is. The people served are the content of any service environment whatever. The *meaning* of the service is the relationship that it forms with the person served. The *message* of the service as a man-made medium is the totality of its effects.

> A kink in his arts over sense.
>   James Joyce, *Finnegans Wake*

Alderman Sewell expresses the complex interplay of forces when encountering a new *ground* or environment while that *ground* transforms the political process. The residual bits and pieces of the organization chart still impose their "message" of fragmentation by reducing his role in the community to a job in bureaucratic isolation.

BIG BUREAUCRACIES AND BIG BUSINESS ARE NOW INSEPARABLE, IF ONLY BECAUSE BIG BUSINESS IS BUREAUCRACY

When, however, government sources attempt to foster industrial development in "backward" countries, the ordinary pattern of complementarity is reversed. In the age of electric information environment, all "backward" areas exist against a *ground* of highly developed knowledge industries. Such was not the case in the nineteenth century. Colonialism was the transnational form of bureaucratic development. Colonialism was the means of extending new services to "backward" areas, in return for which these areas temporarily yielded up their raw materials. Now the "colonials" are coming "home" to roost. It is easy to estimate the disservices created by the colonial services. It is less easy to estimate the disservices inflicted upon "advanced" populations by their acceptance of the services now provided by the new governmental agencies, irrespective of ideology.

From Top Brass to Plain-clothes Bureaucrats

It is necessary to note that these government services, as we experience them in the Western world, are meaningless without the *ground* of private enterprise that precedes them. That is why in underdeveloped countries that attempt to achieve the *effects* of private enterprise by means of bureaucracy, there is a tendency for bureaucracy to become the social *ground*. Both *figures* and *grounds* in such a society are government officials. In the *ground* of an industrial society we are accustomed to "figures" who are "self-made" men. In contrast, many European countries brought their feudal *ground* with them to the very threshold of industrial development. England and America moved more gradually through the industrial phase, slowly eroding feudal forms during a prolonged industrialization. The result was that the bureaucratic cadres of England and America are occupied by business types devoid of the "braid" and the "brass" that are the mark of the abrupt transition from feudal to industrial state.

Ombudsman: The People's Private Eye

Following the Scandinavian example, many industrial countries are introducing the "ombudsman," or people's agent, who may freely cross all bureaucratic bounds to deal with complaints against government administrators.

The "comic-opera police states" like the "banana republics" lack government officials who have undergone a long apprenticeship in a sophisticated industrial community. Naturally, they are ill at ease when assigned the task of creating industrial communities where nothing of this sort has existed previously. The government functionary assigned an industrial role in an agrarian community is somewhat in the position of the contemporary computer-system specialist attempting to introduce electric speeds and functions into an old industrial structure. A computer-system specialist is as helpless in modern industry and government as an industrial engineer in a nonindustrial country.

Computer Systems as Comic Opera

It is to be noted that the dilemma of the computer-system specialist who tries to speed up mechanized processes of production and management alike has a parallel in the previous age of mechanization, when industrial engineers moved into agrarian culture. This phase can still be observed in Russia and China, where technologists still struggle with the tenacious peasantry. Meantime the United States moves into a period of "inefficiency" and breakdown resulting from the application of electric speeds to mechanical processes. The computer-system specialist, in practice, is entirely a product of old literate and mechanical training. He thinks of electric technology as a quantitative increase in the performance potential of the old mechanized systems. In practice, what occurs is that the old system is simply shaken to pieces by the "vibes" to which it is subjected:

> Speech moves at the speed of light: writing moves at the speed of the
> alphabet.   James Stephens

In the Western world the movement of mail has long been subjected to telephone and Telex speed-up and interruption. If anything is really important today, it is phoned first and written later. (Newspaper copy long ago ceased to be moved by mail.) At the same time, mail services have slowed down greatly. Letters that used to be mailed in the morning and get delivered in the afternoon are now likely to take much longer. In England, until World War II, ordinary homes received several deliveries a day, including one after dinner (like India today). As speed-up in the environmental services occurs, there is a slowdown of the old system. Inefficiency is the natural accompaniment of all speed-up, simply because it shakes the old system apart. As the old system begins to shake loose, experts are called in to buttress it with the latest technologies. Starting with the pickup truck, and then air-mail delivery, speed-up moved toward impasse in the sorting sector.

In prewar Dublin, for example, a friend employed in the post office tells of how, during the sorting process, a strange item—say a letter for Mrs. O'Brien with insufficient address—would be waved aloft by one of the sorters who shouted the name around the room. He was typically answered with volunteer information: "She lives on Victoria Road. That letter is from her daughter-in-law in County Downs." He said further that there were very few insoluble cases in a situation where they could pool their corporate experience by direct oral methods. The postmen on the routes took their turn at sorting the mail. Mere separation of those functions ensured slowdown. This type of separation of functions was further increased by the introduction of a supervisor who specialized in speeding up the fragmented work process. Backtracking for corrections, easy at low speeds, becomes disastrous at high speeds. In the computer world mistakes become "impossible" in all senses. *Whereas mechanical "dehumanization" wrecked the person, electric super-"humanization" wrecks the entire system.*

It is no longer necessary to labor this type of example, since the attempt to introduce the computer into various services, from banks to schools, has jeopardized their very existence. The dissatisfactions with postal systems are so pervasive for employees and customers alike that there has been an extensive return to private couriers. EXTREME CENTRALISM OF INPUTS BREEDS DECENTRALISM OF OUTPUTS. No "hardware" power or process of mechanical type can withstand the decentralizing power of electric information. That is why the postal breakdown cannot be shored up by any system of "reprivatization." In all processes of innovation, while the immediately preceding technology is scrapped, its earlier forms are retrieved in the cliché-archetype pattern.

Matching in Echoland

In *The Age of Discontinuity,* Peter Drucker stresses the incompatibility between "governing" and "doing," and he advocates

> the nongovernmental institutions of the society of organizations for the actual "doing," i.e., for performance, operations, execution. Such a policy might be called "reprivatization. . . ."
>
> Government would be seen as society's resource for the determination of major objectives, and as the "conductor" of social diversity. . . .
>
> The real role of the capitalist is to be expendable. His role is to take risks and to take losses as a result. . . . Business is the most adaptable and most flexible of the institutions around. It is the one that has a clear, even though limited, performance test. It is the one that has a yardstick. . . .
>
> Therefore, it is the one best equipped to manage. For if there is a yardstick for results, one can determine the efficiency and adequacy of the efforts. . . . It is the only institution where control need not be an emotional or a moral issue, where in talking "control" we discuss "value" and not "values."

"Performance," borrowed from the car industry, finally reaches the common denominator of bucks only. The box office becomes the ultimate measure of performance, just as the car has become show biz.

Management by Myopia

What Drucker ignores is that the nineteenth-century *ground* of mechanization enormously increased the separation of "thinking" and "doing" in government and business alike, whereas today's *ground* of information speed-up has reversed this trend. *Now, thinking is doing.*

The "reprivatization" cure is like handing the railways over to the airlines, or trying to prop up declining Hollywood by calling in NBC and CBS. *What is in conflict is not human efficiency or motivation but technologies of incompatible speeds.*

Now Speed-up Etherealizes Old Securities

The stock exchanges in America are in the same fix as the postal system, even though they are not government bureaucracies. Stock exchanges parallel the rise of the labor-commodity market. Whereas the labor market offered the private services of individuals to corporate enterprises, the stock exchanges offered the corporate services of public enterprises to private individuals. Both became commodities in a competitive market of prices. The actual distinction between making and implementing policy had already vanished by the time its ghost became clearly visible in the rear-view mirror. Drucker's prescription of more market medicine serves more as a "lift" for old myopic management than as a stimulus for new institutional vigor. The disease is specialized fragmentation. But Drucker insists upon more fragmented specialism as the remedy, just when the needs are for total involvement and the return to human scale.

What H. A. Innis calls the "penetrative power of the price system" has had strange effects upon both the labor and stock markets. Pricing systems originate in uniform and repeatable commodity services. Without the uniform mechanized processes of industrial society there would be no base or *ground* for the *figure* of "securities." That is why, in the age of electric information, which dissolves the old *ground* of mechanical production, the entire basis of stock-market superstructure is undermined. When information services supersede in scope the old "hardware" infrastructure provided by rail, road, car, plumbing, and the like, then the superstructure of the stock market is assailed by intolerable pressures of speed.

"Hardware" Softens as "Software" Hardens

The old "hardware" basis for prices has gone. In the new "software" world of design and information, the stocks and securities that had imperceptibly assumed the status of "hardware" commodities crumpled under the impact of radio in the twenties and TV in the sixties. The gilt began to drip off the edges of the securities. Their real character became palpable once more. The stock exchange, which had originated in the world of the new dailies of the steam-powered presses, gradually became a major source of news. At first the product or creature of news services, it came to dominate news and politics after the telegraph, and then succumbed to improvement and enlargement of news in the age of radio and TV services.

In the 1960's, stock-market sales were occurring at a speed in excess of existing means of transferring and storing securities. Like the postal system, which had been subjected to similar strains by the new speeds, the stock exchange began to close down in order to catch up. As a corporate service for distributing corporate services to private individuals, it is self-liquidating.

With telephone and TV it is not so much the message as the sender that is "sent." It is not so much the receiver who gets the message as the receiver who is brought simultaneously to the originating point of the message. The paradox is that in the age of "hardware" the message was relatively light and abstract. In the age of electric information, that which is transmitted or transported is both thing and person. In the mechanical age of "hardware" the "message" was relatively soft and light, witness *The Reason Why*. A mere misunderstanding of a scribble released a historic "hardware" explosion, "the charge of the light brigade."

Tomorrow Is Our Permanent Address

Today, the satellite environment has scrapped the entire nature process of the planet. This was not the result of an inadvertent blooper but of a relentless pressure for more speed of information. The resulting increase of environmental information has in effect scrapped everything known as human organizations while at the same time retrieving innumerable forgotten forms of human organization from the most remote and prehistoric past. The things we assumed as the *ground* for human existence have simply been canceled.

5

Hard Experience v. Soft Knowledge

Inner Ideals and Outer Goals

The information world drives the corporate organization inward. What it had previously pursued as a tangible product it now tends to regard as an *ideal* of service. Formerly, the "ideals" had merely been carefully specified procedures. They corresponded to Plato's "ideal forms" or archetypes. With the rising tide of information flow around us, the patterns are no longer incidental or external to the operation, but integral. They become the main activity.

In other words, as the corporation internalizes its goals, it acquires the character of the older centralized universities. The universities in turn have tended strongly toward the selling of outer goals for growth and production. Their facilities have become theaters for entrepreneurial exploitation. The climate of enterprise inside a big modern university is like the fabled "jungle" of nineteenth-century business. No contemporary business could sustain the uninhibited slaughter among these academic Jasons in pursuit of the "golden fleece." The new Argonauts are not the "land-grabbers" but the "grant-grabbers." The accumulated spoils of generations of ruthless money specialism now nourish new escalations of academic specialism.

The New Golden Fleecers

This major merger of the old commercial jungle and the new groves of academe manifests a much greater transformation. The universities and the business world become mere *figures* against a much bigger *ground* that has been created by the same forces of old wealth and new knowledge. This *ground* is nothing less than the transformation of the traditional aims and directions of the Eastern and the Western hemispheres. Under the impact of Western "hardware" the Orient shifted its interest to the *outer* world almost in exact ratio to the transfer of Western interest to the *inner* world.

Not only did the nineteenth century discover the unconscious of the private citizen; its anthropologists and archaeologists explored the collective unconscious of preliterate societies, "the people who dream." The Japanese, for example, awakening from the corporate tribal dream of centuries, were only too conscious of the technological causes from the West.

The Western world, fascinated by the meeting with the East and with tribal societies of high culture, became increasingly unaware of the role played by its own electric technology in initiating and reinforcing the "inner trip" that the whole society was now committed to. The East became much more self-conscious and individual in its encounter with the electric age, which had the reverse effect upon the Western world.

Management by Self-Deception

Somnambulism is the normal response to new knowledge. The West pays a price of somnambulism and loss of self-awareness as it extends its power over the world. Many would consider it a terrifying fate for a conqueror to fall asleep in the very moment of conquest.

In the age of the new knowledge industries the paradox of somnambulism amidst vast new acquisitions of knowledge was amply documented by Alexander Pope in *The Dunciad* early in the eighteenth century. He lived when it was quite observable that floods of printed materials had lowered the levels of conversation and social awareness to the point where a universal DULLNESS covered all. We now know that sleep and dullness can be the effects of overstimulation and excess of data. Max Picard has devoted an entire volume to this subject. It is called *The World of Silence*, and he says: "Man, however, who has become a mere appendage of verbal noise, believes decreasingly in the reality of his own existence." But the "sonorous silence" of Joyce is the *ground* for discovery, just as noise is the source of music.

What Max Picard missed in his rich study of silence as the *ground* for speech and all emergent institutions was the haptic or tangible, tactile character of silence. It is the interval in the *figure-ground* relation of sound and silence. The very structure of the age of information is inevitably the structure of discontinuity and resonance. The critics of audile *discontinuity* as the new electric structure too often ignore that the visual age of continuity was the age of nuts and bolts and hang-ups. The structural components of the new age of discontinuity will be instant awareness of the events in the total field. This cannot be a *visual* so much as an *acoustic* awareness, conferring much empathy and sympathy for the diversity and language of forms. It will be an age of intuitive and artistic preferences. The West has already begun to explore and conquer that fabulous and mythic realm brought into expression by the arts of the great Oriental cultures. Starting where they left off, we are likely to move very swiftly into even more dazzling dimensions. We may join the Balinese in saying, "We have no art; we do everything as well as possible."

GOVERNMENT AS THE MOST EXTENSIVE FORM OF HUMAN ORGANIZA-
TION NOW YIELDS TO ECOLOGY AND TO THE PROGRAMMING OF SPACE-
SHIP EARTH AS AN ECO-BOX.

The future of government lies in the area of psychic ecology and can no longer be considered on a merely national or international basis. The bureaucratic hierarchies, structured to distribute old "hardware" services piecemeal, depend upon an earlier industrial ground for their form but not their efficacy. Satisfactions enjoyed by the bureaucratic hierarchy are less related to the work performed than to the status enjoyed by the members of the hierarchy. The notorious example of the welfare agencies is analyzed by Daniel Patrick Moynihan in his report *The Negro Family: The Case for National Action.*

Lee Rainwater and William L. Yancey, in *The Moynihan Report and the Politics of Controversy*, discuss many implications of the report and note that it seemed to be

> . . . an attack on the welfare establishment's approach to Negro problems—its implicit message was that they had not cared enough ever to really understand the problem. . . . The bureaucracies themselves were incapable of solving the problem. The welfare establishment was hamstrung by its history and by the necessity to defend existing programs.

Moynihan is well aware of the President's power to put on a public, his "power to bless: if he talks about a subject, he can make it respectable for discussion."

Automated Cold Charity

In his article "The Crisis in Welfare" in *Public Interest* (Winter, 1968), Moynihan quotes Governor Rockefeller, who considers the increase of welfare dependency with the rise of prosperity as "the most serious economic paradox of our times." Moynihan adds:

> The present welfare system is the social equivalent of an automated factory: the input goes in and the output comes out untouched by human hands. If anything goes wrong it is the machinery that is to blame. . . . [There is] growing evidence that the more prestigious forms of casework and counseling had relatively little effect on the clients, however much they enhanced the status of the counselors.

Moynihan concludes: "The true issue about welfare is not what it costs the taxpayers but what it costs the recipient." Moynihan both substantiates and provides the key to the paradox: *the more effort that is exerted to get welfare to the needy through bureaucratic procedures, the more encumbered and futile the operation.*

GAS OR GARB?

The Return of the Longhouse

Speculation is rife on just how soon the annual cost of supporting welfare bureaucracies, whether private or public, will exceed the cost of a guaranteed annual salary to provide subsistence for all. In the *ancien régime* aristocrats were already herding into hotels, forced "to eat cake" in Paris. Now, the kids are in effect demanding immediate guaranteed annual room and board. On October 3, 1970, Ken Romain reported from Vancouver to Toronto's *Globe and Mail*:

JERICHO ARMY BASE STAYS OCCUPIED
AS YOUNGSTERS DEFY ORDER TO QUIT

The provincial Government has been subsidizing part of the cost of the food that is being brought to the building twice a day by a Vancouver welfare organization known as Inter City. And, with the order to close yesterday, the federal Government apparently is now washing its hands of them, although it has said it would have subsidy grants available for the establishment of hostels in the city.

The educational and welfare establishments are of the same character. The more ardently educators seek to convey their packages to the uninstructed, the more peremptory their rejection by the young. In the case of both the needy and the ignorant, there are new and unacknowledged environments of affluence and information that render meaningless the old services of welfare and education.

When the Young Teach and the Old Learn

No one has ever learned from the past how to live in the present except in an oral society, where the past is now. The kids intuitively grasp the wisdom of the primitive. They drop out from "visual" hierarchies to get in touch with "acoustic" harmonies. *Time* (August 17, 1970) notes that "50 per cent of all collegians now belong to an alienated culture, hostile to service and technology."

It is affluence that creates poverty, just as learning creates ignorance. These old and familiar adages take on a completely different character at present, when multibillion-dollar service environments of travel and entertainment are freely available to all. This does not concern mere charter flights and cheap tourist fares. Far more significant is the fact that the TV viewer is actually at the point he is viewing, and what he is viewing has become the actual environment.

JOBS CREATE UNEMPLOYMENT

No Role Player Need Apply

If payment were proportional to the degree of "labor productivity," children learning their mother tongue would automatically be the most highly paid members of society. Both their motivation and their involvement are total, and their achievement correspondingly exceeds the performance of any other social group. It has long been recognized that the acquisition of one's mother tongue evokes faculties associated with the actions of genius. Just as the vast majority of mankind has always leaped into the act of learning the mother tongue, so, be it noted, are there few if any "backward" children with learning problems in preliterate society. By the same token, a pregnant mother would be highly paid for her creative role in producing a new member of the community while nourishing and instructing her social dependents and associates. As science reveals the work of necessary social purgation performed each night by sleeping citizens, they, in turn, would be suitably paid.

In the same way, the elders of the community—the social liaison with past experience—provide the means of continuity and adaptation, a role that the very young are ill-suited to perform. Those who are acquiring their earliest experience have no means of comparison and contrast to relate themselves to social innovations. For the young, innovation erases identity. For the mature, new service environments merely ruffle their equanimity (cf., Margaret Mead's *flexible elders* and *rigid youth*).

"The Royal Divorce" (*James Joyce*)

Whereas the reading public defines areas of culture by divorcing EYE and EAR, Adam Smith, in the eighteenth century, redefined the realm of Nature as laws of the market. The examples given in the preceding paragraphs are by way of reminding ourselves that the main employment of the community is not contained within the pattern of any marketable job whatever. The real work, now as ever, is done not by highly paid job holders but by deeply involved role players. No role player could be hired to do for pay what he gladly does for nothing. Returning from this aspect of society to the specter of unemployment, it is plain that it is an artificial creation designed to expedite processes by fragmentation that translates roles into jobs. These jobs are for sale. They are products of a contrived market mechanism. Once more it appears that the dominion of market pushed to its limits recalls the kingdom of man and revokes the market regime.

Instant Expectations and Practical Wasdom

The popular approach to the "unemployment problem" in the confines of the market system is for "instant" or immediate jobs. This expectation is a built-in pattern of a specialist, fragmented culture. Toronto's *Globe and Mail* carried these two headlines on the same day, January 29, 1971:

SEARCH FOR INSTANT HAPPINESS SEEN BRINGING WIDER DRUG USE

DAVIS REJECTS "INSTANT POLICIES" IN CAMPAIGN FOR PREMIERSHIP

To the degree that people have become alienated from their work by extreme specialism and noninvolvement, they assume that employment, like any other service such as water or electricity, can be turned on or off.

Especially in the electric age, people expect "instant" effects in all sectors of their society, whether in entertainment or education or politics. *It is precisely the instant dimension of "electric" living that constitutes both the problem and the solution.* The hang-up is to transfer the instant character from the new information environment to the old "hardware" world of the assembly line. This is where confusion naturally occurs in any sudden transition from one structure to another.

A "comic" grievance is expressed in the story of the puzzled child watching his father change a flat tire in the mud and the rain: "Daddy, why don't you switch the channel?" Father: "Look, this is not TV. This is for real!" The confusion between the old "hardware" and the new "software" worlds illustrated by this anecdote pervades the adult world today. The "instant" job wisher expects to see the old work supplied as a package but presented on the new medium of his electric world, as if he were turning on an old silent movie on his TV set. The first use of a new medium is always a replay of an old one. To solve unemployment by replaying the old work and job patterns in the new information environment is the natural impulse of all "practical" men with their feet on the ground.

Quantum Leap from Package to Process

The "quantum leap" into the new instant world of pattern recognition is not for them. Rather, they are inclined to find ways and means of getting out of their running shorts without taking their feet off the ground. Instead of replaying the old "silents" as a way of creating new jobs in the TV age, there is totally new work to be done. The new services, such as TV, create not only a few extra jobs but vast new publics to be served and the need for totally new programs. The new "work" and the new "jobs" are in these new services. Neither the jobs nor the publics bear any relation to the work and skills exercised in the preceding "hardware" world. The gap is as great as that between the traditional craftsman and the first assembly lines. This electric gap, however, is constituted in a totally different way. The old assembly-line worker is now conned into role-playing activities, which offer even more human satisfactions than the traditional crafts that were scrapped by the assembly line. UNLIKE THE OLD SPECIALISM, CONTEMPORARY FORMS OF HUMAN EMPLOYMENT DEMAND THE CREATIVE POWERS OF DESIGN THROUGH PATTERN RECOGNITION AND INCLUSIVE SOCIAL AWARENESS.

"CREATIVITY" AS SUPERJOB

The Right of Everyman

For those who understand the nature of the new age of information, work and learning and leisure now tend to merge in a single process of continuous fulfillment.

"Ancien Régime"

What about the *ancien régime* of industrial production and markets? Paradoxically, the word *"régime,"* which arose from the spread of military regimentation, has long been used to describe the relics of the feudal system, buried by the French Revolution (1789). It is natural to perceive the old in terms of the new, and vice versa. The huge regimentation and homogenization imposed by the French revolutionaries by means of the "metric system" accelerated the industrial revolution. Yet this metrification, so necessary to "hardware" production and marketing, is far from complete in the 1970's. North America and England are now moving to liquidate traditional features of currency and measurement as a means of linking themselves to new markets. Maximum effect and trauma are being registered on the old industrial front, while the "economic" action has shifted to the new information environment. Such policies, however, typify interim measures of transition, which are mistaken for major confrontations with the new reality.

The User Is the Content

It is appropriate, while mentioning the *ancien régime* and the liquidation of royalty, to observe that royalty as a service environment has become a new democratic possibility in the electric age. Just as the work of royalty had always been to *grow up* into a hereditary role, so the work of the "electronic" child and adult is increasingly and typically characterized by the learning and growing process itself. As explained in *From Cliché to Archetype,* the process of the new environmental form of technology includes the dynamic of retrieving and restoring very old forms of human organization. Whereas the old "star system" created the "queen for a day" as a consumer commodity, the new age of electric-information role playing restores "leadership" as a service environment."

The Work Force of the Electric World Is a Community of Learning

LEARN BABY LEARN

The new university cannot be located geographically, neither can it be restricted ideologically in an information environment. Subjects and departments become as irrelevant as bricks and mortar and lectures. Newman caught a hint of this coming development in his *Scope and Nature of University Education* (*Everyman, p.* 122):

"I protest to you, gentlemen, that if I had to choose between a so-called university which dispensed with residence and tutorial superintendence, and gave its degrees to any person who passed an examination in a wide range of subjects, and a university which had no professors or examinations at all, but merely brought a number of young men together for three or four years, and then sent them away, as the university of Oxford is said to have done some sixty years since, if I were asked which of these two methods was the better discipline of the intellect—mind, I do not say which is *morally* the better, for it is plain that compulsory study must be a good and idleness an intolerable mischief—but if I must determine which of the two courses was the more successful in training, moulding, enlarging the mind, which sent out men the more fitted for their secular duties, which produced better public men, men of the world, men whose names would descend to posterity; I have no hesitation in giving the preference to that university which did nothing, over that which exacted of its members an acquaintance with every science under the sun."

New York *Times* Service, Watts, California, February 23, 1971

The teacher, by definition, is a role player and not a job holder, except by accident. The abrupt demand of the young that their teachers be totally involved may appear to be matched by the student "teach-ins" and "sit-ins." The students protest against the fragmentation of the learning process into specialized packages by usurping the scraps and dregs of bureaucratic power, such as still exist around the educational establishment. On the other hand, the student response to the electric environment is to demand a deepening of insight into their studies, and to ignore the administrative functions as too trite to be worth attention. Two reports by William Johnson in Toronto's *Globe and Mail* (February 2, 1971) reveal these conflicting trends:

SINGING STUDENTS HALT MEETING AT U. OF T.

Students at the University of Toronto tried to sing their way to parity of representation with faculty members yesterday at a meeting of the general committee of the Council of the Faculty of Arts and Science.

STUDENT SEATS GO VACANT ON BOARDS AT CARLTON

Carlton University students expressed a thundering indifference to sharing in university government yesterday as three-quarters of the student seats to be filled in annual elections went vacant for lack of candidates.

The teachers themselves are the "community of learning." If their dialogue is interrupted by excessive specialism or excessive administrative work, the level of intellectual employment sinks. As that level rises, the total impact of the teacher in his function of communicating knowledge by dialogue (rather than by lecture) reaches ever new intensities.

It is the same with the city, the government, and the business world today. The "wired planet" has no boundaries and no monopolies of knowledge. The affairs of the world are now dependent upon the "highest information" of which man is capable. (In the world of information theory, the

word "information" means *pattern,* not raw data.) The boundaries between the world of affairs and the community of learning have ceased to
exist. The workaday world now demands encyclopedic wisdom. Ecology is
the simultaneous awareness of the interplay of the total field of processes.
This simultaneity pushes the most banal situations into high relevance.
Under these conditions, the old form of specialized job has lost meaning. It
was meaningful only at very low speeds, but it has now been *assumed* into
patterns of electric speeds. This change of pace from "production line" to
"on-line" computer programming has been ignored, just as the shift from
"hardware" to "software" accelerates, making the old categories meaningless.

One way of perceiving the transition from the older organization of work
into the new community of learning is to observe the manifold varieties of
"moonlighting" that mark the course of this change. There is also today's
growing retrieval of old skills and ancient artifacts with new relevance (the
cliché-archetype pattern). The complex and complementary patterns of
dropout and drop-in as effects of speed-up in electric information flow are
central themes of this book.

Slaves Look Up While Freemen Look At

Job stability pushed to extreme creates instability. Reuter (February 22,
1971) reports from Stockholm on what is happening in "one of the world's
most stable democracies":

STRIKE-TORN SWEDEN

Most welfare aid and legal proceedings have been stopped. . . . The
widespread dispute was further complicated following a dramatic
Government announcement Friday that as of March 3 a large number
of officers would be locked out of their barracks over wage demands.

Charles A. Reich, in *The Greening of America,* comments on what is
occurring in "the world's greatest consumer society":

The first signs of consumer revolt are beginning to appear. . . . On
the New York commuter railroads, which constantly break down, people have been known to refuse to pay their fares. When the telephone
company changed to digit dialing, there were minor rebellions. There
have been local revolts against prices in supermarkets, and mutterings
against the airlines. One day in New York a subway train broke down,
and the passengers were asked to get off and board another train. But
the people, silently and quite spontaneously, simply sat there and refused to leave. Small signs, but ominous.

What Reich does not mention is that the *Greening* is "The Cooling of
America" via TV (see *Time,* February 22, 1971).

For industrial man, unprepared for leisure, loss of job means loss of identity, which leads to violence. But for youth born in a surround of global services leisure is the *norm*. Such youth are like gentlemen with no visible means of support.

The growing clamor for more jobs and more pay heralds the obsolescence of job classifications and pay scales alike. The main action is now shifting beyond production for market to global role playing. In this new situation the market itself has returned to theater—a place to haggle rather than a place to stand (as Cyrus the Great remarked more than two millenniums ago).

GNP IS A BILL OF GOODS

The dream of reason produces monsters.
Goya, *Caprichos*

Nineteenth-century economists like J. M. Keynes introduced the term "gross national product" as a means of relating the older functions of government to the old "hardware" economy. The GNP is not only outdated but consumer-oriented. The term began to be used absent-mindedly to include both services and disservices. In estimating GNP there was no possibility of taking into account the disappearance of satisfactions resulting from innovation. In the GNP the matter of defense expenditure was as much a major item as the hospitals for war victims. How to estimate "products" such as emotional security or belligerent euphoria was as impossible as putting a price tag on the national image. In the age of instant information, satisfactions resulting from all kinds of nationalism have become elusive and even illusory. Yet the budget for these items is constantly increasing. They are considered justified on the grounds of "morale" boosting. When the disservices and dissatisfaction of a growing GNP obviously exceed the services and satisfaction, the whole concept of GNP crumbles like the Dow-Jones index. The GNP can no longer be measured by the currency it creates.

"LE GNP EST MORT"
"VIVE LE ROI"

Prominence Is the Harbinger of Obsolescence

If the GNP has become an obsolete tool, it is another way of saying that it has just begun to penetrate the entire system. It has become the national icon. "Return on investment" (ROI) has met a similar fate. Meanwhile, econometrics, the latest application of mathematics and computer technology for measuring the economic performance and cost effectiveness of government and private business alike, relies on the foundation of these old clichés.

Robert Duffy, reporting from London to the Toronto *Globe and Mail*, September 22, 1970, headlines the uncritical use of "modern measures":

THE BATTLE TO SAVE LONDON LANDMARKS

Standards of Cost Effectiveness Are a Hazard to
Many of London's Famous Buildings

It is not enough to apply current values in deciding whether or not it is worth saving a piece of architecture. Fifteen years ago Victorian buildings (like Scotland Yard) were little prized; fifty years ago nobody cared about Georgian ones.

With the disappearance of "modern measures" as valid criteria in political economy and private business, we revert to the immediate human encounter with fluctuating services and disservices of regions and cultures, all of which are now becoming simultaneously accessible. Mere growth, whether of GNP or dinosaur, means simplification by specialism—today's formula for dying hard.

EVALUATION IS HOMOGENIZATION

Transforming Common Sense into Common Denominator

In *Behind the Executive Mask*, Alfred J. Marrow considers the heart of the problem:

> In the past, managerial control rested on the authority-obedience relationship between the manager and his subordinates. But in these days we see that tight control has the effect of limiting rather than stimulating productivity; and greater efficiency, profits, and growth seem to call for a different kind of approach. Today's manager, whether the head of a huge corporation or the supervisor of eight delivery men, is learning the limited power of control by coercion, for such control eventually causes conflict, apathy, and resistance.

To Be Uncritically Engaged in Doing What Everyone Else Is Doing Is the Accepted Human Use of Human Beings

What has come to be called the "Hawthorne effect" is the sort of thing that Marrow would have us heed. Although the Western Electric Company (A.T. & T.) carried out the experiment in its Hawthorne plant during the 1930's, its meaning was little understood. The experiment set out to discover the kind of physical conditions that would increase work output, *i.e.*, what sort of "input" would increase product output. In other words, a purely quantitative "hardware" approach.

Where It Was at Hawthorne

What baffled the experimenters was the improvement of output, regardless of what *physical changes* were made in the "input." Both worse lighting and heating and better lighting and comforts led to increased physical output. There was a nonphysical hidden environment that had been unintentionally created by the experimenters. It was the environment of attention and observation, which upgraded the workers, making them actors in a new drama. This dramatic situation released new impulses and energies of the workers through participation. All forms of "new management" in various and diversified patterns seek to activate precisely this drama as the alternative to mere authoritarian command structure.

Commando Module

Another illustration of this principle of participation can be taken from military experience. During World War II, commando raids called for a new kind of aggregation of human resources. This in turn related to great speed-up in the movement of human personnel as well as great increase in the portability and firepower of weaponry. One man could carry enough explosive power to destroy a dam. He had to know where to place the charge. Increased demands of knowledge go with decrease in the amounts of "hardware." The dynamics of both miniaturization and "etherealization" call for an inclusive awareness of total situations. Before a commando raid was mounted, the practice was for officers and men to confer as equals. The military staff-and-line pattern of command was effaced. What was here suspended was the entire structure of military organization, which had been transferred to the commercial establishment at the end of the nineteenth century. Instead of approaching the problem from any particular point of view, they swarmed over the problem as a group, using their total knowledge to encounter its many unexpected facets. This procedure was in direct contrast to General Staff plans prepared by experts to meet all conceivable eventualities. The "blueprints and specifications" were scrapped. As in an Operations Research séance, these men stormed the problem from all sides. The individual expert yielded to the wider range of perception provided by the corporate dialogue. The nineteenth century would have said: "Many hands make light work." The twentieth century translates this: "Many minds make much light."

THE LAW OF IMPLEMENTATION

There is still a widely held assumption that the most advanced discoveries can be translated into action only by the older forms of organization. *The "Law of Implementation" is that the newest awareness must be processed by the established procedures.* In the commando conference, those who were to implement the decisions were present and helped to make the discoveries that became the *action*. The commando team did not "delegate" but acted as a uniform task force. Its dialogue became dramatized. There was no question that once they had begun to confer they would then fall back on the old command structure for implementation.

"Ca'canny"—"Work to Rule"—Speed-up Creates Slowdown

In contrast, consider how the insights of dialogue of "commando" teams in our workaday world are handed over to committees and bureaucracies for implementation. Had the commando unit been required to seek budgetary resources and to manufacture its own weapons before going into action, there would have been the same kind of delays and miscarriages with which we are familiar in every area of our institutions.

The discrepancy in business between "R and D" and "Operations" ensures that every valuable insight will be reduced to a grotesque parody of itself.

Uncontrolled Roles for Production Unlimited

Economy does not need an actuary; it needs a visionary.
Antony Jay, *Management and Machiavelli*

A notorious example of the "commando" approach to war production was the firm of Jack and Heintz. These entrepreneurs discovered that while launched on a program of conventional war contracts a startling transformation occurred when they ventured to involve their total personnel in an unstructured swarming approach to the problems of increasing output. All "time-and-motion" controls were discarded. Men could work as long or little as they chose. There was no uniform schedule imposed. Everybody improvised and shared their discoveries for maximizing output. Production soared.

Controlled Jobs for Production Limited

When the war ended, an attempt was made to methodize and formalize the process that had achieved the phenomenal production records. The "Law of Implementation" ended the play. The quantitative approach was used for embalming what had been a spontaneous performance. The production engineers had moved in to regularize the situation by reducing it to the old pattern. They went back to work. The fun was over. Production fell.

If World War II as an environment favored involvement and eager energy, the much greater strain placed on old structures by speed-up and "electric rim spin" today seems to have the opposite effect. The dropout succeeds the enthusiastic participant. During World War II industrial personnel could have a dramatic sense of role playing. The expedient of "job enrichment" merely attempts to remedy fragmentation by handing a man a few more fragments to assemble. A watchmaker, instead of handling a spring, is allowed to manipulate a few wheels as well. *Job enrichment is no substitute for role playing.*

Here Comes Everybody

Judson Gooding, writing in *Fortune*, July, 1970, about "Blue-collar Blues on the Assembly Line," describes the current situation:

> The absentee problem is especially severe in the automobile industry . . . with old, ultrasimplified methods originally designed not only to avoid waste motion but to accommodate unschooled immigrant labor and farm youths. . . . Since pay alone does not work, management must study the lessons offered by absenteeism.

The Incentive Illusion

Money is the most expensive means of communication.
Current saying

The same principles fail in the same way in the entire area of take-home pay and fringe benefits. The president of a company receives what is technically known as "compensation," not merely a salary or wage. Today, the incentive of wages is like the incentive of more parts in "job enrichment," that is, pure illusion. Even if the watchmaker had the entire watch at his disposal, it is still a fragment of a much larger fragment. The satisfactions of role playing can never be found by enlargement of this kind. Organized labor, like organized management, is trapped by the "Law of Implementation": everything must be processed through an irrelevant and backward mechanism. All the "wage" hikes and "compensation" demanded and desired cannot confer the relevant controls and satisfactions. The top executive has no control over the kind of society in which his youngsters or his organization operates. The new speed-up in the whole social organization makes it precarious to relate anything to anything. Anxiety undermines all the fragmentary satisfactions previously deemed adequate to the "good life."

The Rear-view Mirror That Cracks

Since our concern is with human organization, it is necessary to ask what kind of organization will suffice under these new conditions. Bigness will not serve, since it alienates the individual. The human scale adds new effectiveness in the age of speed-up. As "hardware" yields to miniaturization and etherealization, the giant organizational structures become helpless dinosaurs incapable of maneuvering in the new environment. Specialism and inadaptability are the fate of all large structures. They have no meaning relative to a fast-changing environment. The dinosaur had no option whether to drop in or drop out. He died hard in his tracks. The piranha can swallow the whale.

Time was when the big structure created its own environment and dictated the ground rules to many other organizations. The new electric rim spin ends that. Electric-information movement means that you are here and we are there simultaneously. Under these conditions everybody is drop-in and dropout impartially. There is no part of the world in which we do not participate, whether we know it or not. And there is no part of us which is not equally invaded by everything in the world. "Nipping in" and "nipping out" anywhere in the world now involves responsibilities for having altered that part of the world. The drop-in and the dropout alter the situation totally.

COMMITTEES, CONFERENCES, CONVENTIONS

Interpersonal play is the name of the game.
                    New saying

The Committed Executive

A committee of multidisciplinary specialists, ostensibly working on a particular problem, creates both a mask and an "in-group"; it simultaneously reassures an "outside public" and serves as a catharsis for its members. Committees, like conferences and conventions, are a form of social life that has become a major aspect of bureaucracy, whether in business, politics, education, or science. Members engage in professional "gossip," batting around their knowledge without touching their ignorance. Committees always discover more and more of whatever it is they are studying, be it poverty or violence or pollution. They often find more effects than they imagined possible but only the RVM *figures*, never the invisible *grounds*. Insights sometimes occur "by accident," but they are not "for the record." Since insight is never a point of view, it fits no specialist category. DISCOVERY COMES FROM DIALOGUE THAT STARTS WITH THE SHARING OF IGNORANCE. Today, committees, conferences, and conventions at the peak of their popularity are clearly "past times."

He who runs may read.
                    Old saying

THE MYSTERIES OF COMPENSATION

Its usage in the business world has confirmed the meaning of the word "compensation" as payment for *top* executives. They are paid to stay in one position, even though this deprives them of many opportunities. At the opposite end of the hierarchy there is workman's compensation. This is payment for deprivation of limbs, faculties, or satisfactions attendant upon his actions in the line of duty.

The Employment Paradigm

The term "compensation" by complementarity applies to the extremes of the "employment paradigm." There is a kind of impressive testimony to human perception in the consistency of this terminology. No mere classification approach could have hit upon so unlikely a term as common to the opposite members of the same structure. It is noticeable that the penalties for which the top executive is compensated are psychic deprivations of power and prestige, whereas the disservices for which the workman is compensated tend to be physical.

We are also reminded of the case of a contract cost estimator, who, bored by lack of contracts to estimate, demanded a raise. Got it, and didn't drop out.

EXECUTIVE MOBILE

If payment can be received at both ends, dropping out can also occur at both ends. Robert C. Albrook, writing in *Fortune,* November, 1968, discussed the mystery of the fantastic increase of executive dropouts:

TURNOVER AS A WAY OF LIFE

Executive turnover has risen fivefold since Korean war years; losses are highest among the younger generation of college trained men. . . . Neither power, money, nor position count as much as moving upward from job to job in hope of increasing their competence as executives.

And as Eugene Jennings noted in *Psychology Today* (July, 1970):

MOBICENTRIC MAN REPLACES THE INSIDER AND THE ORGANIZATION TOADY

For him, success is represented less by position, title, salary or performance than by moving and movement.

Mobility itself has become a form of compensation for a great proportion of executives today. The old phrase "Join the navy and see the world" (*i.e.,* through a porthole) seems to fit their specialist job predicament only too well. The job itself has become unbearably confining and fragmenting in an all-at-once world. It is worthy of note that the new mobility is not mere rivalry or career competitiveness. Until recently employers said: "If you once leave our company, you can never return."

Use Competitors for Continuing Education with Pay

Today, the prodigal sons who formerly had been spurned and despised are now welcomed back. Typical of the inability to disguise this new situation is the trend of palliatives offered. As Albrook explains:

These men need not be lost forever. Gellerman proposes what he calls a "visa" program, under which valued departing employees would, in effect, be told: If you decide you want to come home at any time in the next five years, you will have a priority for any opening here, and you will be welcomed back with the same compensation you might have achieved had you remained with us.

Compensation in today's world of fantastically increased opportunities and diversities cannot be measured on the old scale.

The Sender Not Only Gets Sent; He Gets Taken

Mr. Albrook's article describes the new *figure* or pattern of "job hopping" minus the hidden *ground* that provided the motivation. In the new service environment of information, transportation has taken on a new dimension altogether. Electrically, *"you* are there" and *"they* are here." It is the viewer or knower who is "transported" with all electric media. In effect, this instant transportation scraps the entire structure of job positions. Nobody, whether he be a student, a professor, or an executive has a *position* any longer. Job placement at its peak manifestation (endless agencies for this purpose) flipped into total "job" mobility. Students began to form "instant" cities. Professors became "grant-grabbers" and "globe trotters." And executives simply drop off the "organization tree." It is not only the increase of physical travel facilities that creates this situation. Travel agencies, like job placement agencies, are slated for disappearance. The active experience of *being* in all parts of the world by instant electric means greatly undermines all existing "hardware" services for transporting the population.

Unqualified Success in Search of Qualified Audience

Fred "Waldo" DeMara, "the great imposter," found masses of unused power everywhere. Like Hitler, DeMara never muddied a lie with truth. He was a "fake" who was driven into role playing by the sheer triviality of the occupational patterns of our world. The same fragmented character of job structures drives many people frantic with frustration. DeMara simply had enough resource to invent roles where other people were simply seeking jobs. What he lacked was an audience that could adopt a proper role toward him.

The "Backward" Wave of the Future

Another reciprocal relationship is seen in the executive quest for the exotic relief of new work and new work environment, on the one hand, and, on the other, the transfer of the "backward natives" to privileged and specialist areas that the executive now shuns. In *cliché-archetype* terms, as we shape an environment of job structures, we retrieve the much older forms of feudal loyalty and service made possible by the presence of the people who have been relatively untouched by the specialist service environments. Today, Malaysians and West Indians are in the role of the vestigial feudal retainers of eighteenth-century Europe. (These feudal-retainer types, formerly plentiful in the American South, have been specialized and alienated by urban living.)

Emasculation by Integration

The phantom of "integration" for the American Negro has offered us the image of the black man against a white *ground*. The interplay between these two would produce a neutral grey pattern of integration—a reasonable facsimile of a white man. The Negro in this grey mode is of course deprived of the satisfactions of both the white and the black.

The Black-White Perplex

The interface of black against white *ground*, in fact, intensifies the characteristics of both. The black man is endowed with power and "negritude" by his confrontation with the white man. The white man is enriched by the discovery of the unique characteristics of the black man as well as by the recognition of his own limitations. The way in which the black-white syndrome applies to the frantically mobile "job hopper" is that both *figures* exist against the *ground* of the new electric-information culture, which simply dissolves the physical, psychic, and social structures inherent in all the preceding situations. This fact can be verified in the current context of the automobile industry.

In his *Fortune* article, "Blue-collar Blues on the Assembly Line," Judson Gooding writes:

> Both young blacks and young whites have higher expectations of the jobs they fill and the wages they receive, and for the lives they will lead. They are restless, changeable, mobile, demanding, all traits that make for impermanence—and for difficult adjustment to an assembly line. The deep dislike of the job and the desire to escape become terribly clear twice each day when shifts end and the men stampede out of the plant gates.

In line with the upper middle class from our educational establishment, these lower-middle-class operators in the old "hardware" world "vent their feelings through absenteeism, high turnover, shoddy work, and even sabotage." It is very important to note that the effects of the new information environment influence all age groups, ethnic groups, job categories, and economic "classes" in the same way. Gooding notes:

> Of the 740,000 hourly paid workers building cars today, 40 percent are under thirty-five. The automobile industry, justly proud of its ex-

traordinary record of past accomplishments, is totally committed to the assembly line which comes down from that past, and its heroes are veteran production men who know how to "move the iron." At the plant level, managers are trying to build cars by the old methods with new workers they don't understand and often don't much like. While at headquarters top executives are beginning to worry about "who's down there" on those assembly lines, what "they" are like, what "they" want from their jobs, there is still a comprehension gap.

The diagnostics and cures offered for the universal malaise have the forlorn features of the pollutant disposal programs. Gooding points out:

> Somewhat belatedly, perhaps, management is attempting to ease its labor problems in a variety of ways, from sensitivity training for supervisors to the greatly increased degree of automation being built in at G.M.'s new Lordstown, Ohio, plant.

Sensitivity training, on the one hand, merely guarantees a more complete destruction of identity than the machine had been able to achieve. Suppression of identity in turn ensures a backlash of physical violence. The automation "rim spin," on the other hand, ensures the collapse of the old nineteenth-century plant and procedures as such. This type of response to new challenging development is par for the business round in general. The automatic impulse to squeeze more and more out of the old fruit does not foster a supply of new fruit.

As Bruce Hutchinson puts it in his column for Toronto's *Globe and Mail* (November 25, 1970):

> The trouble, in a word, is that the 17th-century stone mason could help Wren build a cathedral in honor of God, but no assembly-line worker supposes, in his wildest imaginings, that he helps General Motors build an automobile in honor of the GNP.

6

Conglomerate Emperors in Global Theater

GENERAL MOTORS THE BIGGEST MANUFACTURER

"Moving the Iron" and Oblivious of the Environments Created

What is good for General Motors is good for America.
"Engine Charlie" Wilson

Shining Knights of the American Dream:
A History of Benign Mergers and Malignant Takeovers

Alfred P. Sloan, Jr., a hero of the assembly line, takes us on a nostalgic tour of what happened in *My Years with General Motors:* "A car for every purse and purpose." To do battle with Ford's static model of utility car, selling at the lowest possible price, GM opted for diversity—"the annual model, the spirit to which the organization must respond or die." GM adapted "the internal combustion engine . . . to a wide variety of power needs, notably the airplane and the locomotive." Mr. Sloan notes that "I put no ceiling on progress. . . . Growth, or striving for it, is, I believe, essential to the good health of an enterprise."

Longer, lower, larger, and more power gives the people what they want through putting them on.

Whorled without aimed. A-man.
James Joyce, *Finnegans Wake*

Management by a Constellation of Stars

In 1908, what had begun as a sport took shape as an industry. Henry Ford initiated the Model-T era, and William C. Durant incorporated General Motors. It is typical of market forecasting that when the motorcar arrived, the coachmen feared no loss of business. They could foresee "making a pot" pulling cars out of ditches. Nobody foresaw that cars would "make" the motor roads and create suburbia. Nor did anyone anticipate that roads would put a "concrete kimono" on the community and destroy cities.

In *My Years with General Motors*, Mr. Sloan observes:

> Both Mr. Durant and Mr. Ford had unusual vision, courage, daring, imagination, and foresight. Both gambled everything on the future of

the automobile. . . . They were a generation of what *I* might call personal types of industrialists; they injected their personalities, their "genius," so to speak, as a subjective factor into their operations without the discipline of management by method and objective facts.

Ford, the mechanic, was typical of the extreme centralizer, while Durant, the racer, was an extreme decentralizer. With products, Ford was the apostle of uniformity, while Durant was the prophet of diversity.

What Eli Whitney had achieved in the manufacture of guns with interchangeable parts, Henry Leland set out to accomplish with General Motors. As an alternative to *management by command*, Sloan developed

SLOAN'S PARADOX

An Organization Co-ordinated in Policy and Decentralized in Administration

Mr. Sloan sought to achieve maximum decentralization of day-to-day operations consistent with control of expenditures and limits of authority in policy questions. He points out that this form of organization has not only worked well for GM but has become standard practice in a large part of American industry. What Mr. Sloan does not mention is that

Size by Itself Creates High-rise Pathology

Specialism is a product of need to create status hierarchies. Mr. Sloan's experience confirms that "if you can describe the function of the whole, you have laid out a complete working organization, for by implication the apportionment of responsibility for decisions at various levels is contained in the description."

The Organization Chart Is the Medium as the Message

It is a technical solution for a human management problem. The basic elements of control are financial, whereas specialism increases dependence on the employer for the "sitting duck."

For Mr. Sloan, the ideal incentive compensation for executives should combine potential earnings lost with a bonus for corporate profits earned. He did not expect anyone to accept a promotion *instead* of a salary increase. Like Gilbert and Sullivan's *Mikado:*

> He wished all men as rich as he
> And he was rich as rich could be.

Mr. Sloan also notes that "The role of personality can be so important that sometimes it is necessary to build an organization, or rather perhaps a section of it, around one or more individuals rather than to fit individuals into the organization."

Today, we hear a growing rumble of discontent from the human *makers* upon whom the assembly line is imposed as a *matching* mechanism. When work goes down, compensation goes up: payments for pains—physical, psychic, and social—due to lack of roles in the global theater. Speed-up creates slowdown.

What Mr. Sloan did not recognize was that speed-up of information flow in the electric age would transform his previous exceptions and assumptions into new ground rules.

COCOON CUDDLING CURVES OR TIGER TANK?

When Disservices Exceed Services, as Everyone Can Plainly See

The shock treatment for *motivated somnambulism* is when the neglected children strike back at the successful parent. The last hero becomes the latest villain. The standard response: Don't learn how to anticipate effects with causes; react with a sledgehammer, too late!

The Growing Revolt Against King Auto

Robert Bendiner reports in the New York *Times* Service (August 26, 1970):

> Henry Ford the elder described his first gasoline buggy as "something of a nuisance, for it made a racket and scared horses." Its descendants make 75 per cent of the racket in major U.S. cities and scare a lot more people than their forerunner ever did horses.
>
> So frightening indeed has the automobile become that a major rebellion against its dominance is in the making—and it is by no means a rebellion of the restless young. A full decade ago San Franciscans successfully rose up against an Embarcadero freeway that would have blighted their waterfront and since then plans for concrete royal carpets to accommodate King Auto have been aborted in half a dozen cities from New Orleans to Boston.
>
> #### CAR-FREE EXPERIMENT
>
> New York, after happily banning the automobile from Central Park on weekends, has been timidly experimenting with car-free thoroughfares on Saturday in the heart of Manhattan and the lowly pedestrian is promised similar moments of glory elsewhere in the city.

The London *Observer* Service (August 21, 1970), reporting another aspect of the return to human scale, cites Ray Bradbury of Beverly Hills, California:

WE AMERICANS WERE AFRAID OF 1984—THEN WE
GO AND BUILD IT

He believes in people getting together, yet they have nowhere in this concrete wasteland to congregate. "Where are the squares of Europe, the plazas, bridges, trees and fountains? Where can people walk and talk?" New York's skyscrapers are no better: "Everyone is piled up like a layer cake, hating each other." He blames architects for playing it safe and business moguls for wanting nothing new. He curses the car for its dehumanizing influence. "You go through your house into the garage, drive alone to an underground parking place at your office, take the elevator to your cubbyhole and drive home at night without so much as waving at a fellow-being."

While Mr. Bradbury warns us that man's whole history is a flight from such boredom, planners prepare for still more high-rises and throughways.

Report from Jet City

While Mr. Sloan exhorts us to put a belt of cars around the world, the fossil fuels have put a "greenhouse" around the planet. Illinois Attorney General Scott has filed suit against twenty-three airlines: "The pollution from one jet is equal to the exhaust of 10,000 cars." (Four jets of an airliner equal 40,000 cars. It figures!) Mr. Scott explains that although all military aircraft are equipped with antipollution devices (costing about $10,000 each), only the threat of severe financial loss will force the civilian airlines to install such equipment. He does not mention noise. Our history begins again.

UNPLANNED OBSOLESCENCE AT PEAK POWER

You've come a long way, baby.
Current ad

Nowhere to Go but Down and In

Obsolescence leads either to extinction or to metamorphosis—breakdown or breakthrough. The choice is a human one. For solutions lie *not* outside, but inside the problems themselves. We can find them by recognizing their process patterns. Both the approach and the patterns are recurring topics of this book.

"Figures" Topple as "Grounds" Shift

It has been taken for granted in the automobile industry that the highway is natural *ground* for the car as *figure*. There will be highways because the open road is demanded by the American dream. What is overlooked is that the highway automatically ceases to exist when the wheel takes to the air. The wheel is to the jet what the horse was to the car. The car put the horse under cover. The plane pulls the *ground* out from under the car as *figure*. The horse returned on a much greater scale as sport and entertainment. The car is already becoming an art form in the same mode of obsolescence. The car is now becoming costume.

Hot Pajamas for Cool Cats

The car has moved steadily from "hardware" to "software" status by the continued stress on picturesque costumelike effects, hence the increasing value of old cars. As we recall some of the great beacon slogans of the car past, and as General Motors proceeds into history, we can hear the voice of Henry Ford giving the old raspberry to his rivals: "History is bunk!"

AMERICAN TELEPHONE AND TELEGRAPH
THE BIGGEST CORPORATION

Communicating "Bits" Hung Up in Wired World Unaware of Magnetic City By-pass

Communication is what gets out of one mind and into another.
                    Frederick R. Kappel, chairman, A.T. & T.

A.T. & T. had to begin as a monopoly whether it liked it or not. You cannot be partially "electrified" in the communications world. If you tune in, you are turned on, and then you drop out. A.T. & T. has now completed this circuit.

Tuning In

The tuning-in process for Bell himself was inventing the telephone. As Joseph C. Goulden relates in *Monopoly*: "Bell was an early student of the human voice and how it produces sound. Accident and an ignorance of German started him toward the telephone. . . . To Western Union, Bell's telephone at first was a joke."

It is instructive to note that Bell was trying to improve old telegraph technology when he discovered the new telephone medium. It was also quite natural for him to offer his invention to Western Union, which then dominated the American telegraph business. The following extract from the minutes of a meeting set up by Western Union in 1877 to consider his offer is a classic example of conventional management reaction to any major innovation:

1. The telephone is so named by its inventor, A. G. Bell. He believes that one day they will be installed in every residence and place of business.

2. Bell's profession is that of a voice teacher. Yet he claims to have discovered an instrument of great practical value in communication which has been overlooked by thousands of workers who have spent years in this field.

3. Bell's proposal to place his instrument in almost every home and business place . . . is fantastic. . . . The central exchange alone would represent a huge outlay in real estate and buildings, to say nothing of the electrical equipment.

4. In conclusion, the committee feels that it must advise against any investment in Bell's scheme. We do not doubt that it will find users in special circumstances, but any development of the kind and scale which Bell so fondly imagines is utterly out of the question.

Western Union reasoning was well founded on principles of sound business management. But events soon proved that they had not asked themselves the right questions. "The humor soured as the phones became a public fad" (Joseph Goulden, *Monopoly*).

The tuning-in process for A. T. & T. was the great patent struggle through which Bell secured the basic telephone patent. A. T. & T. owed its existence to a 4-to-3 ruling of the United States Supreme Court, which credited Bell with the invention. It allowed him to assign his patent rights to develop the telephone commercially.

Turning On: Hello Central!

The next stage in the innovation process was to centralize the "hardware"-making connections through telephone centrals. "The system" had moved from archetype to cliché—from the business of art to the art of business.

Bell Drops Out as A.T. & T. Drops In

Then began, in the words of one United States judge, "the most important, the most protracted litigation that has arisen under the patent system in this country." And Goulden relates: "At the outset of the patent suits Bell withdrew . . . saying he was through with telephones. . . . He took no active part in the business after 1878. Bell's interest turned to flying machines, among other things."

Fessenden, the Forgotten Father of "Wireless" Telephony

Not so fortunate was Reginald Aubrey Fessenden. Alan Edmonds, writing in *Maclean's* Magazine (September, 1969), describes how on Christmas Eve, 1900, Fessenden transmitted the human voice from place to place for the first time without wires. Radio was born. By Christmas, 1906, he produced and broadcast the world's first "radio" show for an audience of ship-and-shore station operators. At his death in 1932, with five hundred patents to his name, the New York *Herald Tribune* said: "It sometimes happens, even in science, that one man can be right against the world. Professor Fessenden was that man."

Like Western Union before it, hung up in the old wires, A.T. & T. missed the new by-pass of the electric field. In winning its *reason* A.T. & T. had lost its *resoun.*

Allen F. Demaree, writing in *Fortune* (May, 1970) on "The Age of Anxiety at A.T. & T.," observes:

> A.T. & T. is more than the biggest monopoly in the U.S., a corporation controlling greater wealth than any other in the world ($47 billion in assets at the end of 1969). It is also a kind of subculture all its own, encompassing nearly one million employees and filled with its own myths and mores, prides and prejudices, that only momentous events can call into question.

Quite naturally, at Bell all instructions and decisions are in writing.

THE MEDIAN IS THE MESSAGE

The Law of Implementation as the Bell Curve

Demaree continues:

> Bell is a strange, perhaps unique, blend of independence and conformity. In mood and atmosphere, a great gulf separates the operating companies from corporate headquarters . . . as the years go by your head becomes more and more Bell-shaped. . . . If you figure out a better way of doing something, forget it—they'd have to change the manuals.

(The *Bell System Practices* are the hidden environment.) This has ensured that Bell's organization system would be by-passed by every process of electric communication including its own service environment. The largest subculture in the American economy is run on centralist and connected lines of old-fashioned "hardware" efficiency.

ROI Reins

As Demaree points out, the single most important decision that Bell executives have to make is "how much to invest in new capital equipment— the trunks that carry telephone calls, the central offices that switch them . . . $6.5 billion this year . . . or 8 percent of all capital expenditures in the U.S."

SERVICE COMES FIRST

Mother Bell Sounds the Knell

On the other hand, they are engaged in providing a service utterly opposite in character to their own organization. Bell telephone service is acoustic, resonant, discontinuous, and audile-tactile in its very nature.

Bell's Name Is Its Fortune

Yet everything in the service child ensures the demise of the parent system. (The hand of the child has been raised against the parent.) Now, for
the first time, competition is providing buyers with a "yardstick" for beat-
ing Bell's performance. According to Demaree's headlines, POOR SERVICE,
NEW COMPETITION, INEXPERIENCED WORKERS, AND EVEN ITS OWN LIFE STYLE
BESET THE BELL SYSTEM WITH WOES UNDREAMED OF A DECADE AGO.

THE A.T. & T. PERPLEX

Ours is a communications business, not just a telephone business.
John de Butts, vice-chairman, A.T. & T.

If the post office is a kind of bank, then Bell Canada is a kind of collection agency.
Gordon B. Thompson, senior scientist, Northern Electric R and D Labs

The telephone scrapped the letter and retrieved person-to-person communication, not the message, but "you are there" and "they are here" simultaneously. The videophone scraps person-to-person communication of the
telephone and retrieves the group. Instead of the private intruder, the telephone, we get James Joyce's HCE (Here Comes Everybody). The speaker
must go into role: miming, grimacing, and gesticulating like a "rock group."
The kids got there first.

Videophone Hang-up: User as Prisoner
Sending the Whole Environment

The office intercom anticipated the videophone by freeing the speaker to
walk and act while talking. The old telephone had encouraged the nervous
pace and the long cord. Whereas the telephone had provided simultaneity
of presence in *acoustic* space, the videophone encounters the problem of
sequential or alternating presence in *visual* spaces. The videophone automatically becomes a private TV station. The speaker becomes broadcaster.
The videophone is potentially the most colossal toy of the world game nursery. Education, entertainment, and business would become indistinguish-
able in a global theater dominated by the videophone.

The new service outspins the old service to the degree that the movie outdid the photograph, or to the degree that the radio surpassed the phonograph. The birth pains to which this would subject the parent matrix, already swollen, would be fatal.

WHERE ITT'S ATT

They Call It Geneen U.

Conglomerate business is the business of business.

Forbes, May 1, 1968

Everybody's business is nobody's business.

Management saying

ITT was originally the international arm of Western Electric Company. Western Electric is still the manufacturing operation for the A.T. & T. group, with enormous diversities of products. It manufactures everything from the old plug for the switchboard to microwave systems and sophisticated military weaponry.

ITT is a "transnational" conglomerate, familiarly known as "Geneen U." The students at this university are postgraduates from higher levels of the University of Hard Knocks. These men are intent on continuing education. They enter the newly contrived rat race of Geneen U. as programmed dropouts. These men are chosen by Geneen as promising material for higher performance. They are trained under fire—on the job. These men were frustrated. They had tasted success in many fields. They wanted eminence and command "that gives you a chance to either strike out or hit a home run in the world series." They were prepared to scrap modest success and security for a shot at bigger game. An article in *Forbes* Magazine (May 1, 1968) states:

> Surprisingly, turnover has brought ITT ambitious, aggressive men who wouldn't be career employees in *anybody's* company except their own. Eager to make big reputations, they've done quite a lot of good for ITT before they move.

Geneen exacts a high price for his postgraduate training, which merges education and business:

> He sets almost unattainable standards that either stretch a person or break him. . . . His technique is a strange and contradictory one. He gives them authority, at the same time prodding them, pushing them, badgering them, even screaming at them. . . . What is unusual about Geneen is the detail he demands. He demands monthly reports from all divisions . . . an item as minor as a lost order.

Says Geneen: "I delegate, but don't abdicate. . . . Most American companies compete with each other in inefficiency."

NEW CAMPUS FOR OLD CAMP

A recent grad of Geneen's School for Continuing Education is Robert Townsend (the man who got everyone to try harder). In *Up the Organization: How to Stop the Corporation from Stifling People and Strangling Profits*, Townsend manifests the Geneen pattern of hotted-up "camp." If there is one thing that is perfectly obvious about Geneen U., it is that it is a "replay" of some very worn-out organization ploys and patterns.

AVIS HERTZ: SUCCESS AS MARKET MAID

Old Hash at New Speed

Everybody has seen the popularity of "camp" in our time: the recovery with rituals, earnest resuscitation and revival of outworn things that have scarcely been discarded. In Geneen U. the "star" system, which disappeared with TV and the return to dialogue, seems to be the main noun. Instead of a lifetime career, he offers a "five-year contract." All the old specialism and fragmentation of work and achievement are offered to the candidate as a "package deal." Where formerly he had an open-ended career within the corporation, Geneen offers him a closed deal. It is as if he were attempting to include the new "electric module" within the confines of the old assembly line.

Survival Module

At high speed, Geneen's candidates are forced to resort to small-team modular organization within the big structure. Townsend reveals that the real meaning of Geneen U. is for training survivors how to survive. Those who have come through the "hardware" "hard-sell" world of pre-electronic America are being given a refresher course in the old folklore while surrounded by the "software" of the electric age. It suggests a nostalgic reunion of Buchenwald alumni.

"Stars" Without Audience

The Geneen program offers not only a repeat of the miseries of the concentration camp but proffers its experiences to other people. The only satisfaction it offers is that of having survived the miseries. No matter at what point you enter Geneen U. you encounter art forms or relics of a departed culture. Whereas work used to be torture, Geneen U. is more artistic in presenting torture as work. What Geneen has done is retrieve from past forms of human commercial striving all the dissatisfactions and miseries as ends in themselves. While ostensibly striving to intensify the profit lash to stretch flagging human tendons and nerves, Geneen in effect substitutes the whiplash for the profit lash. His candidates have none of the satisfac-

tions of existing in an industrial·*ground* that corresponds to their motivational patterns. Instead, the patterns of their energies represent *figures*
that have merged with the old *ground* of specialist, private goals. All that
remains is the goal or *figure* without the *ground*—a "star" system without
an audience. The electric age has dissolved the *ground* and ground rules for
this kind of "play." That is why such institutions as Geneen U. have all the
characteristics of a "monster born out of due time." *Typical of all dropout
situations is the absence of* ground *for a well-defined* figure.

THE CAPSIZED ORGANIZATION CHART

Bottom-up Management

Let's turn the boat over quickly before it sinks.
Anonymous

FALSE BOTTOM AS END OF THE BOTTOM LAYER
THE EXECUTIVE AS INVERTED DESPOT

The remnant that is escaped . . . shall again take root downward
and bear fruit upward.   Isaiah 37:31

Dr. Edwin A. Menninger notes in *Fantastic Trees* that bottom-side-up
trees

> will develop a mass of fibrous roots that hang down from the branches.
> These roots never reach the ground: they surround the trunk like a
> hula skirt. . . . Their function is unknown. . . . The tree may be
> preparing in some way for its old age.

As T.S. Eliot puts it in his "Sweeney Agonistes" (a spoof of the primitive
pastoral life of sex on tropical islands) :

Under the bam

Under the boo
Under the bamboo tree.

Menninger continues on jacking up businesses from the top:

> A banyan is a fig tree that has developed auxilliary trunks to help sup-
> port the superstructure. The word *banyan* signifies a manner of growth,
> not a kind of tree. . . . Usually aerial roots keep growing downward
> until they reach the earth, sometimes forming great festoons under the
> big tree. They remain fine and slender until they reach the ground and
> then one of these thickens into a stout limb, like a trunk supporting
> the branch.

This is where nature itself performs a *figure/ground* merger, an OUROBOROS*
monster, uniting earth and air.

---

* The worm OUROBOROS, which ate its own tail, is the ancient mythic symbol of a
world that survives by endlessly devouring itself.

THE EXECUTIVE AS FALLOUT

What happens to the swingers in an upside-down tree? Back to the roots! You gotta dig it or hang from the branches of the old family tree.

When the tree goes upside down, the executives fall out of the branches.

REIGNING EXECUTIVES OF THE ELECTRIC AGE

Old Vibes of G.E.

With the advent of computer programming a new group of managers appeared on the scene. We have seen an account of them in Boguslaw's *The New Utopians*. These are the people substituters. In the past, assembly lines and technical-training programs had suppressed people while using them as components in a production process.

New Life Through Accelerated Slow Death

The next stage was simply to by-pass people altogether. When this occurred, people recovered a new importance and a new role in management. After a century of progressive dehumanization of work, the computer had no sooner pushed the process to an extreme than people were suddenly back in the forefront of operations. On the one hand, the top executive, whose new role is oral briefing and explanation of extremely technical two-bit program packages, has arrived. His role is to reveal dramatically the superabundance of possibilities in the package. He also helps his associates adapt these possibilities to their needs.

From Machine Output to Drama Production

On the other hand, at the shop level, the foreman has a parallel abundance of choices. Whereas in the past he had merely to manipulate machinery and interpret blueprints and specifications, now he has to interpret both human possibilities and limitations. The machinery has become so complex that his role has become a complicated and ever-changing assessment of the cast available to him for the operation in hand. Instead of "casting parts," as in the old "hardware" days, he now has to assign human parts or roles to his cast. Like a dramatic producer in rehearsal, he has to explore each part with the members of the cast. Like the movie of still shots, the assembly line, pushed to high speed, becomes a continuous and totally involving experience.

Minding Is the New Business

O the mind, mind has mountains; cliffs of fall
Frightful, sheer, no-man-fathomed. Hold them cheap
May who ne'er hung there.
                    Gerard Manley Hopkins, "No Worst, There Is None"

Now that the "console" is replacing the assembly line, we are putting our minds into the business instead of the old fragmented movements of the body into repetitive operations. We can no longer think in terms of the assembly line and factory as the basic components of production. The change that has occurred in these relations is not unlike the new way of regarding electric circuits and electric wiring. We now live in "wired cities," just as we have drainage systems everywhere in the urban environment. Many people are thus inclined to imagine that electric current is actually contained in a wire, as water in a pipe. It is natural to think of new forms in accordance with older patterns. In point of fact, it is more fitting to think of electric current, and indeed to think of the "wired city" in accordance with a very different pattern. Basically, there is no electric current *in* the wire. Instead, there is a field of electric energy that is structured or guided by wiring. It is the same with the information environment, which is a field of electric energy patterned by a variety of wiring systems or "wave guides."

From Manipulation to Orchestration at the Control Console

In the same way, a business operation at whatever level, whether in design, production, sales, distribution, promotion, or general management, can be conducted from a computer console. As with the old electric keyboard organ, from which the metaphor "console" is borrowed, the computer console can extend simultaneously its chords, harmonies, and controls to a diverse number of areas of operation. More and more, the mind and heart go into the musical score that determines the quality of business service or activity. This is at a great remove from the "hardware" days of specialist functions assigned to quite separate organizations and individuals. The old pattern had been for everyone to mind his own business and to keep out of everybody else's way as much as possible. In the new harmonic scale of the computer console, choral togetherness and harmony will supplant the old separate notes of isolated voices.

In the old pattern the ideal had been "a place for everything and everything in its place." There was "one best way" for anything to be done. Frederick Winslow Taylor made himself famous by his time-and-motion studies and scientific management. Like any other *avant-gardist*, he had one foot firmly planted in the past. This was expressed well by the history student who wrote in his examination that "Petrarch stood between two ages.

While with one foot he saluted the rising star of the Renaissance, he kept the other firmly planted in the Middle Ages." Taylor, while looking forward to "scientific management," speaks of it only in the most antiquated terms of the Gutenberg assembly line. As a method for measuring how much work a first-class man can do in a day, he announced:

> The best way to do this, in fact almost the only way in which the timing can be done with certainty, is to divide the man's work into its elements, and time each element separately. For example, in the case of a man loading pig iron onto a car, the elements should be: Picking up the pig from the ground or pile (time in hundredths of a minute). Walking with it on a level (time per foot walked). Walking with it up an incline to car (time per foot walked). Throwing the pig down (time in hundredths of a minute). Walking back empty to get a load (time per foot walked).
>
> Quoted in H. F. Merrill, *Classics in Management*

Taylor, by pushing this arrested fragmented montage of actions to an extreme point of analysis, was in fact moving from the factory to the film form of organization. As soon as the film form is speeded up, it loses all its jerky still-shot character and becomes an involving experience. This is what has happened with the speed-up of the computer, as its programs are transferred to the world of production. In all areas of the older kinds of specialist organization, such as the one Taylor outlines, the process pattern had been lost in the elements analyzed. With speed-up, the pattern of the process manifests itself again abundantly. The rhythms of the new electrotechnical operations are as pronounced as those of a dance orchestra. Everybody insists on getting into the swing of things again.

GOALS-GOLDS-GAOLS

Alienation Above and Retribulation Below

Scientific management dedicated to the goal of "moreness" through "rationalization" (what any fool can do, another can) had excluded the possibility of pattern recognition of process from the very beginning. At the next level of speed-up it is not the worker who suffers the dehumanization of his function but the manager himself. The illusion and deception of the inverted pyramid is to imagine that speed-up merely turns the previous hierarchy upon its head. In fact, the resulting change is not one of direction but of involvement. Today, as we move from literate to postliterate modes of awareness, speed-up of information flow is the chief determinant in every kind of human activity and organization.

HITHERTO, THE CHARACTER OF ANY BUSINESS HAS NEVER BEEN UNDERSTOOD BECAUSE ITS DETERMINANTS HAVE NEVER BEEN STUDIED DURING THEIR ACTIVE EXISTENCE.

Chapter 8

The Crisis of Identity

Simultaneous Quest for Change and Conformity

TUNE IN

TURN ON

DROP OUT TO GET IN TOUCH

Nowhere to Go but Inward or into Orbit

There must be somebody out there who speaks English.
> Boy astronomer in movie *IF*

Willed without witting whorled without aimed.
> James Joyce, *Finnegans Wake*

> This withered root of knots of hair
> Slitted below and gashed with eyes,
> This oval O cropped out with teeth.
>> T. S. Eliot, "Sweeney Erect"

BIGGEST DISEASE—BEING UNWANTED
> *Canadian Register*, October 30, 1971

Well, if I called the wrong number, why did you answer the phone?
> James Thurber, *Men, Women and Dogs*

Private Premises—KEEP OFF!

Private individual man is a "civilization freak" made possible by the power of the phonetic alphabet to impose visual criteria on the whole of social life and communication. Paradoxically, Western man with his highly specialized and precarious individual ego (or private psyche) has resisted all efforts to study the *effects* of technologies, old or new, upon his own psychic life.

1

Off-Spins and In-Spins

The rim spin of the electric world annihilates the very image of one's self. The paintings of Hieronymus Bosch present the horrors that occur when opposite phases of the same culture interpenetrate one another during rapid technological change. The same thing is happening today with the snatching of conventional goals and patterns from our midst by the sudden lurch from a mechanical to an electric world. The young are deprived of both identity and goals. They react in a kind of narcolepsy or apathetic somnambulism. They regard all aid as unwarranted interference. They submerge in their "yellow submarine."

Babes in the Woodwork

The dream is no longer *inside* but *outside*.
> A hippie

We have seen hippies watching the movie *Yellow Submarine*, made for four-year-olds, and weeping. It's like the astronauts taking Snoopy on their trip to the moon. The Beatles' name is a clue. This generation is like something that crawled out from the woodwork; they afford little possibility of communication. They are a group of immature semiliterates in our Jules Verne period of outdated science fiction. Just as NASA does not understand the "auditory space" of the electric age, they do not realize that the real space of our time is inner space, not outer.

The We Nobody Knows

At the same time, young people today tend to be "grey at three," thanks to the enormous speed-up of information. Any item of news that is moved at electric speeds acquires infinite mass. The resulting "information overload" is a world in which all the patterns stand out loud and clear for the first time. Even children can now detect social forms and patterns long hidden from an adult world that had grown up at slower speeds, as stated in a teen-ager's poem:

> No matter what you see, be silent
> It's not life but only news that's really violent
> or so the hangman said
> be silent.

Apocalyptic recognition of the hidden assumptions of adult activities has much effect in depriving the young of their private identities. A technical revolution for them is much the same as a vast military defeat, such as the Germans experienced in 1918 and after. That tribulation was followed by the retribalization of the German people. It was a new corporate identity, sought by a generation that had lost its private identity and meaning. The massive "hardware" exchange of World War I (mainly a railway war) was followed by the advent of radio and massive exchanges of "software" information with planetary coverage and instant speeds. The Jazz Age was an upsurge of primitive tribal experience that has been greatly surpassed by the allied effects of television. Contemporary teen-agers have had these direct experiences of world war in their nursery playpens, drinking in Armageddon with their mothers' TV. The present apocalyptic generation has difficulty in taking seriously the bureaucratic arrangements of the educational establishment.

SUBURBIA'S BLUEPRINTS FOR THE YOUNG

The Handwriting on the Wall Is Always for Somebody Else

The cover of *New York* Magazine (October 28, 1970) pictures a hippie seated in a wheelchair while his rich mom boasts: "Of course he can walk. Thank God he doesn't have to." In the cover story, "Notes on the New Paralysis," Jane O'Reilly observes: "The kids are playing *Musical Families.*" They are moving down the block or across the tracks as "neighborhood nomads" swapping families. They are "very big on love and ideals, but very short on will." The trouble starts when kids show a "will" of their own. School is the central obsession of the child-centered family: "Your mother and I are worried about your grades. . . . Your English teacher says you could do well if you weren't bored." But nobody seems to care why the school's antiquated "consumer packages" have lost allure. Parents have stopped listening. Taught the same language, but with different meaning, they don't know who their kids are. Suburbia's analytic blueprints exclude all dialogue and insight, all oral-aural modes of awareness, while teachers and parents alike complain: "Junior won't grow up and be a man!" (*I.e.,* drive through with a *will* for the *goals* of *more*—more what?) They say: "We did everything the books told us to do."

Those books were written for children living in a vacuum. Sired by the "sheiks" and "hot mamas" of the radio-booze generation, Spock's spooks have become the "hippies" of the TV-drug generation. In a period of consumer glut kids went into their programmed consumer role without goals, only to encounter the trauma of switching from the old consumer role to the new producer goal. Result: the paralyzed child. Movies, radio, and inflation scrubbed the European identity in the 1920's in the same way that the American identity was scrubbed by TV in the 1950's and 1960's. The enthroned "hippie" is an unconscious expression of the position

THE CHILD AS EMPEROR OF AMERICA,

just as FDR became emperor when he was paralyzed by polio. As long as FDR could stand on his two hind legs, he was just another politician. Seated, he was an emperor. The "hippie" generation is "stoned" via TV— *driven* in, rather than caved in. They are out of the running for *private* goals or jobs. They hope to get in *touch* through *corporate* roles and "communes."

Dickens's Tiny Tim is a cripple in an impoverished family (*i.e.*, physical hardship). TV's "Tiny Tim" instinctively adopts the mask of a "psychic cripple," falsetto and androgynous (caught between roles and goals). In private fact, today's Tiny Tim is an individual with a strong baritone, who yet wears the corporate *mask* of the TV-generation cripple. The cripple in his case is the over-advantaged child of suburbia. This paralyzed problem child has become a much bigger emperor than the one who can stand up on his own two legs.

Private Sensitivity Training

Mama, I learned something at school today from the psychologist. He calls it "spanking."

What had been child training has become a credit course for the child specialist. Spanking is a private form of sensitivity training for the corporate University of Hard Knocks. By encountering the "lines of force" in his world, the child learns "where it's at."

When you say that, smile!
Owen Wister, *The Virginian*

In his report, *Violence in TV Drama*, George Gerbner, of the Annenberg School of Communication, explains:

The fundamental function and social role of ritualized dramatic violence is, then, the maintenance of power. The collective lessons tend to cultivate a sense of hierarchical values and forces. Their conflicts expose the danger of crossing the lines, and induce fear of subverting them. Such symbolic functions of myth and ritual historically socialized people into growing up to know how to behave in different roles in order to avoid, as well as to use, violence.

The maintenance of social power is, in fact, the manifestation of social identity.

The PERSON as EMPEROR

This relates to the power of forms to impose their own assumptions. The human form has the imperial power of creating or of "putting on" environments. The user is the content of any medium or form of organization. Recognition of this basic but submerged fact was given to an explorer working with a team of Cree Indians. Becoming disoriented on the return to camp, he said to the Crees, "We're lost." They replied, "We not lost. Wigwam lost." They were simply pointing out that the environment created by a human being takes precedence over the environment he puts on by means of his artifacts. From this awareness can grow aristocratic *insouciance* and the utter command over mere things. Historically, traditional forms of authority were often based on humility and service, as with the ancient motto of the House of Windsor: *Ich Dien* (I Serve).

The Dominicans call themselves "the servants of the servants of God." Responsible leadership has always been humble, shunning the egotistical appetites of arbitrary and whimsical rule. How to achieve these ends in actual human organization has been the study of many philosophical minds. In our time, such study has tended to come under the name of "management." Whether we consider the *figure* of Frank Gilbreth at one extreme, or Mary Parker Follett at the other, there is the silent assumption that the relevant *ground* against which to consider patterns of human organization is business. Gilbreth, on the one hand, concentrating on "the one best way to do work," and Mary Parker Follett, studying "the Law of the Situation," concur in accepting the functions of trade and commerce as a normal basis on which to mount their meditations on the arts of governing men and things. In the new age of information these "commercial" assumptions no longer cover the ground. The clamor of the young at the gates of the Establishment tells us that the claims of the "inner life" have taken a new priority over "hardware" production and exchange.

Authority and Obedience

Toward the end of the "hardware" regime of specialism and ever-narrowing goals, the question of authority became psychotic. With intense specialism, any basis for rule disappeared. At the very time when all personal authority came into question, when every parent dreaded that he might cast a shadow of paternalism across the spirit of his child, specialist science demanded absolute obedience from the total human community for its conflicting and incompatible goals. It was at this point that there came the existential flip in which both authority and obedience were swept into the limbo of the yellow submarine and a universal sound-light show.

The problem of authority and obedience is inseparable from the quest for identity. If there is no private independent personal substance such as has always occupied the thought of the sages, then all matters of authority and obedience are frivolous, all service and disservice indifferent and equal. If there is no personal identity, indefeasible and intransigent, then human society can only be the "Penal Colony" evoked by Franz Kafka.

OBLOMOVISM

Due to the lack of interest tomorrow has been cancelled.
United States Government ad, *Atlantic*, July, 1969

Large sections of the Russian population in the later nineteenth century collapsed under the psychic pressure of new technology. A great wave of sleeping sickness swept the country. In any "civilized" society human satisfactions depend on a leisurely pace in which to enjoy one's specialty—distant goals that can actually be achieved. Any acceleration of the ordinary social processes makes demands of accommodation that the psyche cannot meet. Deprived of the energy for awareness and understanding, the ordinary person "folds." It is a process that the Western world has inflicted on countless "backward" countries. Today, it is the "backward" cultures that are the "advanced" ones. The dynamic pattern is the alienation of the new EAR people from the old EYE structures. It is the specialist Western culture that is retarded and obsolescent in terms of electric technology. The expert is cut off from enjoying the new environments that his own activities create. The weak point of any man's armor is his ignorance.

Rebels Without a Clue

Bernard Gwertzman, writing for the New York *Times* Service (August 17, 1970), reports from Moscow:

> Roving bands of dropouts from Soviet society, living in self-isolation in Siberia and other distant parts of the country, have become a source of official concern here. . . . They are known as "bichi" . . . "nuisances" . . . former bank directors, builders, disappointed artists, metalworkers, graduates of circus schools, and piano tuners. . . . For months and years, they do not listen to the radio and do not read newspapers. As painful as it is to note, these people exist who have isolated themselves from society, from its moral principles, ethical norms and also its laws.

OUR PRESENT "HARDWARE" WORLD IS IN DANGER OF TOTAL STRIKE

Such are the effects of nineteenth-century technology upon people, regardless of ownership of the "means of production." The new *avant-garde* is the primitive.

The Tough Old and the Fragile Young

Peter Drucker has observed that the captains of American industry read-ily adopted the image of themselves as medieval knights in shining armor. It was impossible for them not to see the huge benefits they conferred upon society at large. They were less observant of the *disservice* environments that accompanied their innovations. Perhaps the wedding between "hard-ware" and idealism, or any attempt to implement ideological programs, must always result in the hybrid horrors of war. Even war is not without its service and beneficial side, as Marshall McLuhan and Quentin Fiore point out in *War and Peace in the Global Village*. The theme of that book is that war is education, just as the theme of B. F. Skinner's *Walden Two* is that education is war. The movie *IF* shows that when the programmed pattern of an institution ceases to have the backing of the dominant forces in a society, education becomes not the conquest of the kingly state of youth, but a matter of open hostilities.

Peter Farb, writing about the Pueblo Indians in *Man's Rise to Civiliza-tion*, comments:

> The tribe is an inherently fragile structure; it possesses no strong political organization or permanent office of control that might give it stability. Instead, the tribe is regulated by a variety of social institu-tions, among them clans, secret clubs, and specialized societies that carry on warfare or perform ceremonials. The tribal "chief" belongs to no political hierarchy or dominant group; he is merely a sort of con-sultant, an adviser who may or may not be listened to. In the absence of political authority in the tribe, the households take unto them-selves the right of self-protection. As in the band, disputes tend to be perpetuated as feuds, with each act of revenge generating a reprisal.

The fragility and insecurity of tribal life lead to violence as a quest for identity in preliterate and postliterate societies alike. The Associated Press (November 24, 1970) reports:

> WASHINGTON—As many as 30 per cent of the children in some ele-mentary schools may be receiving drugs to quieten them down, a Government investigator told Congress yesterday.

When boredom fails to numb, use knock-out drops. Suppress the symp-toms and ignore the disease.

CRY HAVOC

The Unbridgeable Gap When Resonance Yields to Cacophony

When the generation gap widens too far and too fast, abrasion yields to head-on clash, the loss of identity, and the violence of civil war. The Cavaliers and Roundheads, as much as the American Civil War, were a result of technological imbalance and innovation. The British public-school system in the nineteenth century became an accelerated process of "transmogrifying sons of grocers into haughty young bloods." Later, when the goals and objectives of the new industrial elites of England were dislocated and blurred by the invasion of electric-information systems, the ideals of the public schools collapsed. The division that had seemed natural in the nineteenth-century world of plentiful consumer goods became repugnant and meaningless with the transfer from producer to consumer ideals. To illustrate that changeover, from *matching* to *making*, from acquisition to involvement, and from job holding to role playing is the object of the present book.

2

Identity Through Violence

THE RETURN OF THE NATIVE

One of the most bizarre examples of a utopian ideology implemented in our time is told in detail by Bruno Bettelheim in *The Children of the Dream*. It is the story of an ideological technique for abolishing "ghetto" psychology. Just as the British public-school system had rigorously suppressed most of the social backgrounds of its students in order to produce a uniformly polished, gentlemanly product, so, also, in the Israeli *kibbutzim* (collective agricultural settlements), the individualist patterns of child rearing and family life yield to a rigorous blueprint. After the first six months, all aspects of child care are assigned to a *metapelet*. The same pattern was pursued in England a hundred years earlier by the "nanny" system, which isolated children from their mothers.

Bettelheim seems to be completely ignorant of the parallel of the British public-school system to the *kibbutzim*. It is true that the English did not tend toward agricultural settlements and routines, but something equally disrupting was substituted. The English problem was to dislocate the lower- and middle-class children from their sordid urban backgrounds. The *kibbutzim* ideal was to erase all traces of urban "ghetto" from the psyches of their charges. As Wyndham Lewis used to say, "The value of the fox hunter is that he keeps the businessman in his place." But the British public-school system substituted the aristocratic ideals of huntin', shootin', fishin', for the agricultural toil of the *kibbutzim* children. The parallelism between the two forms extends all the way to the attempt to achieve an absolute tribal unity. The British aristocrat shares with the British slum child an entirely tribal or group-oriented pattern of life. In between the extreme of slum and castle is the great "muddle crass" of nobodies. Today, in England, the tribal slum culture, with its ancient roots of communal song and dance, has been retrieved by television and the computer. What is characteristic of tribal man, whether he be a Mountbatten, a "Limey," a Vietnamese, a Japanese, or a member of the *kibbutzim*, is instant readiness to serve the whole community and to die for it without a qualm.

Today, when Jewish tribalism confronts Negro tribalism in the New York slums and when Jewish tribalism confronts Arab tribalism in the Middle East, it is necessary to understand why the children of the affluent in Europe and America have abandoned individual patterns in favor of communal and corporate forms of association.

SLUM RICHES

Wealth Without Measure

It is also important to understand why the conditions of the slum are mandatory both for tribal creation and for tribal maintenance. The artist throughout the ages has expounded the meaning of the slum as a profound, sensuous involvement in the life process. The moment a slum is tidied up, its occupants become disengaged and individualist. A poor man, as long as he is set beside wealth, will readily envisage goals and purposes for himself and his children. However, the wealthy person who provides him with these goals cannot share them. The affluent are helplessly alienated members of the society they create and police. Their children are the first to revolt, when technological innovation permits. And today, as we shift from the old, mechanical world of specialist technology and private goals to the new circuitry with its total service environments, the affluent young cannot accept the objectives of the old mechanical world. They make their own slums. They turn inward, or they go Eastward, even as the Oriental turns outward and Westward under the impact of the same innovations. Conservative Westerners will shortly be sending their children to the Orient to Westernize them.

Retribulation

The old wars versus the new overkill are essentially embedded in all the patterns discussed above. Railway wars from 1860 to 1920 were fought with and for the old, industrial "hardware." The "staff" and "line" organization applied equally to both military and civilian management. Today, both the Salvation Army and the traditional religious orders of the Church Militant have had to abandon managerial hierarchies in favor of guerrilla tactics. No greater change is conceivable at any level of human organization than the change from "inner" to "outer," or from tribal to civilized. Now that electric speed-up has brought all people within a single family relationship, the shock and misery is just as great for tribal societies as for civilized ones:

DON'T LOOK DOWN BUT OUT!

Responding to the new global patterns of retribalization, the Canadian Mohawks and Iroquois are getting off the high steel and heading for the old hunting grounds. They are easily a match for Londonderry's lass, Bernadette Devlin, in their tribulation.

One Pressure Deserves Another

We are the primitives of a new civilization.
Boccioni

It may sound paradoxical to say that as the world retribalizes, those societies that already enjoy the tribal state of family unity also experience severe distress. At the same time that the civilized or individualist (*i.e.,* visual, print-oriented; see *The Gutenberg Galaxy*) world is reduced to communal involvement, nonliterate societies, whether in the Mideast or the Far East or Africa, are brought into much more intense interface among themselves. The new intensity of interface via new proximity inflames tribal man, just as it exposes him to the whole spectrum of consumer values enjoyed by the Western world during the past century.

High-Rise as a Quest for Privacy and Identity Turns Everybody into Nobody

Our image of ourselves varies greatly with our surroundings and associates. Any change, therefore, in technical services or disservices creates new environments that directly interact upon our sensory lives and the shaping of our identity images.

In *The Hidden Dimension,* Edward T. Hall shows that "most of the distance-sensing process occurs outside of awareness." Only the visual sense can be static; all others are dynamic. After examining the activities and spaces related to intimate, personal, social, and public relationships in North America and in Europe, Hall compares differences in what Americans and Arabs consider to be "pushy" in public:

> . . . most Americans follow a rule, which is all the more binding because we seldom think about it. . . . As soon as a person stops or is seated in a public place, there balloons around him a small sphere of privacy which is considered inviolate. The size of the sphere varies with the degree of crowding, the age, sex, the importance of the person, as well as the general surroundings. Anyone who enters this zone and stays there is intruding. . . . For the Arab, there is no such thing as an intrusion in public.

Whereas Americans assume rights to space where they sit, Arabs take on space rights as they move.

A massive space and identity syndrome that concerns the antithetic characters of Europe and America is overlooked by Hall.

North Americans go out for privacy.
North Americans stay home for community.
Europeans go out for community.
Europeans stay home for privacy.

Americans have no privacy at home and indeed the phrase "at home" means open house, whereas *chez nous* or *chez moi* means incommunicado. Thus for the North American his car is a cherished mode of privacy, whereas the European car is a social toy.

RIM SPINS—PHYSICAL, PSYCHIC, AND SOCIAL

The editors of *Time* (June 6, 1969) report an experiment in "Violence: Beyond the Inner Circle":

> "I'm going to approach you now," said Psychiatrist Augustus F. Kinzel to his subject, who stood eight feet away at the center of a bare room. "Tell me to stop when you think I'm too close." . . . and a man with a long history of violence, shook his head. But as Kinzel continued his advance, the prisoner's hands clenched into fists and he backed up, like someone gearing for attack. It was almost as if he felt himself inside an invisible circle into which no one, not even an unthreatening psychiatrist, could safely intrude.

In *The Hidden Dimension*, Hall discusses the effects of crowding not only on various animals but also on people of different cultures. He concludes:

> Apart from the ethnic enclave, virtually everything about American cities today is sociofugal and drives men apart, alienating them from each other. . . . The automobile is the greatest consumer of public space yet created by man. . . . (In Los Angeles . . . 60 to 70 per cent of the space is devoted to cars.)

Congestion leads to a loss of identity and to violence as a means of keeping or establishing identity. Etiquette is a ritualized way of avoiding violence by protecting identity.

By dimming down and homogenizing individual responses to any social pressure whatever, "sensitivity training" now provides the TKO for private identity. James Joyce asks, in *Finnegans Wake*: "Why do I am a look alike a poss of porter peas?" Here, Joyce is recalling Esau, the hunter, who sold out his identity for a mess of "pot."

The UNPERSON is the inevitable result of improved communication. When all barriers of private consciousness are overcome, the resulting collective form of awareness is a tribal dream. Western man experiences it only in his sleep. During sleep the Western community works very hard to process and scrub the inputs that have entered private consciousness during the day. We all become unpersons at night.

In an extreme bureaucratic or totalitarian regime there is intense conflict between the corporate tribal needs and the insurgent demands of private identities. These rebels are treated as unpersons in the new totalitarian regimes. Saints and criminals are in the same cell, and for the same reasons, as far as "the organization" is concerned. These "mavericks" or "originals" are the "tragic flaws" in the corporate structures. Without them there can be no change for the better, only for the worse. When everybody *fits in*, the result is total connectedness or the absolute logic that is *rigor mortis*. Only the flaws or misfits create the needed gap or interval for resonance and "interface" and change or transformation through dialogue.

Both TO-BE and NOT-TO-BE Is a QUEST

Toronto's *Financial Post* (August 22, 1970) interviews Robert Ballon on how the Japanese mind works:

> Ballon: "There is no one more dogmatic about pragmatism than the American. Whereas the Japanese is pragmatic about pragmatism. He doesn't care, as long as it works. . . . There's nothing the matter with planning, but what counts is flexibility. . . . No computing, no forecasting will establish the future."

To-be OR not-to-be is NOT the question

Ballon observes that for the Japanese if the matter that comes up is *not* to be, there is *no* question. All that interests them is what *is* to be. And while we are impressing ourselves with technology, the Japanese are merely using it. When we say all Japanese are "gregarious," we are letting our categories fool us. For the Japanese is a participant, not as an individualist but as a member, just as one arm participates in the whole body.

Mutual Comprehension: Yes OR No?

Ballon stresses that no Japanese would ever try to convince you of anything, and it would be useless to try and convince him. When he says "yes," he means "yes, I heard you," *not* "yes, I agree."

COMPREHENSION IS NEVER MERE CLASSIFICATION. IT MEANS THE PERCEIVING OF TOTAL PROCESSES BY USING EVERY SENSE IN ANY SITUATION.

Walter Deiter, president of the National Indian Brotherhood, is reported by Toronto's *Globe and Mail* (August 19, 1970) as saying:

> "We are fed up with being studied by study groups. . . . We are a little backward in expressing our feelings, and we get a little concerned when someone else tries to plan for us."
> He said it is up to the Indian leaders to motivate their people. "But many want to be left alone. They don't want to get into the economic stream or rat race."

Chief Adam Solway added that Ottawa is trying to make Indians "little brown white men."

BURN, BABY, BURN!

A rioter in Watts, California, said: "THEY know where WE are now!" What the rioters and the public alike ignore is that *pushed far enough, "they" always become "we."*

In Toronto's *Globe Magazine* (November 21, 1970) Barry Came cites three examples of violence as a quest for identity in today's Middle Eastern conflicts:

> *Abu Hassan, captain in the Popular Front for the Liberation of Palestine:* He had been a farmer, he said, in the West Bank until 1967 when he had been driven across the Jordan River with his family by the Israeli advance in June. "When I came here, I could not stand, and I know that if I am to be a man again I must be able to stand."

> *Fuad Farrady, engineer, not a member of any guerrilla group:* "You see, we have been a people without pride for so long that anything that shows the world we exist is a triumph."

> *Ghasian Kanafani, editor of "Al Ada'af," the newspaper of the Popular Front:* Turning on those who accuse him of being a "Nazi," he asks: "When are you people going to understand we don't wear your blinders. We have no history of persecuting the Jews simply because they're Jews. That's your guilt."

Recently, a Kuwait government official, discussing tribal warfare in Southern Arabia, asked one of the authors: "Can any Westerner understand why many Arabs change from Royalist to Republican and back again on the same day?"

Today, the Golden Rule has dropped out. It has become *do unto others what they want done unto them.* This means the right of every man to be himself and to be recognized as such, whereas the Golden Rule assumed that people knew who they were and you did unto them as they did unto you. Identity now changes faster than rules. Who are you at this moment? The kids learn by changing costumes or customs.

CRIME DOES PAY

Today, we all live by our wits. The old denial has dropped out long ago. If an author like Donald R. Cressey can be confused by the tribal patterns of the Mafia, how much easier for a modern manager or educator to mistake the new tribalism within our own Western world for the conspiratorial invasion of an alien enemy. The American illusion of a Communist conspiracy in the world has the same sort of base as the Cressey illusion of the Mafia take-over in the United States.

Anything that is not visually oriented and rationally processed threatens the entire American way of life. Therefore, it is un-American. Since the

United States is the only country in history to begin with print technology as its guideline and pattern for all its establishments, it is, of all countries, the least able to confront the advent of electric technology, which contradicts every facet of specialist rational order.

MAN-OF-WHICH-WORLD

Diehard: when *Ground* leaves *Figure*
Dropout: when *Figure* leaves *Ground*

Whereas the nineteenth-century executive held a position of power in an organizational hierarchy, today's executive creates a vortex of power by putting on his organization as an audience. Now the name of the game has changed from manipulation to participation.

In Shakespeare's day, for the man of the world to "lose face" meant losing both name and role. Hence the anguish of Richard II as he responds to Northumberland's "My Lord—":

> No lord of thine, thou haught insulting man,
> Nor no man's lord. I have no name, no title—
> No, not that name was given me at the font—
> But 'tis usurp'd. Alack the heavy day,
> That I have worn so many winters out
> And know not now what name to call myself!
> O that I were a mockery king of snow,
> Standing before the sun of Bolingbroke
> To melt myself away in water-drops!

Since Richard had no choice, losing his role as King was to lose life's meaning—to be reduced to No-man.

The Ghost of a Salesman

In *McCall's* (July, 1970) Arthur Miller discusses

THE WAR BETWEEN YOUNG AND OLD

In a hundred ways the generations facing each other today have shown that what the older ones value the young despise. And chief among these golden calves of the old are work, war, and sex. . . . The older generation has an investment in waste and self-denial, and when these are mocked, honor is seemingly soiled and degraded. . . . It is not only that the young are wiser than the old—they were born into a world in which there would be no survivors after the next war. The old still imagine war otherwise. . . . What the young are threatening is the very existence, psychologically and spiritually speaking, of the old. . . . Willy knows that if he really starts listening to what his son is saying to him, he will have to, in effect, vomit up a good part of his life.

GLOBAL THEATER ENDS CENTRALIZED JUSTICE

As Public Becomes Criminal, Culprit Becomes Hero

The Associated Press (April 2, 1971) reports from Fort Benning, Georgia:

NIXON ORDERS CALLEY FREED
UNTIL REVIEW IS COMPLETED

Today, as the public participates in the news-making process, it automatically becomes the criminal with its own way of life on trial: "I might have done the same thing myself."

VORTICES OF POWER

Is Your NAME or Your FACE Your FORTUNE?

Once, it was advertised that McLuhan would give a speech on the subject "From Jobs to Rolls." Occasionally, he meditates on the possibility that this boo-boo conceals some deeper truth than the word "roles."

James Joyce discovered that almost any slip of the tongue was likely to yield new insights far deeper than the so-called Freudian slip, *e.g.*, "casting his perils before swains." Ordinary life from day to day tosses up such items as "loogal leap holes," or "the most juice" for "*le mot juste.*" Nearly all successful labels, from "Vat 69" to "Coke," are loaded with implications highly appropriate to the product in question, such as keeping up with the Dow-Jones. Now the "midi" has become "the Edsel of the rag trade." Successful enterprises, without exception, are clad in suitable, if not inspired, styles of resonance. "Proctor and Gamble" might have come from some playful contest in nomenclature, as "Bell" or "IBM" (eye beam, etc., etc., etc.). The world's authority on chemical solutions is W. C. Dampier Dampier Wetham, and he has a cousin, W. C. Dampier Dampier Wetham Botham. Was it not Hazlitt who asked, "How many people by the very force of their names have been compelled to greatness"?

Tribal Mask or Private Face?

What is true of the resonating label is equally true of the masks and costumes (*costume*, Italian for custom or habit) that people devise for role playing. When in role or costume, clothing becomes spatial. It puts on an audience like charisma. Ordinary dress is a private extension of man's skin facing the elements. The "civilized" man uses his private face, like his clothing, in order to hide. The tribal man, on the other hand, wears his face as a mask that he dare not lose. Who are you at this moment?

The Midi and the Hula Hoop

When hoops ran high.
James Joyce

Mini born of hula was a howling success. The midi born of the "rag trade" was a howler. Fashion must be a surprise effect of invisible causes. When causes show, skirts won't get off the ground.

A Costume Puts on an Audience

The hippies hate policemen dressed in blue uniforms, hand on rule book and notebook, eyes roving to detect delinquents and rule breakers. The same hippies dote on the "Cyclops," *i.e.,* motorcycle cop, helmeted, breeched, and leather-putteed. This mythic monster with his single eye beam does not qualify as "fuzz" or "pig." His costume, like that of the judge, hangman, or hippie, indicates that he is involved in a role. The kids do the motorcycle cop the honor of imitating him. The judge puts on his robes (and, in England, his wig) by way of assuming the corporate authority of the community. So bedecked, he is not a private person, and he is not allowed to speak to anybody as a private person until he has removed his costume.

THE HIPPIE IN THE ALTOGETHER IS IN TRIBAL COSTUME

The stripper puts on her audience by taking off her clothes. Thus clad, she is not a private person. Backstage, in whatever situation, she is a private person. Stripped of her audience, she is nobody.

Goldsmith said of the great actor Garrick, "On the stage, he was natural, simple, affecting. It was only when he was off that he was acting." Goldsmith was quite right. No actor is an actor without his audience. Two boxers slugging in private are not putting on a boxing match of any sort. The greatest football teams in the country cannot play a game without an audience. Without a crowd, it would merely be a practice.

Anyone Who Can Fake Sincerity on TV Has Got It Made

In the electric age, all events tend to require and obtain audiences. The movie did not require and could not tolerate a studio audience. TV shows *must* have a studio audience. This difference is a succinct way of indicating the world of difference between the camera eye and the inconoscope of TV.

3

Effluents from Affluence

Putting Off Old Clothes

Jann Wenner, writing in *Rolling Stone* Magazine (January 7, 1971), quotes former Beatle John Lennon:

> I'm sick of all these aggressive hippies or whatever they are, the Now Generation, being very uptight with me. Either on the street or anywhere, or on the phone, demanding my attention, as if I owed them something. . . . They frighten me, a lot of uptight maniacs going around, wearing peace symbols.
>
> The bigger we got, the more unreality we had to face; the more we were expected to do, until, when you didn't sort of shake hands with a mayor's wife, she would start abusing you and screaming and saying "How dare they?"
>
> All that business was awful, it was a humiliation. One has to completely humiliate oneself to be what the Beatles were, and that's what I resent. I didn't know it, I didn't foresee. It happened bit by bit, gradually, until this complete craziness is surrounding you, and you're doing exactly what you don't want to do with people you can't stand —the people you hated when you were 10.

Lennon is expressing the plight of the media giant trying to survive as a little guy.

On Stage in Role

The theme of this book, at every turn, indicates the inevitable new patterns of role involvement demanded by a speeded-up information flow. The new rim spin on the planet, created by the satellite environment, is only an outer and visible indicator of the innumerable inner adjustments demanded of earthly man under this new spinning canopy of information. The entire world has become a global theater with every human being more or less aware of being on-stage and in role. This is like the leap from the movie to TV. Under the old photo regime of universal culture and organization, there was a place for everything and an effort to keep everything in its place. In the West, at least, each man hoped to have a job, based on a skill or specialty. But in our time job has been replaced by role, involvement, and commitment. It is a condition that approximates closely that of caste and may quickly surpass that of the participational patterns of medieval society. We return to what Shakespeare thought of role playing in musical terms, as if each member of society were in a communal orchestra:

> Music do I hear?
> Ha, ha! Keep time. How sour sweet music is
> When time is broke and no proportion kept!
> So is it in the music of men's lives,
> And here have I the daintiness of ear
> To check time broke in a disordered string,
> But for the concord of my state and time
> Had not an ear to hear my true time broke.
>
> Shakespeare, *Richard II*

It is helpful to remind ourselves of both the means and the motives that led our predecessors to create the opposite form of social structure, such as followed the Middle Ages: the discovery that by specialist fragmentation and dehumanization, aggregations of men could perform superhuman feats of industrial production. After centuries of confronting the hidden and twisted motives of social men, it came as a mighty deliverance through mechanization to slough off humanity altogether. The alibi for their gesture was absolute equality, albeit in nonentity. As we return to role playing under the impulse of electric circuitry, we also confront once more the mysteries of both malignancy and magnanimity in the human heart. Work can no longer be organized on the mechanical and specialist equality basis. The transition from the old specialist to the new tribal occupations takes many forms under such names as "team work," "creativity," and "work modules." Now satellites speed past in the RVM of the old jalopy.

In "The Ordeal of Fun" (July 27, 1969), *Look* Magazine cites the *Journal of Social Issues*: "Fun, from having been suspect if not taboo, has tended to become obligatory." The article continues:

> In certain ways, it smacks of an ordeal. But it goes on. At a paradoxical moment when the country seems obsessed with anger, the pursuit of fun is expanding. . . . Already the fun quest has reshaped big segments of the society, turning field hands into busboys and meadows into rest-stop communities. . . . You may find fun elsewhere—but only the fun you bring with you. For that, as every child knows, is where it is at.

The rich man becomes the displaced person.

THE AFFLUENT DROPOUT IN THE EFFLUENT SOCIETY

Paradoxically the new "proletariat" is to be found in the affluent world of the alienated. In a world of "software" the rich, who possess nothing but "hardware," have been dumped, as it were, on the old middenheap of discarded artifacts. They have lost their identity, their goals and purposes, and their satisfactions. In the old "hardware" world the poor retain a satisfactory bond with motorcars and the rest of the obsolete technologies, including the educational establishment. The poor can still pursue "goals" in education, knowing that they will better themselves in the world. There is no way by which the rich can better themselves in such a world. They are in the position of the young lady who "had everything." The only possible gift for such a person is antibiotics. The rich have no role in a "software" society. Role playing for them means abandoning all their consumer values. Thorstein Veblen saw their plight long ago as "conspicuous consumption," where one eats as one is eaten. The satisfactions of conspicuous consumption in the age of "software" are zero. *Homo consumens* in the Western world is dead, just as the *economic man* was killed by Hitler. Today, anyone with $40,000 a year has as much access to the services available to Western man as the billionaire.

The Rich Man as Displaced Person

Give your ulcer a break, Dad; don't fight it.
Outlook of a teen-age daughter

In his frantic endeavors to maintain his wealth, the rich man tries to augment it. As he strives, he loses all the advantages of wealth; he is a dropout. He is like the young man in the ancient parable, who went away sorrowing when asked to sell all he had to give to the poor. He sorrowed because he had great possessions. Possessions in that time did not mean just "hardware"; they meant commitments. He had thousands of people who depended on him. We, also, have the example of the peasant who hangs onto his land—to "hardware" totally, rejecting all "software" as truly insecure. The miser, grasping his possessions, is the image of the man who has no "software" to enjoy.

Canetti's Principle of Power

The crowd, or wealth, craves to become more, and fears that it is becoming less. So the rich man lives in a state of anxiety that he is losing everything. The rich man loses "software" benefits by worrying about the "hardware." The only escape hatch for him is to leave the "hardware" rat race.

The new *ground* created by newly acquired wealth destroys the identity or self-image of most people and leads to violence, or even to madness: *the danger of unstopability*. If you win, then what? Know when to drop out and drop in again, like the sailor prince—*breezy come, breezy go*.

PARAPOLITICAL PARADOX

The hidden service environments that began to permeate the Western world with printing and mass production have been little heeded by the

Marxist theorists. It is embarrassing for them to be reminded that by 1820 the ordinary worker could command public services of travel and information exceeding in scope the greatest resources of merely private wealth. In the information world of the electric age, this ratio has been further altered. The ordinary person can now command multibillion-dollar services of entertainment, information, and travel. This leaves Marxism stranded on the old "hardware" plateau. Marxian dialectics of Nature have failed to go through the Greek "looking glass" to discover existence. In the logic of Robert Benchley: "There are two kinds of people in the world: those that divide the world into two classes and those that don't." What are they *for* or *against?* Where are their premises *now?*

All ideologies based on Western industrial civilization have failed to go "through the vanishing point" for direct perception of "where it's at." Whether starting from "left" or "right," their concepts and private points of view now converge "beyond the fringe" in the nineteenth century. Such ideologies, persisting as "past times" for "critics of critical criticism," are powerless to cope with the patterns of development emerging in today's global theater. The *avant-garde* of the RVM, unable to fit the new processes into the old categories, resort to gloom or to moral indignation, age-old substitutes for perception and understanding. For such people, all *breakthroughs become breakdowns*—FUTURE SHOCK.

Chapter 9

Everyman as Dropout and Drop-in

Failure Through Success
and
Success Through Failure

In my end is my beginning.
Mary, Queen of Scots

In America the rich man is a dropout because he's a beginning, not an end. The rich man who makes it is finished. His sons have to start all over again. The rich man's son does not enter a society where the possession of wealth is meaningful. By becoming wealthy you prove to the world that you justify the American dream by unlimited success. The American dream is now being spoofed. One*up*manship now means one*down*manship.

WHEN THE OLD SUBSONIC AIRCRAFT WENT THROUGH THE SOUND BARRIER, ITS ELEVATORS REVERSED THEIR EFFECTS.

Looka Busy!

The rich are in the same danger as the old of being excluded from the community. Wealth retires people. At sixty or sixty-five the old are dropped automatically by industrial organizations. The rich drop out by starting at the top; then they are fed into the process from the bottom:

> A millionaire doesn't need a pay check. But the fact is that they work like everyone else. Except for an extremely small group of café-society playboys, all America's rich men are busy as bankers, lawyers, executives, or politicians, doing something productive.
> Richard P. Frisbie, *How to Peel a Sour Grape*

The American millionaire can find privacy only by going out to work. The office "pad" is like an academic's study. Only the car (ideally in a traffic jam) affords more immunity to intruders. The millionaire's hotel "pad" affords solitude, not privacy (privacy implies a public). Although the millionaire can afford privacy, he cannot achieve community.

1

Speed-up via Job Mobile

THE NEW JACOB'S LADDER

DROPOUT of BIG as DROP-IN to SMALL
DROPOUT of SMALL as DROP-IN to BIG

The Peter Principle refers to the old situation that is now dead and rotting. The executive no longer gets pushed up to the level of his incompetence. He is continuously educated and given more and more equipment as he mounts. This is the new dimension in management. In the old Peter Principle the executive "did his thing" and was raised to the level of his incompetence.

LBJ drops from the big presidential job into a little professorial job. Vice versa, the professor starts in a little university job and drops into a big business job.

PECKING ORDER PECKED AWAY PACKS UP

RENT-AN-EXECUTIVE
Current Toronto ad

We know from fun books that old management is dead: the executive "steal"—the executive "dragged out"—like top players being grabbed off by other teams. Is the new trading in executives for wizards or whipping boys?

The Economist (September 20, 1969) discusses the services and disservices implicit in the drop-in/dropout executive syndrome—*paying the piper*:

> Nearly two years ago history stood on its head; Henry Ford's grandson, Mr. Henry Ford II, took William Knudsen's dynamic son, Mr. Semon Knudsen, away from GM and made him president of the Ford Motor Company after Mr. Knudsen had been passed over for the presidency of GM. Late last week the board of Ford met to sack Mr. Knudsen, because things "just had not worked out." . . . If a bad year comes, it will be convenient to blame that too on Mr. Knudsen.

The "mobile executive" is rapidly coming to the position where he can choose his place of work. One man's dropout is another man's drop-in, *e.g.*, the consultant chooses his place of action.

The shift in executive concern is toward the global ecological environment instead of merely the individual job—specializing in anything required. It means becoming a hunter and creator of new information and roles.

It's Reigning Executives Everywhere Today

Some *figure-ground* interfaces resulting from information speed-up are seen in student participation in politics. Older monopolies of knowledge, which sufficed to hedge the activities of banks and defense departments, have been eroded by the "rim spin" of global information flow (credit agencies built on discreditable data create credulity gaps). These same data banks, which replace monetary banks, also reveal the power structures of many other service environments. The revelation of top personnel guiding incompatible and conflicting services had long been taken for granted. Lack of specialists of recognized competence once justified their allocation to conflicting roles. In the early days of Hollywood the shortage of actors led to the discovery that six people running a figure eight could make a mob scene. In the same way, big business in its earlier phases lacked sufficient numbers of recognizable players to create a massive effect. A few people had to play diverse roles. As the show developed, the players became stars, putting on ever larger audiences as they developed new vortices of power via the box office or the market place. It often happened that one of the stars "stepped down" from his great eminence in order to develop an even larger role.

Stepping Down or Stepping Out?

When a John D. Rockefeller stepped down to become a *figure* in new *ground*, he brought his old *ground* (or institution) with him as part of his new *figure* or image. That is, when a star "steps down," the image or fame detaches itself from the modest setup in which it grew. The image is transplanted into a richer and wider field. Thus the executive or star as dropout can flourish afresh and more abundantly, as a great actor does, seeking ever-new roles. The actor, like the businessman, carries not only his image but his skills from the roles he abandons to enrich the new role. The mobile executive also transfers his prestige and skill from role to role.

The New York *Times* (December 18, 1969) announced:

> Jack J. Dreyfus, Jr., one of Wall Street's leading financiers, will retire tomorrow from Dreyfus & Co. to devote full time to studying and working with a drug that he believes may have broad implications. . . . In stepping down as senior partner of Dreyfus & Co., Mr. Dreyfus will be leaving the brokerage house that he founded in 1946 and that since then has grown from a net worth of less than $300,000 to more than $50 million.

The executive who "steps down" often prepares the way for sudden increase of the wealth-making process.

THE CLASSICAL CASE OF DROPOUT AS DROP-IN

Breakdown as Breakthrough

The principle of this action is stated by Aristotle in his description of the tragic hero. The hero's suffering or *agon* or struggle for new identity is made possible by a "tragic flaw" or defect. This is the classical case of breakdown as breakthrough. Without this flaw, or gap, he could not *make* the discovery that changes both himself and his actions. As Charles Olson explains in his book *Proprioception:*

> The fault can be a very simple one—a mere unawareness, for example —but if he has no fault he cannot change for the better, but only for the worse . . . he must pass through an experience which opens his eyes to an error of his own.

What Aristotelians have ignored is that the "flaw" is the needed gap that permits "interface" and change. When the individual is entirely at one with his world or organization, he is headed for a hang-up of merging and unconsciousness, which is sterility in life or in business. In the age of instant information something similar to this individual process begins to characterize corporate operations. Indeed, the private star may well yield to the corporation as "star." A corporation may note that many of its resources are unnecessarily static and immobilized in specialized operations. Using the new speed of information access, the corporation team can assume a variety of new roles as a kind of constellation or galaxy of stars. Failure to accommodate to the new speed of information now threatens with by-pass or obsolescence any isolated or stationary enterprise whatever. To classify this new strategy as "conglomerate making" is a mere retrospect of a much slower phase that assumed monopoly, specialism, and stability for its continuance. There are innumerable instances of business-enterprise collapse just at the seeming peak of performance.

Bankruptcy as Speed-up via Dropout

For the historian there will always be the incidence of bankruptcy as a strategy in achieving "liquidity preference." This delightful economic whimsey, with all its bar-room resonance, merely refers to the advantages of having one's resources in readily cashable form. But bankruptcy and default on bonds were for a long time a major means of keeping assets readily accessible instead of having them embedded in sluggish enterprises. A sharp operator will always see a means of using one set of public resources in some innovational form. Before speculative information became available to everybody, bankruptcy was a natural means of transforming a slow operation into a speedy one.

The Iron Law of Eminence

The way up is the way down.
Ancient adage

The bigger the corporation, the more employees it drops out of sight. At the top, on the other hand, the executive is also swallowed by the corporation, knowing less and less about fewer and fewer people and operations: *as work enables a man to put on his public, he puts off himself.* He is like the author who both dedicates and delegates himself to his readers.

The Expendable Executive

Today, an executive is taught that his first job is to select and train several men who can replace him instantly. They often do. The next job is to process all branches of executive function in such a way that a man can be sent to any part of the organization anywhere, anytime, and feel quite at home.

The assembly line has now hit the top brass of management, just as automation begins to supersede the assembly line at the production level. America is rapidly moving into a new phase of simultaneous and many-leveled organization, which brings the enterprise era to an end.

Young Fogies as On-the-Job Dropouts

In the Toronto *Financial Post*, July 25, 1970, Arnold Edinborough reviews three "Marchbank books" by Robertson Davies. About the cult of the young, Davies observes:

> The whole world is burdened with young fogies. Old men with ossified minds are easily dealt with. But men who look young, act young and everlastingly harp on the fact that they are young but who nevertheless think and act with a degree of caution which would be excessive in their grandfathers, are the curse of the world. . . . Their very conservatism is secondhand, and they don't know what they are conserving.

Pushed to extreme, adaptation leads to destruction or to transformation.

THE SUPERADJUSTED PERSON IS A DROPOUT AS SURELY AS THE UNDER-
ADJUSTED PERSON IS A SHUT-IN

Laurence Peter's "victims of promotion" to the level of their own incompetence have only enough power to enfold themselves, as it were, in a cocoon of security or some upper branch of the organization tree. Here they remain safely insulated from the world. Quite otherwise is the case of the superadjusted executive for whom high achievement automatically entails drop out. So also is the question of the superadjusted management specialist.

2

Specialist Ills v. Specialist Cures

CONSULTANT VISITATIONS

In Toronto's *Globe and Mail* (August 1, 1970), management consultant H. J. Mulaner describes a typical case in "How the Executive Got the Axe":

> A young man who walked into the office of the Canadian executive was 27 years old. The executive had been in charge of numerous aspects of his company's operations throughout Canada for 21 years. . . . One hour and 32 minutes later [the young man] recommended the executive be fired. . . . But the most sickening part of this story is my suspicion that the man did not deserve to be fired. His dismissal was a public gesture, a grandstand play on the part of the management consulting firm to demonstrate its supposedly awesome decision-making capabilities. . . . When business historians look back on our era, I predict that they will call it "the Reign of the Consultants". . . . Historians may bestow on us an aphorism, "Never has so much damage been done to so many by so few."

Time (April 13, 1970) cites management consultant Thomas J. Johnson: "Being fired is another part of the executive's job." But bouncing back from being Vice-President of Nothing is the "sternest test."

RESIGN! RESIGN! RESIGN!

> O mother
> What shall I cry?
> We demand a committee, a representative
> committee, a committee of investigation.
> > T. S. Eliot, "Difficulties of a Statesman"

The editors of *Time*, June 1, 1970, observe:

> Whether to quit or not to quit, and when, in a disagreement over policy is a dilemma not confined to people in government. . . . Lord Caradon, Britain's Ambassador to the U.N., proposes these criteria for the resignation of a Cabinet member: 1) he must be directly involved in a policy that he opposes; 2) he has suggested a viable alternative that has been rejected; 3) the issue is a continuing one. "The sad truth is that the man who stays to fight runs the risk of losing both his case and his honor."

Lord Caradon is suggesting old ways as *the* pathways for avoiding "the effectiveness trap." But in today's environment of accelerated information flow THE VIABLE IS ALWAYS INVISIBLE.

Back to the Halls of Akademonium

Ann Rhodes, discussing the "middle-aged dreamer on the campus" in the *Financial Post* (August, 1970), notes:

> Enrolled in Canadian universities today are several thousand full-time adult students—men and women who have quit careers in midstream. . . . The main problems you'll face as an adult scholar . . . are isolation, loss of self-esteem, strained relationships with fellow students and instructors, and difficulty in thinking academically.

Unaware of the changing ground rules, these "older-than-average students" have returned nostalgically to old *camp* on the new campus—no longer a place to walk and talk. They are trapped again by narrow specialist means for broad human aims, like the monastic orders.

Taking the Veil in Vain: The Religious Dropout

The early Christian was a new, small *figure* against a vast pagan *ground*. The body of pagan practice and tradition was too vast to tempt him to adaptation. After centuries of Christian scriptural and theological study, the Christian *figure* not only enlarged, but the pagan *ground* contracted. The Christian enlargement included a great deal of the pagan heritage of arts, letters, and philosophy. The confusion of *figure-ground* became possible. The Christian is always most discernible as a missionary against a pagan *ground*. However, in the West today there is another dimension for the dropout, namely, speed. When too much and too many are changing too fast, there is no time to adapt. One has to anticipate or drop out, break through or break down. For most, the demands of adaptation and anticipation are beyond them. They drop out.

SUPERIOR OF ORDER RESIGNS;
SEEKS TO LEAVE PRIESTHOOD

> Father Boyce fought to force change in the church's hierarchy and make the Redemptorists, traditionally rural in outlook, more relevant to modern urban life. "For better or for worse I now feel that I have said and done all that I can for the renewal of the institutional church in Canada and for the Toronto Province of Redemptorists," he said.
> Toronto *Star*, August 7, 1970

For many today, the imposed patterns of motivational organization seem to have no relevance whatever. They see an immediate clash between integrity and mere respectability. Integrity concerns *figure* without *ground* as usurping figure. When the *ground* itself becomes Protean or bewildering in its multiplicity of changes, then the ordinary psyche abandons all hope of relating thereto and retreats to the ivory tower of integrity. The Redemptorist superior who resigned from governing an evangelical order in the Catholic Church, feeling that he could contribute more to the church as a layman, was very much in the position of the corporation president who thinks that he could be of more use to the organization if he could creep underneath the organizational pyramid.

Joining or Relating Old Figures to New Grounds

If the early Christian felt isolated by the size of the adversary—the world —the modern Christian feels outdistanced by the speed. Today, it is inconceivable to the organizer of traditional teaching and instruction how any arrangement could be made for relating the young or the faithful to the ancient church except by arbitrary "authority" and paternalism. Failing to relate old *figure* and new *ground,* he sees no recourse but to join the new *ground.* This is the fatal formula for loss of identity: "*Here lies community R.I.P.,*" as James Hitchcock observes. In the RVM, church unity via centralization of existing bureaucratic institutions *on paper* appears more and more attractive as a technical solution for current organizational problems. Meanwhile, individual people and local organizations are exploring gaps to find new ways of creating religious community *in action* through further decentralization.

THE GREAT TRAINING ROBBERY

In *Education and Jobs: The Great Training Robbery,* Ivar Berg examines the present educational system. In brief, his conclusions are:

> A growing number of workers have more education than they need. . . . Salaries are not necessarily closely related to education. . . . An employee's productivity does not vary systematically with his years of formal education. . . . The rate of turnover is positively associated with high education. Upper- and middle-class employees are not the only ones who are over-qualified for their jobs. . . . Better-educated employees are often rated as less productive. The practice of basing teachers' salaries on the credits they earn toward higher degrees actually encourages teachers not to teach since those who feel overtrained tend to seek administrative positions or better-paying jobs in industry. . . . In the armed forces, it was found . . . that training on the job was more important than educational credentials.

Dr. Berg notes that the degree has become a "badge of stability" rather than a guarantee of competence. In reviewing government employee performance, he remarks that "the nonrational use of formal credentials, which might be taken as a significant symptom of 'bureaupathology,' is more likely to be found in our great private enterprises than in our government apparatus."

Dr. Berg confronts the educational establishment in its "police-state" aspect. What he ignores is that "the great training robbery" took place long before he was born. It was in the nineteenth century that fragmented curriculums were substituted for dialogue and discovery. By then, Newman had already found that someone had made off with the boodle. Newman retrieved the oral tutorial system and got "education" off the book, instead of dishing out concepts, training perception by studying all manner of effects in the man-made environment. *In an information environment the most valuable resource is the recognition of specialists' ignorance.*

Hidden Abdication: The Disappearance of Take-Home Power

Today, in more and more organizations, whether business or government or educational, only marginal funds remain within executive control for incidental projects. The rest is automatically assigned to maintaining existing services. As monopolies of knowledge vanish, these services appear clearly as disservices. The new translucence of *formal* structures calls in doubt all the goals and purposes of every human organization; the services no longer reach their intended beneficiaries. The business of controlling and administering activities has hijacked the operation. Now all that remains of the *process* of education is in the committees or bull sessions.

"Poésie Concrète": Great Expectations and Rude Encounters

Today, as students and teachers alike demand greater support for their various specialisms, we meet increasing numbers of "overskilled jobless" hunting for nonexistent jobs:

> Aerospace experience is not acceptable.
> Recent want ad

The outwaged student says, in effect, "You tell me to attain this high degree, then drop into the real world." The students who have been processed on the computerized assembly lines of the new classrooms, expect to drop off the end of the line into a job. Why else should the line exist? While fighting what they have become, they increasingly become what they fight.

The Environment Drops In
as the Classroom Drops Out

Edward Mortimer, writing from Paris for the London *Times Educational Supplement* (August 7, 1970), reports:

> Mr. Michael Huberman, a member of the Secretariat of the United Nations Educational, Scientific, and Cultural Organization (unesco)

in a paper written for International Education Year . . . argues that
in both developed and developing countries formal education is devouring funds that are needed for other purposes and is failing to
achieve the results expected of it. . . . He argues that education in
the world today is a self-justifying process unrelated to any real human
need.

The hidden assumption underlying the educational establishment is that
there must be a proper place and regular time to serve their puny packaged
courses to needy students. The educational specialist refuses to consider the
far richer fare to be had without restriction in the global electric theater.
Meanwhile budgets for studying education are increasing faster than for
the educational task itself.

Instead of sending the "ne'er-do-wells" off to make their fortunes, send
them out to learn the score—to train perception rather than to master specialist content. They can prepare to transform the old institutions. By returning to form work modules they can by-pass old organizational hang-ups,
using the potential of the new information environment.

MATURITY IS A SOMETIME THING

As fruit on the tree ripens it drops off.

For the nineteenth-century WASP, "maturing" meant *earning power*. As
Dr. St. Michael Guinan in her paper "Maturation and Aging in Religious
Life" (*Donum Dei*, Vol. 8, Canadian Religious Conference, Hull, 1971)
puts it: "One prevalent measure of maturity in the postindustrial Western
world dominated by the Protestant ethic was the equating of the adult's
worth with his capacity for gainful work." The *earner* displaced the Greek
concept of the "mature" man as the thinker, which had supplanted the
cultivator and the *hunter*.

Mod POB as Ghost of Aged WASP
Oblivious of Shift from EYE to EAR

Today, WASPs are vanishing with the horizons of the pre-electric world.
Their spirits have transmigrated into POBs (print-oriented bastards) of
whatever color or creed or politics—all those who still gaze into their RVMs
at what is past rather than what is passing.

EMOTIONAL MATURITY

Early in the nineteenth century people began to ask, "Is he grown up?"
James Hillman's classic study *Emotion* explains:

Emotion is learned behaviour. . . . The child knows little of pity or
mercy or of a father's holy rage . . . the education of emotions is

changing symbolic fixations. Not hate nor desire nor fear are to be changed, but the appropriate symbols . . . which evoke these emotions. The alteration of symbols alters the emotion.

YOU CAN HURT A MAN'S FEELINGS BUT YOU CAN'T HURT HIS RAGE.

T. S. Eliot's poem *Animula* explores the changing relation of symbols and emotions from birth to death:

> The heavy burden of the growing soul
> Perplexes and offends more, day by day . . .
> Pray for us now and at the hour of our birth.

Sentimentality is the indulgence of one emotion at a time. Aestheticism, by the same token, is to indulge in art as a consumer commodity, not as a training in perception. The aesthete "wants his woe to show" on display for anyone to buy. Emotional maturity, on the other hand, is the ability to experience and to savor conflicting emotions—being grown up.

3

Old as New and New as Old

Darwinian Evolution: Supplanting and Extinguishing

There is no longer a measure of maturity except in the sense of retirement—first on the bough ready to pluck. Our idea of maturity has gradually become that of the aging *Man in Bureaucracy* preparing to vacate his place to the next in line. In the old hierarchical regime retirement is automatic. This RVM policy enables the decision maker to lean on "two-bit wit" rather than human understanding.

THE RETURN OF THE CASTAWAYS

Old Skills as New Treasures

Yorick Blumenfeld, writing in Toronto's *Globe and Mail* (November 26, 1970), reports:

> Starting in the late nineteen fifties America began a whirlwind infatuation with its youth. . . . Old age quickly turned into an unwanted commodity. . . . Then, last summer, a reversal began to be seen. As the *Wall Street Journal* noted, many companies found that the "oldster" not only can be counted on to do a better job than the youngster who replaced him but will also "complain less, show up more regularly, and gladly work for less money."

As Dr. Guinan says, "It is an awareness of our human vulnerability which forms an integral part of the wisdom of age." And T. S. Eliot said before: "Old men should be explorers."

PIONEERS OF THE NEW LIFE SPAN

Dr. Guinan explains:

> Today's elders are cultural pioneers . . . they have no present, no tradition to follow. It is the first time in human history that any considerable number of persons have lived beyond the sixties. Longevity, in previous centuries the privilege of the few, has now providentially become the prerogative of the many.

We now see these pioneers proliferating in new groupings, such as SCORE—Senior Corps of Retired Executives.

All are seeking to refurbish old skills to meet the demands of current situations—enrichment through welding the old with the new. The cliché retrieves the archetype.

The Transparent Moment That Snaps the Chemical Bond

The thought of the day when the pretty girl looks through you as if you were a pane of glass is enough to send a shudder through the New York *Times* Service (April 10, 1971):

BEGINNING OF MIDDLE AGE MAY BE COMING 5 YEARS EARLIER

A 40-year-old head of a successful corporation: "I keep feeling more and more depressed, and I can't figure out why. I've gone as high as I can go. There's nothing wrong with my life, but I just can't seem to shake this feeling of, 'So here I am, so what?'"

A 46-year-old manufacturer's representative: "For years you have the idea in the back of your mind, 'If I don't like this, I'll cut out and go somewhere else, change jobs, try a whole new field.' Then one day you look in the mirror and see white hairs, and bags under yours eyes, and you know you've had it. You're not going any place except to the cemetery."

Let's remember the big exec being lowered into the grave in his custom-built white Cadillac while his friends remark, "Man, that's really living!"

THE STRATEGY OF MULTIPLE CAREERS

Moon-lighted, Star-lighted, De-lighted

Hobbies are preferred areas of incompetence.
Anonymous

Peter Drucker's strategy of multiple careers is to knock off at forty and do something different. Drucker has temporalized the whole doctrine of transmigration and put it into this life. "Moonlighting" takes transmigration a step further. The unity of work and residence makes multiple roles possible. The trick is not to get yourself caught in a hierarchy. When things speed up, hierarchy disappears, and global theater sets in.

The Phoenix Pattern: End as Beginning

Fifty years ago great economic success meant a social position. It was a terminus. A man stayed with it. His wife and family enjoyed the fruits of his success as consumers. Today, this is impossible. Consumer ethos is finished. The social hostess no longer exists. The Ivy League school turns out affluent misfits and student activists. The extreme image is Ben Braddock in *The Graduate* and his opposite British numbers in *IF*.

Now that foundations are converting hard cash into art forms, it is hard to imagine a wealthy man in the Western world who is not inclined to use his money for noncommercial ventures. As the old organization structures fall apart, those who had functioned in various corners of the hierarchy drift out into society to become adventurers and privateers. It is an event that has occurred many times before in human history, but never on such a scale. Never before has the entire world been organized on two patterns, both of which are in a state of interchange and simultaneous metamorphosis. The West is going "East" under the impact of speed-up of information movement. The speed of the electric circuit drives man from *outer* to *inner* interests, thus orientalizing the West by means of its own technology. Meantime, the East is going "West" as it acquires more and more of the old Western "hardware" setup. The East, as well as Africa and Latin America, now seeks to create for itself the nineteenth-century world of consumer services and packages that the West is sloughing off via the inspiration of its electric circuitry. Meantime, the East and archaic societies feel the impact of electric technology as well. Where the closely knit kinship systems of tribal man have long survived, radio and TV, far from weakening these forms, reinforce them greatly.

By Embracing Both Horns of a Dilemma Paradox Leads to Discovery

Like Gregor Samsa in Kafka's *Metamorphosis*, all specialists "waging management" are hung up without any means of getting across to their associates. The world is full of alienated and problem-ridden people who want an audience—the principle of the dialogue. For centuries people have been monologuing and expressing their points of view on everything. Alienated people find no satisfaction in expressing points of view any more than industrialists are eager to declare their problems to people who are incapable of dialogue:

VALUE JUDGMENTS DESTROY DIALOGUE, WHICH DEMANDS THE SHARING OF IGNORANCE.

To be able to dialogue with modern people caught in extremely complicated situations requires precisely the encyclopedic range of awareness of the ancient humanist. That is, the complexity of the contemporary world demands a nonspecialist preparation of awareness which is almost poetic in its scope and sensitivity to pattern. The answers to all contemporary problems are to be found in the problems themselves through dialogue in the eco-world: you've got to have somebody to listen to you, just as they need somebody to listen to them. Opposition to the mainstream is for steering past breakdown to breakthrough.

THE EXECUTIVE AS COMPREHENSIVIST

The Bridge Between Old and New Perception

Two complementary modes are thus at work in all parts of the world. Previously, the cultures of the world had known only one of these modes at a time. There had been a stress on "hardware" and weaponry or on "software" and knowledge. These forms are no longer mutually exclusive and the specialist must now become the comprehensivist, whether in Japan or in Idaho.

The part of the world that feels most of the upset is the part which has been the most specialized. It is only where work is highly organized that there can be unemployment, and it is only where there is special stress on goals that there can be boredom. By the same token, when the highly organized forms go out of effective service, they rouse a mixture of feelings that results in "humor" (the word means a special mood). The flood of comic books about the vanishing organization man provides the clue: "A word to the sufficient is wise."

The Fifth Business

In his book of this title, Robinson Davies identifies the components of drama as the hero, the villain, the heroine, the confidant, and the "fifth business," *i.e.*, what is needed to bring about the *dénouement*. The "fifth business" includes both visible *figure* and hidden *ground* revealed by the artist—the perceptive man of integral awareness in any activity whatever. It is not a *science of matching* but an *art of making* that bridges East and West, "hippie" and POB, EAR and EYE.

THE OLD "HARDWARE" STRUCTURES BECOME ART
FORMS IN THE NEW "SOFTWARE" WORLD.

The unstructured and gradeless school of electric information succeeds to the bureaucratic and fragmented school based on the classifications of print technology. In the same way, "hardware" economics based on a money-oriented market is succeeded by the new knowledge industries. This revolution is long past but is still managed as if it were going to take place in the year 2001. For the comprehensivist it is the "noise" of the total environment that he must now convert into the program of his global theater.

RETUNING THE SKY

The moment of Sputnik extended the planet. Something happened to the stellar system at that moment. The possibility of "retuning the sky" was born. Previously, the "extensions of man" related to his body, anything from his skin (clothing) to his nervous system (electric circuitry). Each and all of these extensions affected the transactions between men and their previous environment. The *extension of the planet itself* meant that the technology was not transported by individual or collective man but by his previous environment—the Earth. It became a totally new game with new *ground* rules. Our *ground* now was literally in the sky. An aerial perspective had come to despotize (from the Greek *despotein:* for inclusive vision from above; it is the Greek for knowing something "inside out"). Whereas previous extensions had altered the speed of human motions in a great variety of ways, freely hybridizing with one another, the new extension of the planet seemed to call despotically for a new harmonizing of the spheres of action, influence, and knowledge.

CONCERTMASTER OF GIANT RIM SPIN

Whereas rim spin was a suitable metaphor derived from meteorology and weather forecasting, the *giant rim spin* of the satellite environment reversed the significance of the "weather man" as a guesser. The satellites that transform the planet into a work of art by placing it inside a man-made environment call for something much more than a weather forecaster. They demand a weather programmer. Many have noticed how irrelevant weather is in a city. Whenever the man-made environment is dominant, the whims of weather are impertinent. Weather belongs to the country, not to the city. The erratic climates of opinion and enterprise that accompanied the motions of presatellite Earth, when "old mother west wind" and "old mother Nature" were matriarchs to be reckoned with, have now been retired.

THE NEONOSTALGIC REACTIONARIES

Today's diehards, right, left, and center, strive vainly to reduce the acoustic processes of our electric world to the visual confines of their nineteenth-century conceptual packages. They are terrified to drop out of their "hardware" thinking to get in touch with "where it's at."

The scrapping of Nature by satellites, whether desirable or not, is a *fait accompli.* We cannot go back to the natural state, with or without our innocence. Now that Nature has been discarded, she must be reinvented. We are in the position of actualizing Voltaire's fantasy about God, of whom he said, "If He didn't exist, we would have to invent Him." Voltaire felt he had liberated himself from the divine tyranny. In the same way today many may feel that having liberated ourselves from presatellite Nature, we are free to do as we wish.

Many may think that we are now safely ensconced inside a utopian kingdom like Rabelais's Abbey of Thélème, the fantastic world of do-as-you-like. In fact, we have now to replace nature itself, remaking it as an art form perfectly accommodated to the totality of human needs and aspirations.

Such an enterprise requires nothing less than inclusive awareness of human resources and limitations. Man-made nature, fashioned according to life as art, may tax human creativity far beyond anything levied on presatellite man. Having engineered into existence this giant rim spin around all human transactions, we now have to discover the means of adjusting the speed of this spin in order to accommodate the responsive spins of all the components.

As concertmaster, satellite man would have to audition such selections as the Manhattan Project with exquisite prescience of "audience" effects. The "audience" of satellite man includes the "actors" and is not merely human but consists of all the resonances awakened everywhere. Satellite man no longer inhabits *visual space*, but a resonating *acoustic space* whose boundaries are nowhere. Today, he is an information hunter in ECO-land.

DO-IT-YOURSELF FATE

Everyman as Finn Awake

As all monopolies of knowledge break down in our world of information speed-up, the role of executive opens up to Everyman. There are managers galore for the global theater. By their deeds you will know them—the instant catalysts.

Today, while efforts are intensifying to prop up the old hierarchical structures, they are being eroded and transformed by new modular forms of human organization. Based on dialogue, these modules are where the dropout becomes the drop-in for remaking the clichés while retrieving the archetypes—new treasures for all.

> "To borrow,
>   To burrow,
>   To barrow."
>   H.C.E.
>   with
>   KEYS
>   to
>   GIVEN

ECO-LOG FOR
NAVIGATION

Through the Looking Glass with Many Happy Returns

From Harmony to Harmony
Through all the Compass of the Notes it ran,
The Diapason closing full in Man.

> Dryden, "A Song for St. Cecilia's Day"

The Music Goes Round and Round, and
It Comes Out HEAR!

The "revolution" of *this* age has been a new order in which nature has become the extension of man. The centuries-old pattern had been man as an echo vibrating in harmony with the "natural order." Now nature must play man's tune.

Evolution Is Adapting to Exploration

Ontogeny replays philogeny.
> Ernst Haeckel

Mimesis is the process by which all men learn.
> Aristotle, *Poetics*

Nineteenth-century evolution, Spencer-style, meant small changes finding their place in a "chain of being," as if Nature had the itch to niche. This was the ideal of nineteenth-century man, for whom there was a place for everything, and everything had to be in its proper place.

Eighteenth-century man, Adam Smith–style, had envisaged a micro-ecology, the man-made world of the free market, as a new "Nature." This image of free-market exchange of equivalents in a new "hardware" world of industrial goods and services was the cliché that retrieved the older ideal of romantic primitivism. The hybrid of the new Iron Age paradoxically drove men's dreams into the uninhibited world of poetic romance—the interplay between the private conscious and the tribal unconscious. The iron reality retrieved the Golden Age for poetry.

THE CHAMBERED NAUTILUS

Build thee a more stately mansion, O my soul,
As the swift seasons roll!

> Leave thy low-vaulted past!
> Let each new temple, nobler than the last,
> Shut thee from heaven with a dome more vast,
> Till thou at length are free,
> Leaving thine outgrown shell by life's unresting sea.
>
> Oliver Wendell Holmes

The nineteenth century could make its adjustments to new requirements in art and poetry. Today, in the electric age, instant speeds demand anticipation of new realities, while still burrowing in nineteenth-century thinking. A main obstacle in navigation today is the irrelevance of nearly everything being done by the nineteenth-century minds still in charge of the new electric world.

Outer and Inner Tripping

The Jules Verne mind accustomed us to space voyages anywhere. His was also the age of Edgar Allan Poe's *Descent into the Maelström*, and of De Quincey's *Opium Eater*. By contrast, our time compels us to voyage in a present that includes all times and spaces. Neither evolution nor progress is directional or sequential. EVERY-WHERE IS NOW-HERE IN ECO-LAND.

> We may come, touch and go, from atoms and ifs but we're presurely
> destined to be odd's without ends.   James Joyce, *Finnegans Wake*

Reinventing the World of Yester-Morrow

The familiar idea of "making the news" now yields to making the world itself. For the best part of a century, we have been programming human consciousness with retrievals and replays of the tribal unconscious. The complementary of this process would seem to be the "natural" program for the period ahead: *programming the unconscious with the recently achieved forms of consciousness*. This procedure would evoke a new form of consciousness radically different from former consciousness. Everybody becomes a voluntary participant in creating diversity without loss of identity. Man is the content of the environment he creates, whether of "hardware" or "software," whether of consciousness or unconsciousness. There is therefore no technical alternative to "humanism," even though for many this would include the divine grace of the superhuman. INNOVATION IS OBSOLETE. SO IS OBSOLESCENCE, AS INFORMATION SPEED-UP TRANSFORMS MAN AND HIS WORLD INTO ART FORM.

FINN-AGAIN-ARRAY-SURRECTION!

Bibliography

Adams, Brooks. *The Law of Civilization and Decay*. New York: Macmillan Co., 1895.

Agnew, Neil M., and Pyke, Sandra. *Science Game: An Introduction to Research in the Behavioral Sciences*. Englewood Cliffs, N.J.: Prentice-Hall, 1969.

Allegro, John. *The Sacred Mushroom and the Cross*. New York: Doubleday & Co., 1970.

Arnold, Matthew. *Selected Poetry and Prose*. New York: Holt, Rinehart & Winston, 1960.

Asbell, Bernard. "Can We Survive the Madding Crowd? Science Zeros in on a Neglected Peril." *Think* Magazine, July-August, 1969.

Balazs, Etienne. *Chinese Civilization and Bureaucracy*. Translated by H. M. Wright. New Haven: Yale University Press, 1967.

Benedict, Ruth. *The Chrysanthemum and the Sword*. New York: World Publishing Co., Meridian Books, 1967.

————. *Patterns of Culture*. Boston: Houghton Mifflin Co., 1934.

Berg, Ivar. *Education and Jobs: The Great Training Robbery*. New York: Praeger Publishers, 1970.

Bettelheim, Bruno. *The Children of the Dream*. New York: Macmillan Co., 1969.

Bierce, Ambrose. *The Devil's Dictionary*. New York: Hill & Wang, 1957.

Bloodworth, Dennis. *Chinese Looking Glass*. London: Martin Secker & Warburg, 1967.

Boguslaw, Robert. *The New Utopians*. Englewood Cliffs, N.J.: Prentice-Hall, 1968.

Boorstin, Daniel J. *The Image: Or, What Happened to the American Dream*. New York: Atheneum Publishers, 1962.

Boulding, Kenneth E. "Failures and Successes in Economics." *Think* Magazine, May-June, 1965.

————. *The Image: Knowledge in Life and Society*. Ann Arbor: University of Michigan Press, 1956.

Butler, Samuel. *Erewhon*. New York: Random House, Modern Library, n.d.

Carlyle, Thomas. *Past and Present*. Boston: Houghton Mifflin Co., 1965.

Carpenter, Edward S. "The New Languages." In *Explorations in Communication*. Boston: Beacon Press, 1962.

Carroll, Lewis. *Alice in Wonderland* and *Through the Looking Glass*. New York: Grosset & Dunlap, 1946.

Chandor, Anthony. *Dictionary of Computers*. London: Penguin Books, 1970.

Chesterton, G. K. *Collected Poems of G. K. Chesterton*. London: Cecil Palmer, 1927.

Clarke, Arthur C. *Profiles of the Future*. New York: Harper & Row, Publishers, 1963.

Colie, Rosalie. *Paradoxica Epidemica: The Renaissance Tradition of Paradox*. Princeton: Princeton University Press, 1966.

Cressey, Donald R. *Theft of a Nation: The Structure and Operations of Organized Crime in America*. New York: Harper & Row, Publishers, 1969.

Dantzig, Tobias. *Number: The Language of Science*. New York: Doubleday & Co., Anchor Books, 1956.

De Grazia, Alfred; Jurgens, Ralph E., and Stecchini, Livio C. *The Politics of Science and Dr. Velikovsky*. Reprint of a special issue of *The American Behavioural Scientist*, September, 1963, with subsequent correspondence.

Drucker, Peter. *The Age of Discontinuity*. New York: Harper & Row, Publishers, 1968.

————. *The Concept of the Corporation*. New York: John Day Co., 1946.

Einstein, Albert. *Where Is Science Going?* London: George Allen & Unwin, 1933.

Eliot, T. S. *The Complete Poems and Plays 1909–1950*. New York: Harcourt, Brace and Co., 1952.

————. *The Sacred Wood: Essays on Poetry and Criticism*. London: Methuen & Co., 1948.

————. *Selected Essays*. New York: Harcourt, Brace and Co., 1950.

————. *The Use of Poetry and the Use of Criticism*. New York: Barnes & Noble, 1955.

Ellul, Jacques. *Propaganda: The Foundation of Man's Attitudes*. New York: Alfred A. Knopf, 1965.

Engineering Institute of Canada. Report: *The Engineering Manager—Survival in the Seventies: Proceedings*. Seventeenth Joint Engineering Management Conference, Montreal, 1969.

Farb, Peter. *Man's Rise to Civilization as Shown by the Indians of North America, from Primeval Times to the Coming of the Industrial State*. New York: E. P. Dutton & Co., 1968.

Fishwick, Marshall. *The Hero, American Style*. New York: David McKay, 1969.

Foster, C. D. *Decision Making in National Science Policy*. London: J. & A. Churchill, 1968.

Frisbie, Richard P. *How to Peel a Sour Grape*. New York: Sheed & Ward, 1965.

Fuller, R. Buckminster. *Operating Manual for Spaceship Earth*. Carbondale, Ill.: Southern Illinois University Press, 1969.

Gabor, Dennis. *Innovations*. New York: Oxford University Press, 1971.

Galbraith, John Kenneth. *The New Industrial State*. New York: New American Library, Signet Book, 1967.

Giedion, Siegfried. *Space, Time and Architecture*. 4th ed. Cambridge, Mass.: Harvard University Press, 1967.

Goedel, Kurt. *Goedel's Theorem: On Formally Undecidable Propositions*. New York: Basic Books, 1963.

Goldsmith, Oliver. *The Traveller* and *The Deserted Village*. Edited by W. Murison. Cambridge: Pitt Press, Cambridge University Press, n.d.

Gombrich, Ernst H. *Art and Illusion*. New York: Pantheon Books, 1960.

Goulden, Joseph C. *Monopoly*. New York: G. P. Putnam's Sons, 1968.

Guinan, St. Michael. "Maturation and Aging in Religious Life." *Donum Dei,* Vol. 8. Canadian Religious Conference, Hull, Quebec, 1971.

Hall, Edward T. *The Hidden Dimension.* New York: Doubleday & Co., 1966.

———. *The Silent Language.* New York: Doubleday & Co., 1959.

Hanna, Thomas. *A Primer of Somatic Thinking.* New York: Holt, Rinehart & Winston, 1970.

Havelock, Eric A. *Preface to Plato.* Cambridge, Mass.: Harvard University Press, 1963.

Heisenberg, Werner. *The Physicist's Conception of Nature.* Translated by Arnold J. Pomerans. Westport, Conn.: Greenwood Press, 1958.

Hersey, John. *Hiroshima.* New York: Random House, Modern Library, n.d.

Hillman, James. *Emotion: A Comprehensive Phenomenology of Theories and Their Meanings for Therapy.* Evanston, Ill.: Northwestern University Press, 1961.

Hobbes, Thomas. *Leviathan.* Edited by Francis Randall. New York: Washington Square Press, 1969.

Hopkins, Gerard Manley. *Poems of Gerard Manley Hopkins.* New York: Oxford University Press, 1950.

Howton, F. W. *Functionaries.* Chicago: Quadrangle Books, 1969.

Huizinga, Johan. *Homo Ludens: A Study of the Play Element in Culture.* Boston: Beacon Press, 1955.

I Ching. Translated from Chinese and German by R. Wilhelm and C. F. Baynes. London: Routledge & Kegan Paul, 1951.

IEEE Newsletter, Systems and Cybernetics Group, September, 1967. Reporting on "The First International Symposium on Computer Imitations of Brain Functions."

Innis, Harold. *Empire and Communications.* Toronto: University of Toronto Press, 1971.

Isaacs, J. *The Background of Modern Poetry.* New York: E. P. Dutton & Co., n.d.

Ivins, William M. *Art and Geometry: A Study in Space Intuitions.* New York: Dover Publications, 1964.

Jackson, Denis B. *The Exam Secret: How to Shine in Examinations and Life.* Bungay, Suffolk: Richard Clay & Co., 1954.

Jacobs, Jane. *The Economy of Cities.* New York: Random House, 1969.

James, William. *The Principles of Psychology.* 2 vols. Originally published in 1890. New York: Dover Publications.

Jay, Antony. *Management and Machiavelli: An Inquiry into the Politics of Corporate Life.* New York: Holt, Rinehart & Winston, 1968.

Joyce, James. *Finnegans Wake.* New York: Viking Press, 1959.

———. *Portrait of the Artist as a Young Man.* New York: Random House, Modern Library, n.d.

Kahn, Herman, and Wiener, Anthony S. *The Year 2000.* New York: Macmillan Co., 1967.

Kierkegaard, Sören. *Concept of Dread.* Translated by Walter Lowrie. Princeton: Princeton University Press, 1944.

Kostelanetz, Richard. *Master Minds: Portraits of Contemporary American Artists and Intellectuals.* New York: Macmillan Co., 1969.

Kuhn, Thomas S. *The Structure of Scientific Revolutions*. Chicago: University of Chicago Press, 1962.

Leach, E. R. *A Runaway World*. New York: Oxford University Press, 1965.

Lewis, Sinclair. *Babbitt*. New York: Harcourt, Brace & World, 1950.

Lewis, Wyndham. *The Human Age*. London: Methuen & Co., n.d.

Lovejoy, Arthur O. *The Great Chain of Being*. New York: Harper & Brothers, Torchbooks/Academy Library, 1960.

Lund, Nils W. *Chiasmus in the New Testament*. Chapel Hill: University of North Carolina Press, 1942.

Lusseyran, Jacques. *And There Was Light*. Boston: Little, Brown and Co., 1963.

MacDonald, John. *Strategy in Poker, Business and War*. New York: W. W. Norton & Co., 1950.

Machiavelli, Niccolò. *The Prince*. Translated by Christian E. Dekmold. New York: Washington Square Press, n.d.

Maitland, F. W. *Domesday Book and Beyond*. New York: W. W. Norton & Co., 1966.

Mandeville, Bernard. *The Fable of the Bees: or Private Vices, Publick Benefits*. Edited by Irwin Primer. New York: G. P. Putnam's Sons, Capricorn Books, 1962.

Marrow, Alfred J. *Behind the Executive Mask*. New York: Macmillan Co., 1964.

Marx, Karl. *Capital*. 2 vols. New York: E. P. Dutton & Co., Everyman Library, n.d.

———. *A Contribution to the Critique of Political Economy*. New York: International Publishers Co., New World Paperbacks, 1970.

Marx, Karl, and Engels, Friedrich. *Karl Marx and Friedrich Engels Correspondence*. London: Martin Lawrence, 1934.

May, Rollo. *Love and Will*. New York: W. W. Norton & Co., 1969.

Mayr, Otto. "The Origins of Feedback Control." *Scientific American*, October, 1970.

McHale, John. *The Future of the Future*. New York: George Braziller, 1969.

McLuhan, Marshall. *Culture Is Our Business*. New York: McGraw-Hill Book Co., 1970.

———. *The Gutenberg Galaxy*. Toronto: University of Toronto Press, 1962.

———. *Understanding Media*. New York: McGraw-Hill Book Co., 1964.

McLuhan, Marshall, and Fiore, Quentin. *The Medium Is the Massage*. New York: Random House, 1967.

———. *War and Peace in the Global Village*. New York: McGraw-Hill Book Co., 1968.

McLuhan, Marshall, and Watson, Wilfred. *From Cliché to Archetype*. New York: Viking Press, 1970.

Menninger, Edwin A. *Fantastic Trees*. New York: Viking Press, 1967.

Merrill, H. F. *Classics in Management*. New York: Macmillan Co., 1960.

Milton, John. *Complete Poetry and Selected Prose of John Milton*. Introduction by Cleanth Brooks. New York: Random House, Modern Library, 1950.

Moore, Mavor. *And What Do You Do?* Toronto: J. M. Dent & Sons, 1960.

More, Sir Thomas. *Utopia*. Edited by J. C. Collins. London: Oxford University Press, 1904.

Moynihan, Daniel Patrick. *The Negro Family: The Case for National Action.* Washington, D.C.: Office of Policy Planning and Research, United States Department of Labor, March, 1965.

Mumford, Lewis. *The Urban Prospect.* New York: Harcourt, Brace & World, 1969.

Myers, L. H. *The Root and the Flower.* London: Jonathan Cape, 1934.

Nelson, Benjamin. *Idea of Usury: From Tribal Brotherhood to Universal Otherhood.* Chicago: University of Chicago Press, 1969.

Olson, Charles. *Proprioception.* Berkeley, Calif.: Four Seasons, 1965.

Orwell, George, *1984.* Edited by Irving Howe. New York: Harcourt, Brace & World, 1962.

Pelletier, Wilfred. "Childhood in an Indian Village." *This Magazine Is About Schools,* Vol. 3, Issue 2 (Spring, 1969).

Picard, Max. *The World of Silence.* Translated by Stanley Godman. Chicago: Henry Regnery Co., 1961.

Piel, Gerard. *Science in the Cause of Man.* New York: Alfred A. Knopf, 1961.

Pigou, A. C. *The Economics of Welfare.* 4th ed. New York: St. Martin's Press, Papermac Books, 1932.

Platt, John. "What We Must Do." *Science,* November 28, 1969.

Poe, Edgar Allan. *Complete Tales and Poems of Edgar Allan Poe.* New York: Random House, 1938.

Polanyi, Karl. *The Great Transformation.* Boston: Beacon Press, 1957.

———. *Primitive, Archaic, and Modern Economies.* New York: Doubleday & Co., Anchor Books, 1968.

Pope, Alexander. *Complete Poetical Works.* Edited by H. W. Boynton. Boston: Houghton Mifflin Co., n.d.

Pound, Ezra. *ABC of Reading.* London: Faber & Faber, 1961.

Rainwater, Lee, and Yancey, William L. *The Moynihan Report and the Politics of Controversy.* Cambridge, Mass.: M.I.T. Press, 1967.

Reich, Charles. *The Greening of America.* New York: Random House, 1970.

Report from Iron Mountain on the Possibility and Desirability of Peace, The. New York: Dial Press, 1967.

Rose, J. *Technological Injury: The Effect of Technological Advances on Environment, Life, and Society.* London: Gordon & Breach, 1969.

Russell, Bertrand. *ABC of Relativity.* Edited by F. Pirani. 3rd ed. London: George Allen & Unwin, 1969.

Samuelson, Paul A. *Economics.* New York: McGraw-Hill Book Co., 1961.

Schon, Donald A. *Displacements of Concepts.* London: Tavistock Publications, 1963.

Selye, Hans. *From Dream to Discovery: On Being a Scientist.* New York: McGraw-Hill Book Co., 1964.

———. *The Stress of Life.* New York: McGraw-Hill Book Co., 1956.

Servan-Schreiber, J.-J. *The American Challenge.* Translated by Ronald Steel. New York: Avon Books, 1969.

Sloan, Alfred P., Jr., *My Years with General Motors.* Garden City: Doubleday & Co., 1964.

"Smith," "Adam." *The Money Game.* New York: Random House, 1968.

Smith, Adam. *The Wealth of Nations.* New York: Random House, Modern Library, n.d.

Soule, George. *Ideas of the Great Economists*. New York: New American Library, Mentor Books, 1955.

Speer, Albert. *Inside the Third Reich*. New York: Macmillan Co., 1970.

Sutton, F. X. et al. *The American Business Creed*. Cambridge, Mass.: Harvard University Press, 1956.

Swift, Jonathan. *Gulliver's Travels*. New York: Macmillan Co., 1962.

Thoreau, Henry D. *Walden*. New York: Bantam Books, Bantam Classics, n.d.

Tourneur, Cyril. *The Revenger's Tragedy*. Edited by Lawrence Ross. Lincoln: University of Nebraska Press, 1966.

Townsend, Robert. *Up the Organization: How to Stop the Corporation from Stifling People and Strangling Profits*. New York: Alfred A. Knopf, 1970.

Trevor-Roper, Hugh. *The Rise of Christian Europe*. New York: Harcourt, Brace & World, 1965.

Turner, Frederick J. *The Significance of the Frontier in American History*. New York: Frederick Ungar Publishing Co., n.d.

Turner, William W. *J. Edgar Hoover and the FBI: The Man and the Myth*. Los Angeles: Sherbourne Press, 1970.

Veblen, Thorstein. *Theory of the Leisure Class*. New York: Random House, Modern Library, 1934.

Von Bertalanffy, Ludwig, and Rapoport. Anatol, eds. *General Systems*: Yearbook of the Society for General Systems Theory, Vol. 1 (1956).

Wallas, Graham. *The Great Society: A Psychological Analysis*. Lincoln: University of Nebraska Press, Bison Books, 1966.

Walter, Norman I. *The Sexual Cycle of Human Warfare*. London: Mitre Press, 1950.

White, Lynn, Jr. *Machina ex Deo: Essays in the Dynamism of Western Culture*. Cambridge, Mass.: M.I.T. Press, 1969.

———. *Medieval Technology and Social Change*. London: Oxford University Press, 1962.

Wister, Owen. *The Virginian*. New York: Grosset & Dunlap, 1925.

Wordsworth, William. *The Complete Poetical Works of Wordsworth*. Boston: Houghton Mifflin Co., Cambridge Edition, 1934.

Yale Shakespeare, The. Rev. ed. General editors: Helge Kökeritz and Charles T. Prouty. New Haven: Yale University Press, 1959.

Yeats, W. B. *The Collected Poems of W. B. Yeats*. New York: Macmillan Co., 1954.

York, Herbert F. "ABM, MIRV, and the Arms Race." *Science*, July 17, 1970.

TAKE TODAY
THE EXECUTIVE AS DROPOUT

Marshall McLuhan and Barrington Nevitt

Marshall McLuhan is probably the most original theorist of the postindustrial world. No other contemporary social critic can match the daring of his imagination, the sheer profusion and richness of his insights. McLuhan has been called "the oracle of the electric age" and "the sage of Aquarius." The reason seems obvious: life has already begun to imitate his mantic art.

In *Take Today*, McLuhan, with his co-author Barrington Nevitt, is again concerned with the future. The past, McLuhan and Nevitt say, is too much with us. The world's managers have failed to adapt to "the age of speed-up." They persist in their "hardware" thinking; they are relics of the industrial world of assembly lines and visual space. They become "diehards holding the old management fort." And now their specialized jobs have become casualties, displaced by the electric world of "software" and programming.

The old era came to an end with the launching of Sputnik in 1957. With the new satellite surround, the earth was instantaneously transformed into a global theater, whose inhabitants became not only observers but the observed. They could no longer remain simply spectators. The sudden change made them participants, actors, people involved in role-playing on a global scale. Old experience is no longer relevant. Man must, say McLuhan and Nevitt, reinvent Nature—the old natural order has been scrapped, made obsolete by electric communications and satellites. To this end, the executive will have to drop out of his old organizational structures, whether these are in business, the military, the church, the universities, or government.

Take Today is a major work. Using brilliant aphorisms, striking illuminations, puns, and probes, the authors show how Nature must now be re-created as an art form, "perfectly accommodated to the totality of human needs and aspirations."